# SHAKESPEARE'S STAGECRAFT

*What, a play toward? I'll be an auditor,*
*An actor too perhaps, if I see cause.*

PUCK

# SHAKESPEARE'S STAGECRAFT

BY

J.L.STYAN

CAMBRIDGE
AT THE UNIVERSITY PRESS
1967

Published by the Syndics of the Cambridge University Press
Bentley House, 200 Euston Road, London, N.W. 1
American Branch: 32 East 57th Street, New York, N.Y. 10022

© Cambridge University Press 1967

Library of Congress Catalogue Card Number: 67-13808

Printed in Great Britain
at the University Printing House, Cambridge
(Brooke Crutchley, University Printer)

# CONTENTS

*Introduction*                                                    *page* 1

### I   SHAKESPEARE'S THEATRE EQUIPMENT

1   Shakespeare's Stage                                            7

The flexibility of Elizabethan theatre. The essential Elizabethan
stage. The intimacy of the auditorium. The focus of the
platform. A pair of permanent doors. 'Knocking up the curtain.'
Another level.

2   Staging and Acting Conventions                                28

Convention in Shakespeare's theatre. Properties and symbols. A
wardrobe for scene and symbol. Ranging between naturalism
and ritual. Actor and atmosphere on a neutral stage. A note on
sex and the boy actor. The daylight convention. The localizing
convention. Dramatizing time.

### II   SHAKESPEARE'S VISUAL CRAFT

3   The Actor and his Movement                                    53

Shakespeare as director. Gesture stated and implied. Gesture
and dramatic meaning. Gesture into symbolism. Movement
over the platform. Entrance on to the platform. Alone on the
stage. Playing to the audience. Exit.

4   Grouping on the Open Stage                                    81

Planning for three dimensions. The duologue visualized. Spatial
distinctions between characters. The importance of upstage and
downstage. Speaking to the audience. The ways of eavesdropping. The silent figure.

5   The Full Stage                                                109

Successive entrances. Controlling the visual images. Crowds.
Armies into battle. Two-fold grouping. Grouping, three- and
four-fold. The Shakespearian spectacular.

# Contents

### III SHAKESPEARE'S AURAL CRAFT

6  Speaking the Speech                                      *page* 141

Vocal tones. Uses of tone and rhythm. Repetition and pace.
'For every passion something.' The variation of Shakespeare's
speech. The setting and the solo speech.

7  The Orchestration of Speech                             172

Contrasting patterns of sound. Duologue and duet. Pace.
Crescendo. Variation of tempo. A note on pause and silence.

### IV CONCLUSIONS

8  Total Theatre                                           195

Eye and ear inseparable. The actor's contribution. Building the
action. Shifts of tempo, mood and perspective. Extension into
symbolism and ritual. An 'epic' structure. The audience and
dramatic form. The study of Shakespeare in the theatre.

*Selected Bibliography*                                    232

*Index of Subjects*                                        235

*Index of Proper Names*                                    239

*Index of Scenes*                                          241

The Swan Theatre, London, drawn by Johannes de Witt        10

The Hall of the Middle Temple                              13

vi

# PREFACE

This book is intended to be a guide with which to explore Shakespeare's stage practice. The detail of his work as a craftsman remains to be discovered at closer quarters—in the theatre itself. To make the survey a useful instrument and to put the emphasis in the right place, it seemed best to outline first what little is known of Shakespeare's 'theatre equipment', and the early part of the book therefore reviews much that has already been advanced by scholars of the Elizabethan theatre. The bulk of what follows consists of an introduction to Shakespeare's visual and aural stagecraft.

The text used is that of the *New Shakespeare* of Arthur Quiller-Couch and John Dover Wilson, both because this great edition is now complete and because with its system of theatrical pointing it is such a serviceable text for the actor. Although a start has been made to examine the acting and speaking tradition, the intentions of the 'word-scenery' and Shakespeare's 'gestic imagination', the detailed labour of the Cambridge editors has not yet stimulated close study of the Elizabethan actor on the stage or of the Elizabethan spectator in the playhouse. The need is still to see Shakespeare as the practical man with clear notions about what he wanted his actors to do for their audience, and to find, in Q's words of the General Introduction of 1921, that 'endless reward of curiosity in tracing the experiments by which he learned to master the craft of the stage'.

I have acknowledged my debts to other people wherever I could trace them. Many of the ideas spring from discussion and practical experiment with extra-mural students in Yorkshire and graduate students in Ann Arbor. Those involved will doubtless recognize where their contributions have been gratefully included. More immediately, I owe to Professor G. E. T. Mayfield and Professor Arthur Eastman a great debt for the hours in which they have examined these pages; errors of judgment that remain are my own. Miss Shirley Patrick has done meticulous work on the copy, and, above all, I cannot repay my wife for the time I have stolen from her.

J.L.S.

*The University of Michigan*
*Ann Arbor 1966*

# INTRODUCTION

The account of Shakespeare's stagecraft in this book will not 'solve' many of the problems of Elizabethan staging, although it may suggest a practical director's solution to some of them— the sort of answer found perforce by a busy man of the theatre. As a playwright Shakespeare was daily coming upon difficulties, and as a member of an acting company he was daily helping to solve them. The complexity of his achievement as a theatre craftsman turns on the obvious questions. At what moments did Shakespeare want his audience to use its eyes, and when its ears? When both? What effect had the depth of his platform stage on the kind of theatre he created? What powers did the proximity of the spectator lend the actor? What range of voice did he demand of his actor, and what combinations and contrasts of tone did he exercise? How did the chop and change of scene determine the shape of his action on the swift stage of the Globe? The book tries to clarify some preliminary ideas about the quality of the Shakespearian theatre experience.

The debt to Granville-Barker's way of looking at Shakespearian drama, as an actors' structure of pressures and contrasts directed at an audience, will be seen in the pages that follow. He aimed to blow away the transcendental fog of the nineteenth century, asserting that a dramatic text acquired virtue by its claim to be a prompt book. For the humility of the romantic critics who sought a seer in Shakespeare, he substituted the humility of a director confronting Shakespeare's stagecraft. 'A sense of the stage' in a playwright means his power to judge whether his meaning and intention can be effective with a contemporary audience, and whether the ends of his play can be served in terms of his chosen medium, the theatre, with its actors and physical equipment and circumstances. It implies an ability to be alert in several directions at once, and especially towards actor and spectator.

This seems to make playwriting a work-a-day, business-like matter. Where is the poetry? Words on the stage assume the strength of dramatic poetry according to the spirit in which the actor is animated, the spectator moved and the play's image propagated. To measure this poetry of the theatre (to re-apply Jean Cocteau's apt distinction) is the proper object. Shakespeare deals in the recognizable and particular in order to lead his audience toward the imaginative and universal: he deals in Hamlet and Lear, the fallible men, in order to create Hamlet and Lear, the florescent symbols of humanity. In this way the detailed and particular life of his theatre is the guide to the poetic experience. To examine the manner in which his imagination takes objective form, to gain a close view of the practical man at work with the mechanics of his craft, is to glimpse the depths of that imagination.

The separation of one element in an art in which even a gesture can contribute radically to the whole might be thought an act of presumption. In the process of breaking down Shakespeare's technique of communication in the theatre, it will be the inclusiveness of his dramatic method that will strike us: the eye feeds the ear, and the ear feeds the eye; the words as spoken are inseparable from the movements of the actors who speak them; a character is an intrinsic part of the scene into which he is built; and a scene is nothing outside the sequence to which it contributes. A sense of the stage implies that the playwright is doing many things at the same time, and to undergo an experience in Shakespearian theatre is to submit to a drama which embraces something of the narrative art of the novel and the verbal art of poetry, as well as the musical art of song, its rhythm and tempo and orchestration, with the visual arts of mime and dance, set off by the colour and design of costume. Shakespeare envisages total theatre, and a total image is to be projected.

As the physical particularities of his craft are reviewed, Shakespeare's controlled variety and pattern in the tempo and mood of a speech or a sequence of speeches, a scene or a sequence of scenes, will appear. The dimension of time is of inescapable importance; its passing is one of the conditions of drama. If a play's meaning for its audience resides in part in the temporal accumulation and control of its effects, then such designs as those woven by the rhythm of speech or movement, or the change or intensifying of their tone or manner, must also be indicative of Shakespeare's stage sense. Movement, tempo and mood are not the qualities in a play that are most readily recognized from the printed text, but they are elements without which the drama would not hold. To recognize them is to place proper weight on the quality of the play's impressions on the spectator in the theatre, and the pressures put upon his sensibility and imagination in practice; it is also to take the measure of the play's stageworthiness.

In this activity, the final concern is with the audience. Theatrical communication assumes a largely unconscious scheme of signalling to actor and thence to spectator through the script. The playwright may begin with an idea or a complex emotion, one seen and felt as people animated in time. He has first to particularize them, through a structure of words which suffer the limitations of words as written. His script must be capable of conveying what he thinks and feels, by implicit directions of speech and movement, to the actor on the stage. Finally it must prefigure the impressions the actors project, such impressions in turn being particularized in the evolving image of the play in the mind of the audience. To identify aspects of Shakespeare's code of signals is to begin to map a country of great wealth, and to seek to preserve those permanent elements in his craft which will not change when the shape of a stage changes or when actors and audiences pass on.

# I

# SHAKESPEARE'S THEATRE EQUIPMENT

# SHAKESPEARE'S STAGE

## THE FLEXIBILITY OF ELIZABETHAN THEATRE

The unpredictable variety of Elizabethan playing conditions was a source of real service to the playwrights of the time. The following are the general facts in the case.

1. That the sixty-eight years between the building of the first public playhouse in London, the elder Burbage's 'Theatre' of 1576, and the pulling down of the second Globe in 1644, were years of vigorous theatrical activity and new-born experiments in staging. During such a time the conditions of playing would have changed in both minor and major particulars. The variety of playing conditions found in theatres during the course of the present century suggests an adequate comparison for such growth.

2. That the players had to be ready to play the same piece in a variety of places. A company might from time to time be obliged to desert its permanent playhouse in order to perform at Court, or leave London to play in the provinces at guildhalls and in private rooms, or in some Elizabethan great hall at the command of a noble patron. When London was roused by a plague scare, for example, the players might find themselves on the road at short notice, using a market square or sometimes turning to account the cramping conditions of a posting inn, or private garden or yard, mansion or tavern-room. Even today, amateurs at their drama festivals and professionals on tour know something of what is required of all players—adaptability.

3. That most of the thirty-six plays of Shakespeare's Folio were not first performed at a single theatre of fixed design. Less than half were opened at his own theatre, the Globe, and more than twenty of them at the Theatre and the Curtain, two of the playhouses in use when Shakespeare came to London and before the Globe was built, and at Blackfriars, a more exclusive covered theatre, and at Court on royal occasions. Moreover, their initial

technical planning would have been modified before they went into the repertory. If the methods of production of Shakespeare's plays remain largely undiscovered, it is probably because the players were still trying out new production methods to the end of his career. Why should there have been any intention of fossilizing them, any more than today at Stratford-upon-Avon?

4. That there is nothing in Shakespeare's plays, either at the outset of his career or at its end, that could not be readily fitted to any conditions, from a make-shift to an elaborate stage and equipment. Today Shakespeare makes his appearance in every conceivable place, in the drawing-room, in the cinema, in the open air. No doubt the plays were equally adaptable in their own time. Then, as now, there was always that final recourse, the scissors.

5. That Shakespeare's is, pre-eminently, a drama calling for a liberal imaginative collaboration from the audience. It is hard to conceive a drama demanding less fixed paraphernalia of presentation. In Victorian times, requirements of lighting and scenery, the mode of acting, excessive projection of voice and controlled movement within the picture-frame, could determine a play's success or failure as an effectively rendered piece of theatre. The Elizabethan play could pass in a theatre imposing the minimum of physical limitations.

From these characteristics it is arguable that a prerequisite of a playwright's technique in Elizabethan times was his ability to write a play that could be put on anywhere. Moreover, Shakespeare's theatre practice, the handling of actors and audience, each exploration of the stage's possibilities, suggests that he was fighting to free himself from conventional restrictions. With each new play his drama is enlarged: the actor is forced to review his craft, the spectator forced to a new response, the possibilities of the stage are flexed.

So we must resist the impulse to fix and define the Elizabethan theatre too finally, saying that the stage was like *this*, therefore the play was like *that*. It is wise to allow Shakespeare room for experiment. Yet he did not have unlimited possibilities for staging in his mind's eye when he set about writing his script. He worked from certain assumptions, making his departures from certain broad facts of playhouse life and procedure.

### THE ESSENTIAL ELIZABETHAN STAGE

For the general picture of this stage there are few hard details. The only contemporary drawing of an Elizabethan stage is an awkward second-hand sketch by a man who was no artist, the copy of De Witt's impression of the Swan Theatre of 1596. Nevertheless, as Sir Edmund Chambers decided many years ago, this picture must be the basis for any conjectural reconstruction of the Elizabethan public playhouse. Add to this a few details from the surviving builders' contracts for theatres of the time, those of the Fortune (1600) and the Hope (1613),[1] and some comments from contemporary visitors to London, and there is no other evidence of note external to the texts of the plays themselves. However, if these items cannot confirm all the architectural details deduced by scholars, they are sufficient to establish a general pattern of features which would allow any play of the period to be mounted.

This pattern is made up of very few elements. There was a symmetrically rounded or square auditorium only some 80 feet across, unroofed and surrounded by tiers of galleries. The actors worked on a platform of proportions which were impressive by any standard. The contract for the Fortune required that its stage should 'containe in length Fortie and Three foote of lawfull assize and in breadth to extende to the middle of the yarde', i.e. 43 feet wide by $27\frac{1}{2}$ feet deep, apart from any extension backwards into a conjectural 'inner stage'. It is worth remarking that these proportions at the Fortune, although not necessarily these exact measurements, were based on those of the Globe, since the document in other contexts repeats the

---

[1] For present purposes the relevant details are reproduced in the next paragraph. The full statement of these contracts is to be found in W. W. Greg's *Henslowe Papers*, pp. 4–7 and 19–22, in the appendices to J. C. Adams's *The Globe Playhouse* and C. W. Hodges's *The Globe Restored*, and elsewhere. A. M. Nagler in *Shakespeare's Stage*, ch. 2, provides a neat summary of the arguments surrounding these documents.

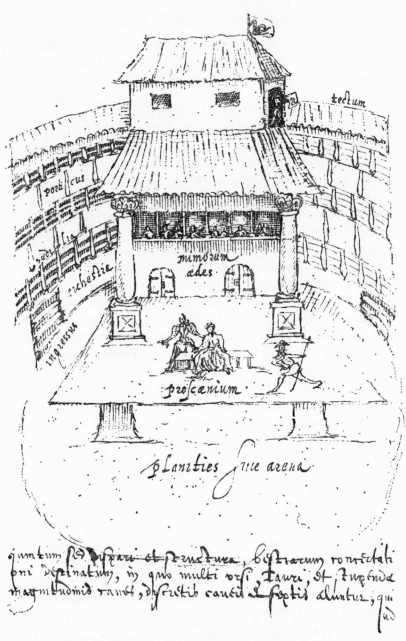

The Swan Theatre, London, drawn by Johannes de Witt

phrase, 'according to the manner and fashion of the said howse called the Globe'. It seems unlikely that this platform was a fixture, since its temporary removal would allow the theatre to be used for other purposes, notably bull-baiting and bear-baiting. This must add to our sense of the flexibility and improvisation characteristic of the Elizabethan playhouse.

The yard which surrounded the platform was occupied by standing spectators. Hamlet comments on the practice of splitting the ears of 'the groundlings' (the play was written in about 1601), and Dekker explicitly describes them as 'the Scar-crows in the yard' in *The Gull's Hornbook* of 1609. If they had to share the yard with some of the spectators, the actors would expect their scaffold to be raised off the ground like the street stages which strolling players quickly set up on trestles in public places. Indeed, when Thomas Platter[1] went to the Curtain, he made special mention of the fact that the players were on 'a raised scaffold and everybody can see everything very well'. Moreover, raising the stage would make possible the use of trap-doors. Thus the immediate condition the Elizabethan playwright and actor had to reckon with was a raised and very prominent acting space, surrounded by the yard and the intimate huddle of the galleries.

These were the essentials, forming a built-in relationship between actor and spectator. Contemporary drawings of the exteriors of the theatres confirm that the hut which housed the flying, lifting and lowering machinery of the Hope's 'heavens' (the Fortune's 'shadowe or cover') was built against one side of the wall of the auditorium. This projection had certainly to overhang at least part of the playing space. There would be an adapted or permanent tiring-house or changing-room behind the façade, situated as close to the acting area as possible: this is De Witt's *mimorum aedes* (actors' house). Upstage doors provided access to the platform, and possibly, by means of simple steps, into the yard as well. A pair of such doors are

---

[1] A visitor from Basle who wrote a fair account of his theatrical experiences in London in 1599. See E. K. Chambers, *The Elizabethan Stage*, vol. 2, pp. 364–6.

shown in the Swan drawing, comparable to the doors in the screen of an Elizabethan banquet-hall, and doors are frequently mentioned in the plays.

Finally, with a gallery extending at first storey level around the best part of the auditorium, there is every likelihood that it continued behind the platform, forming the kind of balcony seen in the De Witt sketch. Such a gallery would lend itself to action on an upper level when a play called for it, or could provide extra seating when it did not. In *Shakespeare's Wooden O*, Leslie Hotson suggests that the lords used this part of the gallery, and that the actors therefore played to them and made their entrances through traps and curtained houses (tent-like structures set up on either side of the platform) from a tiring-room beneath the stage. No doubt Elizabethan actors had a familiar sense of playing 'in the round' under varied conditions, but it is unlikely that they would turn their backs on the majority of the spectators in an asymmetrical auditorium, or enter half-masked from view when doors stood conveniently upstage. On the contrary, the balcony would seem to the players to be part of their stage; and when they found themselves acting in a private hall, they saw there much the same feature in the musicians' gallery above the screen. In addition to this second acting level, a third level was possibly available to the players on occasion: when Samuel Kiechel[1] paid a visit to the Theatre he found 'three galleries on top of one another', a design which is repeated in the Swan drawing.

Thus, in brief, the basic and irreducible ingredients of the Elizabethan theatre which the playwright took into account are four, and this study need not go beyond them:

1. A tight, enclosing auditorium.
2. A projecting platform almost as deep as it was wide.
3. Two upstage entrances on to the platform.
4. At least one balcony.

There is no proof that the theatre consisted of more than this.

---

[1] A German visitor to London in 1585. Again see E. K. Chambers, *The Elizabethan Stage*, vol. 2, p. 358.

The Hall of the Middle Temple, where *Twelfth Night*
was presented in 1602

These features are also all that are needed for an adequate
Elizabethan performance. Indeed, their very sparseness makes
of them the flexible instrument wanted for the multitude of
theatrical movements, relationships and effects to be found in the
plays.

Arguments have been put forward that due account must be
taken of likely production changes for the smaller auditorium of

the Blackfriars Theatre, an indoor playhouse which the King's Men leased in the summer of 1608 as their winter quarters, and for which Shakespeare's late romances, *Cymbeline*, *The Winter's Tale* and *The Tempest*, were written. The Blackfriars had dimensions of 66 feet by 46 feet; these do not suggest that spatial relationships were radically different from those in the public theatres. The platform must have been proportionately smaller, and scenic effects were probably more spectacular. Yet the case to be made for a more intimate style of acting is dubious: intimacy was common to both public and private theatres. Granville-Barker argued that 'bad actors would not shout so much, and good actors could develop new delicacies of expression ...sentiment will become as telling as passion...humour may be less brisk; the pace of the acting in general will tend to slow down'.[1] This seems plausible, but in practice bad actors will shout wherever they are, sentiment was the diet in the spacious Victorian theatres, and humour and pace accelerate in close conditions, as radio has shown. In any case there is nothing in the last plays to show that any of this happened. The real point to stress is that the Globe plays worked in Blackfriars, and the Blackfriars plays worked in the Globe.

## THE INTIMACY OF THE AUDITORIUM

The long view of the basic Elizabethan theatrical elements must reveal their effect on the play, the playing and the response. Above all, the shape into which the spectators were mustered and their physical relationship with the players determined the emotional range of the play, the intimacy or remoteness of the playing and the immediacy or alienation of the response.

The Elizabethan theatre had this advantage, that it was able to capture the spirit of the press of spectators as they thronged round the pageants and mansions (the temporary stages) of medieval street and market-place drama. As a production today tries, by its choice of a smaller theatre, to help the laughter or the warmth of feeling of its drama, so the Elizabethans had this

[1] *Prefaces to Shakespeare, Second Series*, pp. 249–50.

condition of playing built into their playhouses. The development of proscenium arch acting has drained this quality of immediacy from the theatre. Many modern theatres have continued to tier their galleries, but without achieving that sense of having the audience on the point of swarming over the stage.[1]

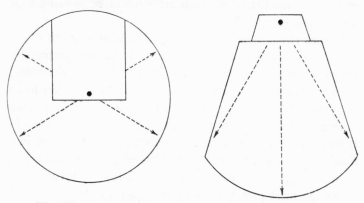

The Elizabethan and Victorian actor/audience relationship

A playhouse which permits at one moment the declamation of an actor, and at the next a whisper delivered in subtle tones but still heard, not only encourages adventurous patterns within a scene or even within a speech, but also promotes the speed of speech, which can make a slight variation of tone or hesitation of voice a moment of exciting drama. Thus there are times when Henry V can be revered from afar, and times when he and the spectator become one.

The pressure which intimacy puts upon an audience is a special factor in itself. The spectator is compelled to pay a closer attention to what is said and done on the stage. In intimate conditions he gives a wider range of attention to the actors, calling upon otherwise untapped sources of sympathy and response.

In his turn the actor must satisfy the range of effects such an

[1] In the Elizabethan theatre some 70 per cent of the house was overlooking the stage from the galleries (J. C. Adams's estimate in *The Globe Playhouse*, 2nd ed., p. 88).

audience asks. He will be required to use his voice in every shade, and his body with great flexibility: there is no better test of acting ability than a mature play by Shakespeare, and, conceivably, no more exacting playhouse than the type of open-stage theatre for which it was written. There would be many moments when the Elizabethan actor would be working as if under a microscope.

In such circumstances, arguments as to whether a few of the audience on occasion sat behind the actors fall into proportion. Down at the foot of the platform, in the middle of the house, the actor would be playing to an audience he would feel to be all about and above him. More than this, he would be playing to an audience in close communion with him, one which would at times revive the medieval sense of physical involvement in a ritual performance, and which would at others invite that actor-audience rapport associated with twentieth-century revue.

For the most part, good sight-lines, good acoustics, a good relationship with the actors: this would sum up the Elizabethan playgoer's assessment of the qualities of his playhouse. Yet these qualities were achieved in a theatre seating almost as many as the largest Victorian theatre built in London—conservative estimates for the Globe provide for over 2,000 spectators.

### THE FOCUS OF THE PLATFORM

It is difficult today to grasp the working conditions of the Elizabethan actors' platform. The modern theatre has little to offer of quite its dimensions, and nothing of its acting depth. Its width compares favourably with any proscenium opening in London today. Covent Garden Opera House has a stage width of 44 feet; this is the widest proscenium opening in London, and compares closely with the Fortune width of 43 feet. Only the width of the wall-to-wall end-stage of the Mermaid Theatre, without a proscenium arch, exceeds this, at 50 feet. But what modern stage can boast a working depth like the Fortune's $27\frac{1}{2}$ feet without a dead area? To sense something of these dimensions, one should stand in one half of a tennis doubles court (39 by 36 feet).

# The Focus of the Platform

Such a platform is not to be considered as an annexe to another acting area, it is no 'apron' attached to a more important and focal part of the structure. It was the space for the play's chief business, reaching into the middle of the house. The merit of the projection of this platform lay in the combination of depth with elevation. De Witt's drawing suggests that the stage juts out at the audience. It was this which allowed the quick access of the actor into the middle of the house, with lines like

> Open your ears; for which of you will stop
> The vent of hearing when loud Rumour speaks?
> (Induction, 2 *Henry IV*)

> Hence! home, you idle creatures, get you home:
> Is this a holiday? (Flavius, *Julius Caesar*)

> Banish'd?...Ha, ha, O Democritus thy gods
> That govern the whole world! (Lodovico, *The White Devil*)

> Gentlemen, have a little patience...
> (Stage-Keeper, *Bartholomew Fair*)

> No bouse? nor no tobacco?
> (Wellborn, *A New Way to Pay Old Debts*)

The platform's vitality derived from this quality of its central control of the house: the immediately felt contact with the spectator, the absence of an inflexible 'fourth wall' of darkness to which actors play in a modern theatre. The audience was not there to counterfeit its participation in the play, like that watching a Victorian melodrama. It was caught up in an act of creative collaboration.

Here also was a stage which could contain its action and yet liberate its movement and strengthen its impact. The players could design their manoeuvres with a balletic choreography in the knowledge that space itself would make visual meaning. We shall see how Shakespeare used this facility, not merely to accommodate the business of battle scenes and street crowds, nor to stage sword duels or dance patterns, nor to exploit the Elizabethan love of pageantry and procession, but to guide a single figure over 1,000 square feet of empty platform, to assert a visual irony by dividing the platform between contrasted characters and groups of characters, enforcing three-dimensional patterns of intimacy and remoteness, and regrouping his players to emphasize changing centres of interest. It has been said that Elizabethan drama tends to be asphyxiated in the proscenium picture-frame: Shakespeare's planning in depth may go some way towards explaining why this is so.

In these conditions the platform was the actor's first piece of stage equipment, the region upon which the great part of his work would be done. The reason why so few stage directions in Elizabethan drama indicate in which part of the playhouse the action was to take place was because it was assumed that the platform itself provided the primary base for effective theatrical communication.

The stage-posts, which in some theatres supported the hut and roof over the stage, do not call for more than cursory reference. The Swan drawing shows pillars on its stage, but according to the contract the Hope was to have its heavens 'to be borne or carryed without any postes or supporters to be fixed or sett uppon the saide stage'. The contract suggests that, although they had served at the Swan, which was the model for the Hope, the posts had become dispensable items, if not for the safe structure of the building, then certainly for the actors. Pillars would not have allowed clear sight-lines, and would clumsily and permanently have segmented the main acting area. Nor is it possible to identify them in Shakespeare's text. Such lines as 'Go, Sir Andrew; scout me for him at the corner of the orchard like a bum-baily' (*Twelfth Night*, III, iv, 180–1), or 'He can come no other way but by this hedge-corner' (*All's Well That Ends Well*, IV, i, 1–2), or 'I'll meet you at the turn' (*Timon of Athens*, V, i, 46) probably indicate corners of the stage. When Cranford Adams and Ronald Watkins urge that stage-posts were used as trees (for pinning up Orlando's verses in *As You Like It*, for example) the argument is shaky, since there is evidence that property trees stood ready in the tiring-house.

The presence of a stage-trap is more certain. From medieval times to those of Faustus's devils and dragons in Marlowe's play written about 1589, a trap denoted an entrance from the underworld and hell-mouth, and was usually associated with the use of thunder and fireworks to make smoke and flame. Scattered through Shakespeare's plays are scenes in which it may have played its part: Joan de Pucell's familiar spirits are 'culled/ Out of the powerful regions under earth' (*1 Henry VI*, v, iii, 10–11); the Spirit that 'riseth' for Mother Jordan the witch is subsequently commanded by Bolingbroke to 'Descend to darkness and the burning lake!' (*1 Henry VI*, I, iv, 39). The trap may have come into play for the Ghosts in *Richard III*, v, iii; for the ghost of Hamlet's father who 'cries under the stage' (*Hamlet*, I, v); for Ophelia's grave from which poor Yorick's skull is pitched and into which Laertes and Hamlet must leap (v, i); for Banquo's ghost (*Macbeth*, III, iv), for Macbeth's Witches and their apparitions (I, i; I, iii; IV, i); for the grave of the wretched Oswald scratched up by Edgar 'here in the sands' (*King Lear*, IV, vi); for Timon's discovery of treasure when he digs for food—'Earth, yield me roots' (*Timon of Athens*, IV, iii, 23); and perhaps even for the sea from which Pericles's fishermen drag the 'rusty armour' (*Pericles*, II, i).

The platform proper was the mainspring of Shakespeare's theatre. He grew aware of the intensifying value for his scene-building of the distance in depth, which could be shortened and lengthened by the movement of the players to and from the hub of the wheel. Borrowing the convention from medieval and Tudor mansion staging, he found he could accelerate the succession of scenes on his stage, and even run two or three in parallel simultaneously, using the eye of the beholder to perceive their irony. He was never under the necessity of having to fill the expanse of this platform with set and lighting, nor aware that his successors might wish that the stage should represent in graphic detail a particular place: his attention could be dedicated to accentuating the value of his characters, whether solo, in pairs or in groups.

### A PAIR OF PERMANENT DOORS

It would be an embarrassment to the modern stage to suffer two symmetrically arranged doors, whether upstage, as in the Elizabethan theatre, or downstage, as in the proscenium arch of the Restoration and Georgian theatres. The conventionality of the Elizabethan stage doors was another indication of a substantially different kind of theatre from our own.

That these doors were in constant use is shown by such common phrases as 'open the door', 'go to the door', 'at the door', and so on. On a number of occasions stage directions refer to the two doors together, when they are to help to formalize the stage, thus:

*Alarum. Enter a Son that hath killed his Father, at one door: and a Father that hath killed his Son at another door.*

(*3 Henry VI*, II, v, 54)

Here the nature of civil war is symbolically emphasized by the symmetry of the entrances.

*Enter, at one door, King Henry, Exeter, Bedford, Warwick, and other Lords; at another, Queen Isabel, the (French) King, the Duke of Burgundy, and other French.* (*Henry V*, V, ii)

In this scene, two opposed sides are visually divided and then joined.

*Flourish. Alarum. A retreat is sounded. Enter at one door Cominius with the Romans: at another door Marcius, with his arm in a scarf.*

(*Coriolanus*, I, ix)

This points Marcius's individual valour at the gates of Corioli. In all such double entrances, the doors divide the players into two groups before they are brought together. Particularly in scenes of war and politics, the doors separate characters according to their place of origin, their roles and attitudes: the English from the French, the Romans from the British. They could also separate characters at the end of a scene, as when Bertram sends his newly married Helena 'home, where I will never come' through one door, and promptly slips away through the other (*All's Well That Ends Well*, II, v).

## A Pair of Permanent Doors

Sometimes they would represent the doors of a house in a realistic way. When Shylock bids Jessica 'lock up my doors' (*The Merchant of Venice*, II, v, 29), and again, 'Do as I bid you, shut doors after you' (II, v, 53), these are an actor's reference to the actual stage doors. Shylock's injunctions transform the façade of the tiring-room into the façade of his house, all in preparation for the scene which follows, in which Jessica throws her father's ducats down to Lorenzo in the 'street' below (II, vi).

At other times the doors could 'disappear' from the mind's eye, especially when they had to serve for entrances through imaginary trees and glades, as in the wood near Athens. The stage direction in *A Midsummer Night's Dream* at II, i, 59 is both amusing and revealing:

*Enter the King of the Fairies, at one door, with his train; and the Queen, at another, with hers.*

Not only is their quarrel suggested by the division, but since the wood is to be thronged with fairies for this formal confrontation, both doors are used to get them all on quickly. The permanent presence of the two upstage doors in their symmetry enabled the actors to behave both ritualistically and naturally, and the Elizabethan stage could mix its elements of symbolism with its realism.

The force of the upstage doors is only to be felt in relation to the depth of the platform. When the actors' term 'an effective entrance' is heard, we commonly think of an actor breaking into the action on the stage by a sudden appearance, the other players so grouped as to throw the eye towards the preselected spot. Every entrance was potentially an effective entrance on the Elizabethan stage, on which the actor might walk the depth of the platform to get into touch with the audience, being given space and time to demonstrate his mood and character as he approached. It will be seen how frequently Shakespeare guides our attention with a 'Look where he comes' at the appropriate moment. And recognizing the effectiveness of the width of the upstage area, with its two widely separated doors, he was free to devise contrasting movements on entrance and exit, on occasion using the 50 foot diagonal depth of the platform to reinforce an effect.

No mention is made in this account of Shakespeare's stagecraft of a supposed 'inner stage' or 'study', thought by some to have been built into the upstage façade. An actor was unlikely to play a scene upstage in a confined space when 30 feet of platform divided him from his audience and stretched invitingly before him. Indeed, throughout the seventeenth and well into the eighteenth century, the actors continued to play downstage to the audience, and not among the flats, or scenic wing pieces, which were later to fill in the background to the acting area.

The idea of an inner stage is convenient because it seems to explain the development of the proscenium arch in Restoration times, and to account for the presence of certain scenes which seem to be representational in the manner of Victorian realistic drama: these are scenes which invite the imagination to supply interiors—a room, closet, pavilion, bower, chapel, cottage, tent, prison, bedchamber, cave or vault; or scenes which disclose a substantial property like a tomb or an altar, a table or a bed. When the word 'study' is found, as in *'They knock and Titus opens his study door'* in *Titus Andronicus*, v, ii, in practice it is an acting direction to the player. Bulky properties were probably pushed out from a stage door or a curtain hung for the occasion. Middleton's *A Chaste Maid in Cheapside* has the striking direction, *'A bed thrust out upon the stage, Allwit's wife in it'*.

The occasions in Shakespeare when some upstage concealment or discovery is called for can be satisfied by the use of such a curtain. In *Romeo and Juliet*, IV, iii, Juliet *'falls upon her bed within the curtains'*—referring either to a hanging or to the drapes of a four-poster. Her tomb in Capulet's vault is set behind a curtain: 'Seal up the mouth of outrage for a while' (v, iii, 216). *The Merchant of Venice* has a curtain to conceal Portia's caskets:

> Go, draw aside the curtains, and discover
> The several caskets to this noble prince. (II, vii)

When in *1 Henry IV* Falstaff hides, he is discovered by Poins 'fast asleep behind the arras, and snorting like a horse' (II, iv, 519). He hides again in *The Merry Wives of Windsor* at III, iii, 85: 'She shall not see me. I will ensconce me behind the arras'. In *Hamlet*, Claudius and Polonius eavesdrop on Hamlet and Ophelia upon Polonius's 'We will bestow ourselves' (III, i, 44) and 'let's withdraw, my lord' (line 54), presumably behind the same 'arras' (mentioned in the First Quarto) through which Hamlet kills Polonius at III, iv, 23. The Folio has the unusual stage direction at the end of the scene, '*Exit Hamlet tugging in Polonius*', as if Hamlet had still to pull him offstage. In *Cymbeline*, II, ii, we find the direction '*Enter Imogen, in her bed*'. A curtain withdrawn would effect this type of entrance most comfortably, like Desdemona's in *Othello*, v, ii.

It is uncomplicated: an arras to sleep or to die behind, a space for an eavesdropper to hide in, a cloak to mask a special property, or (in Jonson's play) a curtain for Volpone to 'peep over' (v, ii)—these needs can be met by a curtain, one either permanently hung from the projecting edge of the balcony between the doors or improvised for the production in hand. In Thomas Kyd's *The Spanish Tragedy*, IV, iii, we read that Hieronimo actually '*knocks up the curtain*' to conceal Horatio's body. There is a danger in making this curtain into a structure of timbers and hangings as immobile as the mythical inner stage itself.

Richard Hosley argues that 'Discoveries in the Globe plays are primarily shows of persons or things themselves inherently interesting. They are never (as in the proscenium-arch theatre) conveniences for the sake of arranging furniture out of sight of the audience'.[1] The curtain might well be a colourful adjunct to the stage wall, but there is no apparent attempt at making it a scenic backcloth, and it is never the traverse or curtain hung halfway downstage within the proscenium arch which William Poel and some other modern directors have used for the spatially destructive convenience of suggesting a scene change. C. W. Hodges has emphasized that no 'important phase of action was

---

[1] 'The Discovery-Space in Shakespeare's Globe', *Shakespeare Survey 12*, p. 45.

sustained *behind* the curtain line',[1] and this is reasonable: the player who could act in depth would not take kindly to acting on dead ground.

To have a permanent balcony built behind their platform must have afforded the Elizabethan players some satisfaction. Enterprising designers today go to great lengths to construct such a second acting level, even on the shallow stage behind the arch: they are content with the visual vitality this lends a production, although they are robbed of stage depth, although the actors may be mountaineering without pointing the play, and although within the arch a balcony seems a piece of representational and obtrusive 'scenery'. Yet a second level is a valuable asset: even to stand on a step or a chair can lend a dominance to the actor's presence and a strength to his speech. A player set on Shakespeare's balcony was sometimes there to bring a touch of *vraisemblance* to the scene, as when a lady stood at a window or a soldier on a wall; he was often there to enhance the significance of a speech other than a soliloquy; but he was never there to provide a change or rotation of acting areas, or that general visual variety we today associate with crowd scenes in complicated sets in musical comedy. Speech from the balcony is essentially linked with the action on the platform.

There is undisputed evidence for this useful feature. A second level was as natural to the medieval pageant as it was to the Elizabethan hall, and it is clear in the Swan sketch. '*Enter above*' or '*aloft*' is a common stage direction throughout the period, sometimes with mention of a '*window*'. The window is probably not a separate acting area, but at most an arrangement for a particular play.

The following selection of examples of the balcony in Shakespeare will suggest the range of uses to which the second level was put. For *1 Henry VI*, I, vi–II, i, the siege of Orleans, we read, '*Enter on the walls La Pucelle, Dauphin, Reignier,*

[1] *The Globe Restored*, p. 54.

*Alençon and Soldiers'*, and Joan cries 'Advance our waving colours on the walls'. When the English have set their scaling-ladders against the balcony, *'The French leap over the walls in their shirts'* at II, i, 38. A company of acrobats would not be ashamed of a leap of some ten feet on to the platform. In *Romeo and Juliet*, II, v, for the scene of Juliet's bedroom, the First Quarto has *'Enter Romeo and Juliet at the window'*, and the Second Quarto *'Enter Romeo and Juliet aloft'*—two terms for the same acting place. At line 42 the First Quarto has *'He goeth down'*. There is no need to assume that the long interview with the family that follows would also be on the balcony: Juliet could join her mother on the platform with 'Madam, I am not well' at line 68. In *Richard II*, at III, iii, 61, Richard enters on the walls of Flint Castle to address Northumberland below, until

NORTHUMBERLAND. ...may it please you to come down?
RICHARD. Down, down I come, like glist'ring Phaethon,

and the platform has imperceptibly become 'the base court' *within* the castle walls. In *King John*, IV, iii, *'Enter Arthur on the walls'*, from which he leaps to his death: 'The wall is high, and yet will I leap down'. For the Forum scene, in *Julius Caesar*, III, ii, we hear that 'The noble Brutus is ascended' (line 11) and Antony is invited to 'go up' (line 65). Where else but to the balcony, commanding the crowded platform? For the scene of Cleopatra's monument, *Antony and Cleopatra*, IV, xv, we read *'Enter Cleopatra and her Maids aloft'* and *'They heave Antony aloft to Cleopatra'* at line 37. There must have been many ways for an ingenious stage-manager to satisfy this latter direction with steps, rostra or other aids, and there is no reason to doubt the use of the balcony which was there available.[1]

The uses of a balcony as a semi-scenic device are clear. When it is not wanted for musicians or trumpeters it can serve a scene

---

[1] J. W. Saunders has ingeniously suggested in 'Vaulting the Rails', *Shakespeare Survey 7*, ed. A. Nicoll, that here *'aloft'* may mean the platform to which Antony is lifted from the yard. However, if space on the balcony is cramped, the scene of Antony's death is one which calls for a minimum of movement, and its ritualistic importance would be pointed by placing it prominently on the upper level.

vividly: Silvia, Juliet, Jessica, Brabantio and Henry VIII need a window; Orleans, Rouen, Bordeaux, Angiers, Harfleur, Corioli and Athens need walls and battlements.

*The Taming of the Shrew*, Induction, ii ('*Enter aloft the drunkard with attendants*') offers a more unusual case, since Christopher Sly is watching and commenting on the platform action as if he were a member of the audience: 'Would 'twere done!'. Such a commentary, partly external to the play, may have found its counterpart in other scenes inviting speech from the balcony, as when Macbeth invokes the night:

> Come, seeling night,
> Scarf up the tender eye of pitiful day...
>
> (*Macbeth*, III, ii, 46)

while 'night's black agents' could be a cue for the Murderers to take up their places on the platform below. Macbeth is in character again, and they are at his command.

In effect, the balcony came naturally to hand when simultaneous staging was wanted, as when Proteus addresses Silvia on the balcony while overheard by the Host and the unhappy Julia (*Two Gentlemen of Verona*, IV, ii), and probably when Diomedes addresses Cressida while overheard by Ulysses and the unhappy Troilus (*Troilus and Cressida*, V, ii). The control of a crowd called for the balcony, as when Richard III must speak to the citizens of London, and probably when the Prince of Verona puts a stop to the street brawling in *Romeo and Juliet*. Scenes of siege would use the balcony, and thus at once identify the rival parties inside and outside the city and extend the spectacle of battle. When a full stage is required, Shakespeare must manage a visually complex acting area, and it is then that he finds the second level helpful.

Twice in Shakespeare the phrase '*on the top*' is found, which suggests that there may have been a third level, a 'musicians' gallery', in the playhouse façade. At *1 Henry VI*, III, ii, 25, '*Enter Pucelle on the top, thrusting out a torch, burning*'. This is Joan's signal to the French from Rouen, with a speech of three lines. At the other end of Shakespeare's career, we read in *The*

*Tempest*, III, iii, 17, '*Solemn and strange music: and Prosper on the top, invisible*'. Thus Prospero dispenses his magic, again with very few words. The notion of another gallery is attractive, since it would make the façade of the tiring-house an acting area in the vertical plane. It would provide a home for the musicians as well as some scenic suggestion of crow's nest, tower or turret. Yet '*on the top*' may be synonymous with '*above*' or '*aloft*', and the idea of a third level remains speculative.

If the use of a high balcony for special visual and sound effects is just possible, the presence of flying machinery in the heavens above the platform was quite likely. Again it is the artlessness of this that offers the playwright his imaginative opportunities. A throne is wanted centre-stage, and as Jonson observes with disgust in his Prologue to *Every Man in His Humour*, it creaks down from above. An actor has to play Jupiter descending from the clouds (*Cymbeline*, V, iv), and he is winched down in a car on the end of a rope.

However, for the Elizabethans the use of the gallery or the heavens was more a matter of convention than illusion. We pass, therefore, from this summary of the Elizabethan theatre's mechanics of staging to its mechanics of belief.

# STAGING AND ACTING CONVENTIONS

## CONVENTION IN SHAKESPEARE'S THEATRE

An efficient staging convention is properly something that the spectator forgets as soon as the processes of theatre are under way. The Elizabethan spectator took for granted matters of symbolism in character or dress, and ignored the play's elasticity of place and time. Dr Johnson testified to Shakespeare's practical art, which required that the rules of neo-classical criticism be amended before the plays should be censured, and that the spectators in the theatre should be the judges of the merit of Shakespeare's rejection of the unities. Johnson's famous dictum, 'The truth is, that the spectators are always in their senses, and know, from the first act to the last, that the stage is only a stage, and that the players are only players', for all it needs judicious qualification, might have been a piece of post-Brechtian criticism. The spectators know that it is theatre, not life, but they choose not to know. When Coleridge pursued the case further, he observed that 'The very nakedness of the stage was advantageous, —for the drama thence became something between recitation and a re-presentation'. He recognized more particularly in these words the framework of convention within which Elizabethan drama worked, one which allowed it to range between symbolism and naturalism.

When in *Macbeth*, I, v, Shakespeare's audience saw Lady Macbeth reading the letter from her husband, they did not pause to consider that now, suddenly, the scene had changed from Forres to Inverness, from Duncan's palace to Macbeth's castle. The change had been accomplished before Lady Macbeth made her entrance. The audience had heard Macbeth say to the King,

> I'll be myself the harbinger, and make joyful
> The hearing of my wife with your approach,

(I, iv, 45–6)

and the playwright would have upset them had the first lady to enter reading a letter *not* been Macbeth's wife, although they would justly have been surprised at the kind of joy they saw her exhibit. Speech and context of situation were imaginatively one whole. It is a modern habit to query the place of the action, here an irrelevance for which Shakespeare cared nothing. He wrote a drama that created its own atmosphere and identified its own locality, if it needed to.

He mocked the exertions of both silly realism and fatuous symbolism in his burlesque of the preparations for 'Pyramus and Thisbe'. Peter Quince needs moonlight for his lovers, so Bottom, keen amateur student of the drama that he is, calls for the real thing:

A calendar, a calendar...look in the almanac...find out moonshine, find out moonshine. (*A Midsummer Night's Dream*, III, i, 48–9)

Quince has a second problem, to provide a wall with a chink for the lovers to talk through. Again Bottom is quick with a ridiculous solution, although this time a symbolic one:

Some man or other must present wall: and let him have some plaster, or some loam, or some rough-cast about him, to signify wall; and let him hold his fingers thus... (62–5)

To see Robin Starveling or Tom Snout smothered in real plaster is to understand the muddle of ideas in Bottom's head.

In holding his mirror up to nature, Shakespeare was reflecting general truths for his audience to recognize with the minimum of imaginative acrobatics and distracting obstacles. When he wanted to show actuality, he did so with that compulsive particularity found so often in his work: to measure cruelty and pain, blood must spill when Gloucester's eyes are put out; for Rosalind to enact a girl in love, she must see Orlando's verses pinned to a tree. Having caught the spectator's attention by particularities, he swiftly shows him human responses in their general image. The detail of verisimilitude in Shakespeare is not an obstacle but a directive for the imagination.

The simple sweep of the Elizabethan platform not only lent the playwright the freedom he wanted, but also cleared the mind of the spectator for conjuring up visions. By its nature, Shakespeare's was a stage which invited the spectator to 'play with his fancies', as the Prologue to *Henry V* puts it. It is when the imagination is unrestricted that the playwright's skill in curbing and directing it takes on qualities of magic. The actor's convention and the poetic drama are in this way joined; the playwright is the go-between diligently arranging the match, exploiting first the actor, then the spectator; first the wooer, then the wooed.

'It is essential that a work of art should be self-consistent, that an artist should consciously or unconsciously draw a circle beyond which he does not trespass: on the one hand actual life is always the material, and on the other hand an abstraction from actual life is a necessary condition to the creation of the work of art'. So wrote T. S. Eliot in criticism of the conventions in Elizabethan drama. 'An actor in an Elizabethan play is either too realistic or too abstract in his treatment.'[1] Nevertheless, the freedom of Shakespeare's stage and his lack of consistency, in Eliot's sense, permitted his play to pass between particularity and generality, between the real and the abstract, building an experience measurable against the detail of real life, yet finally moving into those areas which constitute good theatre.

## PROPERTIES AND SYMBOLS

This flexibility is seen at its simplest in Shakespeare's handling of two less abstract elements of theatrical convention, properties and costume. No theatre has done without properties, whether scenic set-pieces or devices to help the actor create the action. The Elizabethan theatre was no exception. Shakespeare inherited a lively tradition of using scenic emblems, which he used like other conventional equipment, both as adjuncts to acting and aids to the imagination. When he wanted, even a hand property could have its significance intensified to point his theme, the spectator's attention being drawn to it until the object acquired formidable moral or political qualities.

[1] *Selected Essays*, pp. 111–12.

Glynne Wickham suggests[1] that a tent used emblematically in the medieval way could be transformed into a throne, a pavilion, a house, a palace, a temple, a castle or a city by some decorative device like a vane or a shield. Mansion staging (the setting of localized stations upon the same stage) along such easy lines would be in keeping with our image of the fluidity of the Elizabethan stage: it permitted the kind of real-and-unreal setting of the stage and released the platform for simultaneous scene playing without crushing it with the weight of carpentry; it enabled stage-hands to shift a property while the players were still on, and kept the mechanics of production and décor light and mobile. The traditional thinking behind mansion staging, which permitted the arena to represent parts of the globe or the Kingdom of God, was readily assimilable to the planning for the formal outlines of the platform. With its symmetrical doors and permanent balcony, the platform supplied a spacious neutral acting space over which the actors could pass, freely creating meaningfully localized areas. The Elizabethan stage could embrace effects of simultaneous staging, linking all its scenes without changing the formal appearance of the platform and the façade behind it.

It was also traditional to introduce scenic tokens convenient to the stage: trees, arbours, pavilions, monuments and thrones, as well as many others found in Henslowe's inventory of the properties he kept in his Rose theatre in 1598 and in the Revels Office books, those accounts of costumes and properties supplied by the Master of the Queen's Revels for performances at Court. The solidity of these properties need not be doubted: a tree and an arbour had to be substantial enough to seem to bear a hanging man (as in *The Spanish Tragedy* and *Every Man Out of His Humour*), and strong enough to climb (Berowne in *Love's Labour's Lost*, IV, iii). The box-tree in *Twelfth Night*, II, v, was probably sizable enough to conceal Toby, Andrew and Fabian, all three.

Yet in Shakespeare's hands the objective limitations of the

---

[1] *Early English Stages*, vol. II, part I, p. 298.

properties are transcended, and as symbols their meaning grows. His was the same theatrical imagination as Christopher Marlowe's, whose Faustus hears the striking of a clock while in imagination he counts the minutes of an eternity in hell. So for Shakespeare a property was a dramatic opportunity—think only of Macbeth's dagger, the real weapon slung at his waist, the 'air-drawn' fantasy a chance to plumb his mind and compel us to visualize the murder we do not actually see.

*Richard II*, IV, i, is a scene in which Shakespeare seems to be experimenting with his properties as cues for poetry. Thus the King's business with the mirror:

> Give me that glass, and therein will I read...
> No deeper wrinkles yet? hath sorrow struck
> So many blows upon this face of mine,
> And made no deeper wounds? O, flatt'ring glass,
> Like to my followers in prosperity,
> Thou dost beguile me!...
> A brittle glory shineth in this face,
> As brittle as the glory is the face,
> For there it is, cracked in a hundred shivers.     (276–89)

Here he dashes the glass to the ground. This is an actor's piece, climactic with the rhetorical repetitions characteristic of Richard, and the property mirror is a first-rate aid to him. Yet for the sense, the property is especially apt: the speech is of self-scrutiny, and Shakespeare supplies a visible symbol for a self-conscious and over-sensitive man. Later, other sensitive men, like Cassius and Hamlet, speak also of the glass with which to 'see the inmost part', but for them Shakespeare is content with verbal imagery. For Richard he has made the feeling of the actor and the point of the speech theatrically objective.

The royal crown of the King of England was an early and obvious symbolic property, both for Richard in his contest with Bolingbroke (*Richard II*, IV, i, 181 ff.) and for Prince Henry. Hal moralizes upon it in the presence of his dying father, for whom it is the 'troublesome bedfellow', a 'polished perturbation', the 'golden care' (*2 Henry IV*, IV, v, 21 ff.). Its momentary theft starts that great discussion between monarch and heir apparent on the responsibilities of rule.

*Hamlet* is a play imbued with the imagery of mortality, and this is pointed by the Clowns who dig Ophelia's grave. The property skulls prompt Hamlet's comments, first cynical, then of feeling and understanding, as he fingers all that is left of Yorick. When he realizes it is Ophelia's grave, he speaks with genuine sorrow, in his anger modulating into a parody of Laertes's high-flown expression of grief. The acting, the illustration of a theme, the development of the action and the particularizing of the character, first in his intimate relationship with Yorick and then by reflection with Ophelia, whose remains would match his and lie in the same place, are married in the scene by the use of the properties.

The mature plays are mature in their handling of such objective emblems, and the control of the handkerchief and the taper in *Othello* is particularly sure. Coming at the right moment in Othello's progress to corruption, the handkerchief, that 'trifle light as air' and one so casually dropped, is magnified fantastically by the tortured mind. Its meaning is reinforced by the exotic poetry that seems to weave the magic in its web. It obsesses Othello to the last, while its triviality increasingly belittles the nobility of the soldier we first met. Again, the actor takes up the taper which is at once to mark the dead of night and the Moor's impulse to offer prayer, and its visual suggestion of light and darkness becomes associated with the issue of the life and death of a Christian soul and the murder of a young woman in her vital beauty:

> But once put out thy light,
> Thou cunning'st pattern of excelling nature,
> I know not where is that Promethean heat
> That can thy light relume. (v, ii, 10–14)

This taper makes of her death-bed a sacrificial altar, one upon which man's love of life and hope of heaven are annihilated.

33

### A WARDROBE FOR SCENE AND SYMBOL

No theatre has ignored the contribution to mood and meaning that costume can make, and in Elizabeth's time the actor's wardrobe was lavish. A rich tradition of splendour of costume had been handed down through Tudor times, deriving from the pride in presentation belonging to the craft guild players of the Mystery Cycles. Nor could there be amateurishness in an intimate theatre: conviction of authenticity prevailed.

However, enough is known from Henslowe, the Revels Office, contemporary German accounts of English tours and from internal evidence for it to be said that, while the players cared much for magnificence, historical or national accuracy did not bother them. Hamlet wore doublet and hose, and Cleopatra dressed like a wealthy Elizabethan lady. Although for mockery a particularly topical note might be introduced, as for Le Beau and Osric, a non-committal contemporary dress stressed both the relevance and the timelessness of the subjects.

Where a play or a scene is distinguished by straightforward contrasts of attitude, costume underlines the differences for immediate apprehension by the spectator. *The Merchant of Venice* hints at the Elizabethan view of Venetian luxury which the Gentile merchants displayed; and set against them are the sombre gaberdines of Shylock, Tubal and the Jewish community. Shakespeare marks the contrast at the Battle of Agincourt in *Henry V* between the tired English in their 'war-worn coats' and 'the confident and over-lusty French' boasting of their splendid armour, a familiar theatrical preliminary to the ironic victory of the Englishmen. A visual contrast between opposing forces was a commonplace in the chronicle plays, as also between the Scots and English in *Macbeth*, the Romans and the Volsces in *Coriolanus* and the Romans and the British in *Cymbeline*. *Antony and Cleopatra* offers an interesting extension of this principle. Costume reminds the spectator constantly of the play's seesaw issues when the formal Roman soldiery is visually opposed to the colourful Egyptians. Dress is a visible reminder

34

throughout the play of a masculine Rome at discord with a feminine Egypt.

The playwright probably had less control over this selection of costume than the wardrobe master, but in particular matters of dress Shakespeare revealed his eye for the effect that colour and cut can imply. There is no forgetting the comic entrance of Juliet's Nurse to the cries of the young gallants, 'Here's goodly gear! A sail, a sail!' (*Romeo and Juliet*, II, iv, 98). In visually conceived scenes he demonstrates his flair for using costume to dramatic ends. King Henry V strikes a note of personal distinction from both the English and the gaudy French when he borrows Sir Thomas Erpingham's cloak (*Henry V*, IV, i) to humble himself and his thoughts with the prosaic soldiers round the camp-fire. The colossus Caesar shows himself subject to human weakness when he appears clad in a night-gown to hear of Calpurnia's nightmare (*Julius Ceasar*, II, ii). He is seen following a scene of conspiracy made sinister by thunder and lightning and dangerous men with hats 'plucked about their ears,/And half their faces buried in their cloaks' (II, i, 73-4). In another vein, Malvolio cuts a wildly comic figure in his night-gown when he bursts upon Sir Toby's drinking party in the middle of the night (*Twelfth Night*, II, iii).

The situation at the court of Elsinore is immediately apparent as Hamlet sits apart in his 'inky cloak', the mourning of his 'nighted colour' making its persistent rebuke to the showy, oblivious court that lives 'too much in the sun' (*Hamlet*, I, ii). Moreover, when the Prince adopts the undress of his antic disposition, as described by Ophelia (II, i, 74 ff.), both words and dress mock the proprieties of Polonius. Isabella in the white habit of a novice confronts Angelo in the black robes of a judge (*Measure for Measure*, II, ii). Othello the Moor visually denies Iago's cynical description of the 'black ram...tupping your white ewe' when he makes his entrance into a familiar setting dressed like a prince from a remote sun-scorched country (*Othello*, I, ii). Cleopatra robes herself for the stroke of death and her noblest gesture (*Antony and Cleopatra*, V, ii), and both outwits and outshines her enemy. Coriolanus, previously seen only in military finery, must stand proud and angry before the citizens in his despised 'gown of humility'; the incongruity between his soldierly presence and the costume itself is a neat stroke for drama as he stands alone to face an ordeal he loathes (*Coriolanus*, II, iii).

Shakespeare takes the conventional equipment of property and costume and uses them as a way of speaking to the audience. Their strength is sustained for as long as they are displayed on the stage.

### RANGING BETWEEN NATURALISM AND RITUAL

The mixing of naturalism and ritual is also to be seen in the acting conventions. It was typical of the traditional pattern to break through convention altogether. In the Mystery Plays the amateur actors not only addressed the spectators but played among them and spoke for them. In Henry Medwall's highly formal disputation *Fulgens and Lucrece* (1497), a naturalistic link with the real audience is made by the presence of two youths 'A' and 'B', who at the beginning of the play emerge from the crowd of guests at an imaginary banquet, and like the real audience discuss the play about to be seen. In the role of comic servants to the noble suitors wooing Lucrece, their task is to burlesque their masters. This is a descent to naturalism and a manner of burlesque that extends in Shakespeare himself from the drunken presence of Christopher Sly throughout *The Taming of the Shrew* to Falstaff's intimate parodies of warfare, which establish a similarly close link with the spectator.

In the compact Elizabethan theatre this link was always potentially present, and Shakespeare regularly stresses the actuality of the play's experience by naturalistic means. An aside to the audience, a sudden allusion to some topic of the moment, a chance for the company's clown to extemporize, the courteous appeals of Prologue and Epilogue for attention or applause—these bear witness to the direct contact between player and spectator.

Naturalism and intimacy are not interchangeable elements, but the history of the theatre has indicated their interdependence. The physical nearness of the street audiences of the Mystery Plays encouraged a homely and often incongruous demonstration of the Scriptures, as well as a streak of farce. At another extreme, the impact Shakespeare has on television audiences derives from those moments of familiar speech and conduct scattered through his work. Television, from one view the most intimate dramatic medium, cannot accommodate the delivery of ritualistic speech and the photographic representation of formal battle scenes, but the balance has often been redressed by a soliloquy spoken quietly and naturalistically into the camera's eye.

A theatre which could permit both the rant and the whisper encouraged Shakespeare to develop a structural technique which exploited both: early in his career he applied astringent touches to romantic comedy, introducing unsophisticated workmen, for example, into the moonlight of *A Midsummer Night's Dream*. It was predictable that Falstaff and the companions of The Boar's Head should supply the 'control group' of normality for his social study of politics and politicians in *1 Henry IV*. In his early tragedies he learned with what effect simplicity of utterance or silence could mark moments of emotion:

JULIET. Romeo!
ROMEO.          My niëss!
JULIET.                    What o'clock tomorrow
    Shall I send to thee?
ROMEO.                    By the hour of nine.
JULIET. I will not fail. 'Tis twenty year till then.
    I have forgot why I did call thee back.

                              (*Romeo and Juliet*, II, ii, 167–70)

The actress's exercise is to place the pauses in this reproduction of a shy girl's inability to leave her lover. The lyricism had lifted the balcony scene into a region where now these commonplace lines reflect a natural human beauty.

On the other hand, the ritualistic tradition of Shakespeare's forerunners and contemporaries was the Elizabethans' special delight and Shakespeare's forte. He knew how to have his actor strike an attitude: a speech from the throne by Henry V or Caesar, or in comedy a fairy-tale ceremony like choosing a husband by casket as Portia does in *The Merchant of Venice* or by dance as Helena does in *All's Well That Ends Well*; or in tragedy a ritualistic end for Macbeth or Hamlet, where pageantry lends that sense of finality long after the real crisis has passed:

> Let four captains
> Bear Hamlet like a soldier to the stage,
> For he was likely, had he been put on,
> To have proved most royal.     (*Hamlet*, v, ii, 393–6)

So speaks Fortinbras, and '*Exeunt marching: after the which, a peal of ordnance are shot off*'. The dead must be carried off the Elizabethan stage; an added dignity is given to Hamlet's death by the practice of a stage ritual.

### ACTOR AND ATMOSPHERE ON A NEUTRAL STAGE

Whether in naturalistic or ritualistic terms, Shakespeare is quick to anticipate his scene's mood and atmosphere, and for this reason it is difficult to separate descriptive effects from acting opportunities. Every actor must be ready to pass temporarily outside the action of the story. He has to do more than play in character: he has also to play as if he were a chorus, setting and lighting the stage and prompting a response to it. Any character may be called upon to report the place and the time, and even a major character may find himself made the excuse for a word-picture. This convention has the effect of bringing together the action on the stage, the thoughts of the character and the spirit of the scene, ensuring that the final image is received as it was conceived—as a whole.

Shakespeare practises this technique from his earliest plays. *Titus Andronicus*, II, iii, is a scene depicting the adulterous love of Tamora, the revengeful murder of Bassianus and the rape of Lavinia, but these horrors are prepared with simple irony by Titus's incongruous woodland sketch:

> The hunt is up, the morn is bright and grey,
> The fields are fragrant, and the woods are green... (II, ii, 1–2)

This is echoed and enhanced by Tamora herself:

> The birds chaunt melody in every bush,
> The snake lies rolléd in the cheerful sun...
>
> (II, iii, 12–13)

A generation later, he opens *The Tempest* with an enacted ship-wreck, but a minute later is still filling out the impression by choric speech:

> The sky, it seems, would pour down stinking pitch,
> But that the sea, mounting to th'welkin's cheek,
> Dashes the fire out...
>
> (I, ii, 3–5)

Words here take precedence over action, but the supernatural quality of the storm poetry is also a calculated prelude to the island's magic, and is the more fearsome on the lips of Miranda in her pity for those aboard the ship. Word-scenery, character and situation are integrated.

The visualizing power of language is rarely absent, but Shakespeare knows to inform it with a strength drawn from the dramatic situation. A static line of description from Arthur Brooke's *The Tragical History of Romeus and Juliet* reports the dawn thus:

> As yet he saw no day, ne could he call it night,
> With equal force decreasing dark fought with increasing light.

Shakespeare seizes upon this and charges it with urgency. He stresses the conflict of night and day by associating it with the opposing attitudes of a reluctant Juliet and an anxious Romeo, while making more particular the twilit colour of the original:

> JULIET. Wilt thou be gone? It is not yet near day.
> It was the nightingale, and not the lark,
> That pierced the fearful hollow of thine ear...
> ROMEO. It was the lark, the herald of the morn;
> No nightingale. Look, love, what envious streaks
> Do lace the severing clouds in yonder east.
>
> (*Romeo and Juliet*, III, v, 1 ff.)

He puts the moon in the sky at the beginning of *A Midsummer Night's Dream* and sustains its presence by some eighteen reminders throughout the play, incidentally indicating its importance by playing variations upon its range of associations from chastity to romance. By skilful implication, the forest in *As You Like It* is represented as a different kind of place from the wood near Athens. It becomes a 'desert inaccessible,/Under the shade of melancholy boughs' (II, vii, 110–11), suiting the mood of a love-lorn Orlando and creating an Arden that is ambivalently civil and uncivil.

The mature tragedies are more particular in their atmospheric effects, as befits their specific patterns of emotion. The 'civil strife in Heaven' prepares the audience for the civil strife of the politicians in *Julius Caesar*, and this storm is pursued through the night of the conspiracy, to be sharply contrasted with the quiet of Brutus's meditations in his orchard and the dawning of the Ides of March with its reiterated warnings by Artemidorus and the Soothsayer. The preparation for the events of *Macbeth* is scarcely less striking. In supernatural colours the Witches paint and enact the thunder and lightning, the rain and the fog, and make the heath their own. As in *King Lear*, many of the play's characters serve its atmosphere. Through Banquo,

> There's husbandry in heaven,
> Their candles are all out. (II, i, 4–5)

or Macbeth,

> Now o'er the one half-world
> Nature seems dead. (II, i, 49–50)

or Lady Macbeth,

> It was the owl that shrieked, the fatal bellman. (II, ii, 3)

or through the Porter, Lennox, Macduff, the Old Man, Ross, and later through the Murderers themselves, Shakespeare repeatedly strikes the same note, until darkness, evil and the unnatural night impregnate the theatre.

### A NOTE ON SEX AND THE BOY ACTOR

Not unrelated to Shakespeare's way of identifying the spirit of a scene is his handling of women's parts, since he must make a like effort of suggestion to accentuate their femininity. With boys playing the major roles of his heroines—and Rosalind and Cleopatra are as demanding in point of complexity of speaking and acting as any male character he drew—he sought to seduce the spectator with oblique impressions of their sex. He uses, as might be expected, poetry as commentary. The spectator's image of Imogen is seen through Iachimo's sensuality:

> How bravely thou becomest thy bed! fresh lily,
> And whiter than the sheets!... (*Cymbeline*, II, ii, 15 ff.)

To give the opposite effect, he will drench a character in repulsive sexuality, as he does Gertrude on Hamlet's tongue:

>                      Nay, but to live
> In the rank sweat of an enseaméd bed
> Stewed in corruption, honeying, and making love
> Over the nasty sty.          (*Hamlet*, III, iv, 91–4)

The femininity of some of the ladies of the comedies—Portia, Beatrice, Rosalind—is given wings by their buoyant repartee. He will point a few particulars of their sexual individuality, like Juliet's innocent pertness or Lady Macbeth's negative sexuality, and write on as if there were never a doubt that they are women, as modern actresses can verify.

Nevertheless, all the women have to play out their parts with warmth, and sometimes with coquetry. Kisses abound. For the sexual relationship is repeatedly Shakespeare's concern, and it is a Victorian myth that the boy actors were not centrally involved in a sexual situation. Isabella's forbidding habit in the presence of Angelo's lust hardly suppressed the fact of her sex; Desdemona's whiter skin than snow, so admired by black Othello, unquestionably stressed the theme of miscegenation; Cleopatra with her reputation as a bewitcher of emperors, Marina in the loathsome brothel, Imogen in imminent danger of rape, Miranda seeing a young man for the first time—these instances suggest that conveying sexual attractiveness was a condition of the boy player's art.

Here again is Shakespeare substituting for the actuality a

broad theatrical symbolism. The transvestism of the 'breeches parts' in Restoration times and after offered the actresses merely an opportunity to reveal their legs, which were otherwise draped. Shakespeare's transvestism, on the other hand, revealed femininity by emphasizing the differences of mind and behaviour between man and woman, helping us to see something as familiar as sex in a fresh light, through Portia's delight in tricking Bassanio, Rosalind wooing circuitously or Viola pathetically frustrated.

### THE DAYLIGHT CONVENTION

In the public theatre, Shakespeare's drama was played in afternoon daylight, the theatre open to the sky. Yet it is curious to recall that a high proportion of his scenes are set at night-time, whether indoors or out. The whole of *Macbeth* is characteristically a play of shadow and night. Such an effect might seem reasonable had the playwright been able to call upon the skills of the lighting engineer in the modern theatre, but a perverse *tour de force* when it had to be played on a possibly sunlit stage.

The justification is not far to seek. In the terms of the theatrical experience, the overall lighting of an open-air theatre is equivalent to its unlocalized setting. It could suggest everything or nothing, and equally freed the visual imagination of the spectator. Just as radio drama engages the helpful blindness of the listener, so daylight was a challenge to the poet to conjure special illusions. Moreover, if his play was performed indoors, as at Court, the stage and the auditorium were again lit overall, and the same brush which painted Macbeth's 'black and midnight hags' would serve him as well.

A careful use of candles, lanterns and torches assists the verbal creation of the night scenes. These properties would in addition draw attention to the important entrance: Romeo into the vault, Brutus in his orchard, Iago rousing Brabantio from his sleep, Othello approaching Desdemona's bed with the light on his black face, Banquo and Fleance walking into their ambush, Lady Macbeth in her sleep-walking, Gloucester's discovery of

Lear on the heath and Iachimo's sly invasion of Imogen's chamber, where

> The flame o'th'taper
> Bows toward her and would under-peep her lids...
> (*Cymbeline*, II, ii, 19–20)

Shakespeare may also introduce sounds offstage, owls and clocks, bells and cocks, to strengthen the scene's impression; but he never relies upon realistic properties and effects alone.

His ability to call up darkness displays itself from the outset, and it is worth remarking that several of these scenes in the early plays create the night in order to achieve a subsequent contrast of light or day. Richard III's nightmare before Bosworth is built up by many calculated references. The mood of a tormented night prepares the spectator for the appearance of the Ghosts, but it especially creates an ironic tension before the activity of the dawn:

NORFOLK. Arm, arm, my lord; the foe vaunts in the field.
RICHARD. Come, bustle, bustle. Caparison my horse...
> (*Richard III*, v, iii, 288–9)

He so accustoms the spectator to the nocturnal mood in *A Midsummer Night's Dream* that the dawn of the May morning arrives in IV, i with a winding of horns as a surprise and a revelation. In *Henry V*, 'the foul womb of night', as evoked by Chorus and character and camp-fire, creates a quiet suspense before the battle and provides an apt setting for the King's heart-searchings and his prayer to God; but again the audience is roused with the shock of

ORLEANS. The sun doth gild our armour. Up, my lords!
DAUPHIN. Montez à cheval! My horse! varlet! laquais! ha!
> (IV, ii, 1–2)

So completely may Shakespeare conceive a scene in terms of light and dark, that in *Hamlet* he marks a critical moment in the unmasking of Claudius by his cry, 'Give me some light—away!', echoed by Polonius's 'Lights, lights, lights!' (III, ii, 269–70). The confusion of the court and the scurrying of torchbearers have deluded the audience into accepting that nature is subject to the whim of the poet. After the scene in *Macbeth* in which bells and shouts and bold movement stir Macbeth's castle, Shakespeare practises another risky device. He has Ross remind the audience of the daylight convention with the words

> Thou seest the heavens, as troubled with man's act
> Threatens his bloody stage: by th'clock 'tis day,
> And yet dark night strangles the travelling lamp:
> Is't night's predominance, or the day's shame,
> That darkness does the face of earth entomb,
> When living light should kiss it?          (II, iv, 5–10)

This would be overweening did Shakespeare not feel in command of his theatre. His skill here again is a visualizing one, and such chiaroscuro effects are his response to the challenge of writing for the daylight convention.

### THE LOCALIZING CONVENTION

When Shakespeare makes no localizing suggestion in his lines, it is because he requires his arena to remain neutral for dramatic or symbolic reasons. The general emphasis is on costume rather than scenery, on actor rather than setting. The players can quickly create and dismiss the background, so that the spectator may feel directly the confidence between the actor and himself, or apprehend an essential relationship between two or more characters.

Any player is used to place a scene instantly:

> ROSALIND. Well, this is the forest of Arden!
> (*As You Like It*, II, iv, 14)

Often, however, setting and place are indicated economically in the bearing and language of the player in his character: for all that *Antony and Cleopatra* chops between Egypt and Rome, there is never any doubt where the scene is, even if dress did not show it. Antony embraces his mistress with

> Let Rome in Tiber melt, and the wide arch
> Of the ranged empire fall! Here is my space.
> (I, i, 33–4)

and Octavius Caesar greets the spectator with

> From Alexandria
> This is the news: he fishes, drinks and wastes
> The lamps of night in revel. (I, iv, 3–5)

Location is implicit. A fairy embodies in his voice and movement the nature of the lovers' moonlit wood:

> Over hill, over dale,
> Thorough bush, thorough briar...
> (*A Midsummer Night's Dream*, II, i, 2–3)

and by similarly immediate means Ariel captures the spirit of Prospero's island:

> I come
> To answer thy best pleasure; be't to fly,
> To swim, to dive into the fire... to ride
> On the curled clouds... (*The Tempest*, I, ii, 189–92)

Nor in our admiration for the way Lear conjures up his heath in the storm should it be forgotten that others have their share, particularly in such physically racing lines as Edgar's

> Away! The foul fiend follows me!
> Through the sharp hawthorn blow the cold winds...
> (*King Lear*, III, iv, 45–6)

Under the fluid conditions of the Elizabethan stage, to change an imaginary location presented no problem, and players pass without fuss from the 'inside' to the 'outside' of a building (as in *The Merchant of Venice*, IV, i–ii), or from the 'outside' to the 'inside' (as in *Romeo and Juliet*, I, iv–v), from a 'street' to 'the Capitol' (as in *Julius Caesar*, III, i), or from a 'bedroom' to a 'street' (as in *Othello*, IV, ii). Representational drama must account for the place where the actors find themselves. Presentational drama asks only that the actors adjust their relationships with each other; the stage they stand on remains the same. Romeo departs, and Juliet's orchard goes with him; Lady Capulet enters, is joined by Juliet, and Juliet's chamber has passed from the balcony to the platform (*Romeo and Juliet*, III, v).

The stage is as empty or as full, as anchored or as shifting, as particular or as anonymous, as our fancies make it. When

Claudius greets his Council of State, actors and costumes display the pomp of Elsinore and words supply the formal speech for the occasion; but with '*Exeunt all but Hamlet*', the Prince is alone, and where is he then but in a world of obsessive brooding? Again, for how long in the central scenes of *King Lear* does the King remain on a particularized heath before we have been caught up in his despair?

As a problem, the convention of place seems hardly to have entered Shakespeare's conscious mind. That relationships and not localities matter is well illustrated by the scene in which Othello accuses Desdemona of being a whore (*Othello*, IV, ii). The text may suggest that this scene must be acted in some private room—until it is found that it seems to end inappropriately with an exchange between the conspirators Iago and Roderigo. They are joined by Othello, Lodovico, Desdemona and Emilia, and then Desdemona is left to undress for bed (IV, iii). What were Iago and Roderigo doing in her bedroom? By the power of his imagery, Shakespeare had translated the platform into a room in hell, into which Iago fits exactly, and it is in a kind of hell that the innocent wife is unpinned. There is no change of place and no pause in the playing.

There are scenes when Shakespeare's impressionistic localizing puts setting and atmosphere at odds with character and situation, the poet painting his scene in incongruous detail. Thus, by his instruction to his Page, the County Paris prepares the gruesome place in which Juliet's beauty is to shine:

> Under yond yew-trees lay thee all along,
> Holding thin ear close to the hollow ground;
> So shall no foot upon the churchyard tread,
> Being loose, unfirm with digging up of graves,
> But thou shalt hear it.     (*Romeo and Juliet*, V, iii, 3–7)

Whether it is the romantic Rosalind restless in the restricting court, or the courtiers incongruously disporting themselves in Arden; whether the inflexible Octavius Caesar caught awkwardly in the exotic world of Cleopatra and Egypt, or Cleopatra visualizing her humiliation in the streets of Rome; whether Polixenes and old Camillo bemused by the youth of the Bohemian country-side in *The Winter's Tale*; whether the chaste Marina trapped in the sordid Metaline brothel in *Pericles*—contrast nourishes the drama, and place and setting are its servants.

Shakespeare's localizing exists for the life of the drama. The spirit of place invades Hamlet's Denmark, or Macbeth's Scotland, or the Vienna of *Measure for Measure*: but in these, Denmark, Scotland or Vienna are used to point the play, dealing in corruption, or violence, or licentiousness. This is not unity of place, but unity of atmosphere.

## DRAMATIZING TIME

For Shakespeare a theoretical 'convention of time' would have had little meaning, and only on a few, careful occasions is time required to enter the conscious mind of his audience. It is a modern habit for an audience to fasten a time pattern upon a play: if a scene is localized and if it is set up with the details of actuality, automatically the drama assumes a chronological time-scheme. Naturalistic presentation thus controls the action in a way which the Elizabethans would have found intolerable. Shakespeare's plays are long one-act plays, and time exists in them only for exploiting. Tempo matters, because plays are written in the fourth dimension, and the speed with which the action passes before the eyes is important; but the clock and the calendar are there only when needed.

A facility for suggesting the mere passage of time was always his. The night passes to the horrors of *Richard III* or the chase of *A Midsummer Night's Dream* by the pointing of a few lines. Even in this early drama, however, such pointing, whether Radcliff's

> The early village cock
> Hath twice done salutation to the morn.
> (*Richard III*, v, iii, 209–10)

or Puck's

> night's swift dragons cut the clouds full fast,
> And yonder shines Aurora's harbinger.
> (*A Midsummer Night's Dream*, III, ii, 379–80)

is also always to direct the audience toward the dénouement to come: Richard's fate at the hands of Richmond, or the hasty pairing of the Athenian lovers. Even such time effects as these are not there for their own sake.

A straightforward temporal pressure is exerted in *Romeo and Juliet*, in which Shakespeare displays his early skill. Arthur Brooke's *Tragical History* dealt in a leisurely narrative covering nine months; Shakespeare's play has its lovers assaulted by time, and its audience with them. Three days are all that Romeo and Juliet are granted, while Juliet's father jocularly fires her suitor's ardours:

CAPULET. ...bid her, mark you me, on Wednesday next—
   But soft, what day is this?
PARIS.                          Monday, my lord.
CAPULET. Monday, ha, ha; well, Wednesday is too soon;
   O'Thursday let it be—o'Thursday, tell her,
   She shall be married to this noble earl.          (III, iv, 17–21)

Subject to a grim irony, a confident daughter asks her father's pardon, only to find that he lops off a further precious day, one which proves fatal:

> Send for the County: go tell him of this.
> I'll have this knot knit up tomorrow morning.
>
> (IV, ii, 23–4)

Shakespeare continues to press the point with repeated reminders: 'we'll to church tomorrow'——'prepare up him/Against tomorrow', while the Friar vainly tries to warn Romeo in time. Chance will blast the fortunes of the lovers, although time has been tightening the net since the Prince banished Romeo in III, i. It seems not a moment before the wedding morning is upon them, and old Capulet bustles in to rouse the family with

> Come, stir, stir, stir! The second cock hath crowed.
>
> (IV, iv, 3)

until the stage is alive with the servants of an excited household. All this in twenty minutes' playing time.

Time becomes an instrument of Shakespeare's theatre, and

its passing is regularly linked with the emotion of his scenes. By hints and suggestions the night passes in the scene of Cassio's undoing (*Othello*, II, iii), but a scene which begins lightly with dancing, sport and the celebration of Othello's nuptials grows swiftly to a crisis of drunkenness, brawling and the ringing of bells; its mood changes with the anger of an Othello brought from his bed,

> My blood begins my safer guides to rule. (201)

until Iago, his design accomplished, is left with Roderigo his agent upon a quiet and sinister stage, hugging himself:

> By th'mass, 'tis morning;
> Pleasure and action make the hours seem short. (370–1)

Freedom with time lends freedom for symbolism. In *Antony and Cleopatra*, suspense is prolonged and the battles are clocked by the passage of two unusual nights. In the first (IV, iii), Antony 'drowns consideration', while the soldiers who guard him guide the audience's appropriate response to the eery noise-off indicated in the direction, '*Music of the hoboys is under the stage*': this prelude to the fighting is marked by its sly presage of Antony's fate. The second (IV, ix) interrupts the fluctuations of battle, and 'the hand of death' is vividly present in the melancholy Enobarbus, who takes his own life while all except sentries are asleep.

Shakespeare measures the hours by the needs of his drama, matching the tempo of a sequence with a chronology of the imagination, catching a symbolism of life in its flux and flow, as in *The Winter's Tale*, whose seasonal sheep-shearing scene suggests the progress of the natural world as Perdita suggests the progress of the human, making of 'Time, the Chorus' a protagonist who has only to 'turn his glass'. This kind of time will be anarchical, especially in the Elizabethan theatre, unless its meaning is stressed. It is delicately manipulated in *Othello*. That here it is 'contracted and expanded like a concertina'[1] gives the lie to those who feel that its twenty-four hours between

---

[1] H. Granville-Barker, *Prefaces to Shakespeare, Fourth Series*, p. 11.

marriage and murder makes it the most formally classical play in Shakespeare's repertoire. The telescoping of the action after the happy arrival in Cyprus is used to make the spectator sense the contraction of the horizons of the jealous mind, suggesting the swift development of Othello's passions when once strongly roused, and that he had little time to check and prove Iago's hints. The Moor's downfall is accomplished with rare speed as Iago's poison does its work, so that neither he nor the audience stops to consider that Desdemona and Cassio had no opportunity to commit adultery in any case. Yet this play also introduces a new trick of the clock: time is used to cheat the spectator. Upon Othello's decisive words,

> Strumpet, I come!
> Forth of my heart, those charms, thine eyes, are blotted;
> Thy bed lust-stained shall with lust's blood be spotted.
>
> (v, i, 34–6)

Shakespeare appears to stretch time. A short sequence of spectacular action, which includes the stabbing of Roderigo and the wounding of Cassio, tautens the suspense before Othello's next entrance to his defenceless wife, and puts the defenceless spectator under the strain of anticipation.

# II

# SHAKESPEARE'S VISUAL CRAFT

# 3

# THE ACTOR AND HIS MOVEMENT

## SHAKESPEARE AS DIRECTOR

In spite of the demands upon him as a writer, Shakespeare continued as an actor in the Chamberlain's company and took a day-to-day hand in its affairs: he was involved in the life of the theatre. He may even have directed the players. A German visitor to London, Johannes Rhenanus, writing in 1613, reported thus on playhouse procedure: 'As for the actors, as I noticed in England, they are given instruction daily as if at school; even the leading actors expect to take instruction from the playwrights.' Shakespeare was not a director of his plays in the modern sense, but if he was on hand, and often on the stage, during rehearsal, this must have placed him in much the same position. However, his company ran a 'repertory' theatre, varying the plays in the programme each week. Therefore when time for rehearsal was short, hints toward the manner of speech and movement in the lines must have been of help to the players. The liaison between two of the parties to the play, author and actor, encouraged a happy conspiracy, which may also account for the paucity of stage directions. In no case is a stage direction indispensable, other than for entrance and exit.

Instructions to the actors are always found built into the text, rooted in the words selected, and our notion of Shakespeare as director starts from that. The Ghost in *Hamlet* must move in a special way: 'See, it stalks away' (I, i, 50). Juliet must approach Friar Lawrence's cell with 'O, so light a foot' (*Romeo and Juliet*, II, vi, 16). Shakespeare has seen and anticipated what a character looks like, how two characters react to each other, where best on the stage he can show them to advantage.

Even allusive imagery may have the power to guide the actor's body as well as his voice. Antony in his frustration after the seafight enacts the rage in the verse, speaking a 'gestic' poetry:

> The shirt of Nessus is upon me: teach me,
> Alcides, thou mine ancestor, thy rage:
> Let me lodge Lichas on the horns o'th'moon,
> And with those hands that grasped the heaviest club
> Subdue my worthiest self...The witch shall die.
> To the young Roman boy she hath sold me, and I fall
> Under this plot: she dies for't. Eros, ho!
>
> *(Antony and Cleopatra*, IV, xii, 43–9)

It seems as if the maddened Antony writhes with the shirt of Nessus scorching his flesh, and the rising anapaestic treatment of 'Let me lodge Lichas on the horns o'th'moon', with its sense of over-powered emotion, encourages him to fling up his arms as he seeks release from the torture of mind and body. The actor seems to feel the weight of Hercules's club as he fights his anger in the subsequent low-toned lines, 'And with those hands...', until the Alexandrine beginning 'To the young Roman boy...' marks his sweeping exit. A moment later, Shakespeare supplies the contrast. It is the other, the moody Antony who speaks these lines:

> Sometime we see a cloud that's dragonish,
> A vapour sometime like a bear or lion,
> A towered citadel, a pendent rock...     (IV, xiv, 2–4)

Now the hesitant verse reflects the slow pace of his thought and his feet, while the imagery suggests his premonition of death.

The visualizing playwright is one who has an eye for the stage itself, trying the uses to which he can put its depth, seeking a constantly contrasting movement with which to stress its action. The familiar scenes with which the play *Macbeth* assaults its audience from the outset are precise in detail, swift in exposition, sharply imagined. First, effects of thunder and lightning subdue the audience, until the Witches emerge through the trap, briefly chanting their ambiguous dirge to evil, shrouding the platform in mist and dancing their grotesque round:

> Fair is foul, and foul is fair:
> Hover through the fog and filthy air.     (I, i, 11–12)

As they 'vanish', we may conjecture that the bleeding sergeant staggers his twenty or thirty feet down to the foot of the platform, where he falls. A trumpeted alarum is sounded and all heads turn upstage to the other door, from which the King and his sons, rich in regal armour, enter with their noblemen as after battle. Duncan sees his wounded soldier: 'What bloody man is that?' (I, ii, I). The royal group frames the striking figure of the sergeant, who tells his story. In muscular poetry he forges a first image of 'brave Macbeth...Disdaining fortune' (6–7). Shakespeare has seen the advantage of his deep stage for the solo entrance of the sergeant, contrasted it with the splendid entrance of the King's procession, which in turn is at odds with the grimacing of the ancient women who have cast their shadow over the scene. All this is in the nature of Shakespeare's theatre: as drama, built brick upon brick, its command of the auditorium is asserted by the mixture of sight and sound. Some features of this persistently visual stagecraft are the subject of the next chapters.

## GESTURE STATED AND IMPLIED

Occasionally the players describe the gesture of a silent companion, as when the Countess of Rousillon reflects Helena's private heart-ache in *All's Well That Ends Well*:

> When I said 'a mother'
> Methought you saw a serpent. What's in 'mother',
> That you start at it? (I, iii, 137–9)

Some speeches anticipate the figure an actor must cut upon his next entrance, as do Angus's lines,

> now does he feel his title
> Hang loose about him, like a giant's robe
> Upon a dwarfish thief. (*Macbeth*, V, ii, 20–2)

which guide the actor who plays Macbeth toward the precise tone and stance of despair for

> Bring me no more reports, let them fly all. (V, iii, I)

as he feels his authority falling from him.

However, Shakespeare's identification with his character worked so strongly within him that physical gesture forced itself upon the lines, moving the actor to reproduce its muscular activity. Shakespeare wrote a gestic poetry. Most human speech carries with it the picture of a physical attitude. The language of the good dramatic poet especially carries the submerged imagery of gesture and movement. While the sound of his words could caress the theatre to match a soothing image:

> How sweet the moonlight sleeps upon this bank!
> (*The Merchant of Venice*, v, i, 55)

or could scourge the listener with lines catching at Hamlet's anger:

> Who calls me villain, breaks my pate across,
> Plucks off my beard and blows it in my face,
> Tweaks me by the nose, gives me the lie i'th'throat
> As deep as to the lungs? who does me this?
> (*Hamlet*, ii, ii, 575–8)

Shakespeare rarely projects sound effects for their own sake. It is implicit in these lines that he possesses a sense of stillness and movement on the stage, and his blank verse justified itself increasingly by its kinaesthetic qualities.

The connection between the movements of the body and the impulses of speech is to be seen in Ariel's 'to fly,/To swim, to dive into the fire', or Edgar's 'Away! The foul fiend follows me'. These are balletic lines, Ariel's in his tripping syllables, Edgar's in his more forceful, leaping words. By contrast, an actor can be transfixed by the repetitions of a ritualistic verse. After speeches of feverish self-mortification, Richard II finally resigns his crown, but in these solemn terms:

> With mine own tears I wash away my balm,
> With mine own hands I give away my crown,
> With mine own tongue deny my sacred state,
> With mine own breath release all duteous oaths.
> (*Richard II*, iv, i, 207–10)

The ceremonial of this patterned and end-stopped verse has pointed a crisis in the play as the King poses statuesquely

centre-stage. In *Romeo and Juliet*, Shakespeare even borrows
the formal sonnet, rich in its own amorous allusions, and makes
it serviceable to the actors:

> If I profane with my unworthiest hand
> This holy shrine, the gentle pain is this:
> My lips, two blushing pilgrims, ready stand
> To smooth that rough touch with a tender kiss.

(I, v, 93–6)

This sonnet not only conveys a tone suitable to an idealized
encounter, but also precise indications of gesture and attitude.
In Juliet's reply,

> Good pilgrim, you do wrong your hand too much,
> Which mannerly devotion shows in this:
> For saints have hands that pilgrims' hands do touch,
> And palm to palm is holy palmers' kiss... (97–100)

Shakespeare contrives to signal the withdrawal of her hand from
his lips and indicate her modesty as she perhaps turns aside with
the cadence of the last lines. Romeo does not dance with Juliet,
but the flirtatious approach and retreat of the quatrains coincide
with the pattern of the court dance, whose movement itself
symbolizes the pursuit of the lover and the coy reluctance of the
lady in courtship.

Especially transparent in intention is a line which embodies
a direct instruction for the use of a weapon; it commonly
indicates exactly when and at what pace the blow is to be struck.
Such a line demonstrates Laertes's sudden pass at Hamlet in the
duel: 'Have at you now!' (*Hamlet*, v, ii, 300). The gesture is
swift and upon the 'now' the blade goes home. For a contrast,
Antony falls upon his sword with deliberation as he stands over
the body of Eros: 'to do thus/I learned of thee' (*Antony and
Cleopatra*, IV, xiv, 102–3). Yet even here the break in the line
denotes precisely when the wound is made. Or with no weapon
at all, Leontes feels the pang of jealousy as if it were a knife in
his heart: 'Affection! thy intention stabs the centre' (*The
Winter's Tale*, I, ii, 138), and for gesture his hand must fly to his
breast.

Often a short line indicates, and by the break allows for, mime and gesture. Desdemona's 'Come, come' at *Othello*, III, iv, 94, has a line to itself as she tries persuasion on her husband: Shakespeare gives her time for a feminine gesture. The speech of Leontes below includes a remark addressed to his wife, mixed with an aside to the audience, as well as some delineation of her behaviour with his rival as she walks upstage with him away from the audience:

> To your own bents dispose you: you'll be found,
> Be you beneath the sky...I am angling now,
> Though you perceive me not how I give line.
> Go to, go to!
> How she holds up the neb! the bill to him!
> > (*The Winter's Tale*, I, ii, 179–83)

In the middle of this many-purposed speech, the short line, 'Go to, go to!', expressing Leontes's ugly disapproval, is little more than a grunt: it is the actor's moment to mime his jealousy.

### GESTURE AND DRAMATIC MEANING

Shakespeare instinctively uses gestures great and little to bring life to his stage; in an important scene a small detail was not beyond his concern if it could suggest the scale of the main action. When *Julius Caesar* is almost at an end, when Marc Antony's army is on the point of victory and the moment comes for Brutus to take his own life, Brutus calls the soldier Strato to his side and asks him to hold his sword so that he may run upon it. Strato has a single line, one gesture which makes him human:

> Give me your hand first: fare you well, my lord.     (V, v, 49)

By this is Brutus's grander gesture made real to us.

This detail of behaviour reinforces the content of the lines. An instance is to be found in the scene in which Hermione persuades Leontes's friend Polixenes to prolong his stay. All unthinking of the consequences of her gaiety, she speaks a verse as lightly built as this:

> Verily
> You shall not go; a lady's 'Verily' is
> As potent as a lord's.
>
> *(The Winter's Tale*, I, ii, 49–51)

Implicit in the phrasing is the charm of her dancing step towards Polixenes when he tries to withdraw. Returning to the attack, she pursues him next with a verbal image: perhaps he must be made her 'prisoner'? This sally proves to be her undoing.

> Will you go yet?
> Force me to keep you as a prisoner,
> Not like a guest; so you shall pay your fees
> When you depart, and save your thanks. How say you?
> My prisoner? or my guest? by your dread Verily,
> One of them shall you be.                      (51–6)

The point must be stressed by gesture: she has taken him by the arm and holds him her prisoner in affection. This sign is enough to turn Leontes's head and start that jealous train of thought which provides the drive of the action.

An unusual example of the force of particularity in gesture in a scene of otherwise abstract thinking occurs in the first act of *Hamlet*. Shakespeare wishes to suggest how the Prince, distraught and rising from his knees after listening to the long harangue of the Ghost, collects his whirling thoughts. His response to his father's plea to 'remember' him begins again with a verbal image:

> Remember thee?
> Yea, from the table of my memory
> I'll wipe away all trivial fond records.      (I, v, 97–9)

'The table of my memory' seems to call to mind the note-book in which an Elizabethan youth would commonly enter quotations from his reading, whereupon Hamlet takes his from his pocket, and an actual hand-property replaces the verbal concept:

> My tables, meet it is I set it down
> That one may smile, and smile, and be a villain.   (107–8)

When he has snapped shut the book with 'So, uncle, there you are' (110), it seems to the spectator that his thoughts are at last collected ready for prayer, words pointed by visual gesture.

Business and gesture are the index of the character's mind, but Shakespeare also uses them in ironic counterpoint with the urgency of a situation. This technique he practises in the scene before the battle in *Antony and Cleopatra*, a scene of his own invention. Cleopatra gaily helps to arm her general:

CLEOPATRA.                Nay, I'll help too.
  What's this for?
ANTONY.        Ah, let be, let be! thou art
  The armourer of my heart: false, false: this, this.    (IV, iv, 5–7)

Antony protests, but his mistress persists in her game:

CLEOPATRA. Sooth, la, I'll help: thus it must be.
ANTONY.                      Well, well,
  We shall thrive now...
CLEOPATRA. Is not this buckled well?
ANTONY.              Rarely, rarely...    (8–11)

He humours her whim, with perhaps a trace of irritation in his voice at her feminine playfulness. Yet the spectator may not forget that this pretty incident has been preceded by one suffused with ominous music from beneath the ground.

The courtship of the Lady Anne by Richard of Gloucester has disturbed critics since Johnson and Coleridge. The wooing scene was a fair test of a playwright learning to control his players and tease his audience. The vanity of Richard's impudence is a delight to the spectator, and has half subdued the lady before he has begun; his brazen lying is done with a zest the audience shares and a flattery which allows Anne to indulge her scorn. This scene is alive with gesture by which the two may enjoy their perverse pleasure, and none more pointed than that with which she '*spits at him*':

ANNE. Would it were mortal poison, for thy sake!
GLOUCESTER. Never came poison from so sweet a place.
(Richard III, I, ii, 145–6)

Yet the master-stroke in this unnatural scene, and the visual confirmation of what has been heard, follows after he has handed her his sword and fallen upon his knee. The stage direction reads, *'he lays his breast open : she offers at it with his sword'*. Her hesitation and her action of letting the weapon fall from her hand are decisive. When *'she falls the sword'*, the gesture insists that the turning-point has passed. In such an instance as this, we sense that stage business is assuming symbolic qualities.

### GESTURE INTO SYMBOLISM

With simple, concrete detail Shakespeare delineates the scene in which Cordelia wakes her father from his madness. The delicacy of the gestures announces this scene as one of intense naturalism—a domestic scene played on the intimate downstage area of the platform. Such lines as these,

LEAR. Where have I been? Where am I? Fair daylight?
  I am mightily abused; I should e'en die with pity
  To see another thus. I know not what to say.
  I will not swear these are my hands: let's see;
  I feel this pin prick. Would I were assured
  Of my condition!
CORDELIA.        O, look upon me, sir,
  And hold your hand in benediction o'er me;
  No, sir, you must not kneel.      (*King Lear*, IV, vii, 52–9)

exactly convey the physical posture of Lear in his chair, the inflexions of his head, the pathetic detail of the hands. They also borrow and refine a visual idea from the source play. In *The True Chronicle History of King Leir*, father and daughter kneel to each other several times. In Shakespeare's play, Cordelia drops to her knees for Lear's benediction once only, whereupon Lear kneels to her himself, a more emphatic gesture than if he is prevented. In this way the author symbolically reinforces the verbal implication that she is an angel from heaven, 'a soul in bliss'.

The ceremony of kneeling was common on the Elizabethan stage: we remember the poignancy of the King's prayer before Agincourt (*Henry V*, IV, i, 285). Its use is notably extended in *Coriolanus*. As a gesture of respect from Roman son to Roman mother, it is introduced first when Caius Marcius returns home triumphant from his war at Corioli (II, i, 167). When he joins the Volscian camp, Cominius, his former general, is reported to have 'kneeled' to him to beg him to return to Rome (V, i). When, therefore, the women come pleading to him, the spectator has been prepared with the meaning of the gesture, almost anticipating it, and it is especially meaningful that at first he remains seated before his mother. This is borrowed from North's Plutarch, but the kneeling is all Shakespeare's as Coriolanus's upbringing conquers his bitterness:

> You gods! I prate,
> And the most noble mother of the world
> Leave unsaluted. Sink, my knee, i'th'earth...
>
> (v, iii, 48–50)

When Volumnia herself drops down before him that she may 'unproperly/Show duty' (54–5), the effect is shocking:

> What's this?
> Your knees to me? to your corrected son?
> Then let the pebbles on the hungry beach
> Fillip the stars...                                (56–9)

Then a moment later Coriolanus sees with pride his own son, the young Marcius, kneel to him: 'That's my brave boy' (76). As much as by words, the force of this gesture strengthens the spectator's notion of the bond within the Roman family, and Shakespeare's gift has translated simple stage business into a repercussive symbol. Hardly less effective is Volumnia's early wish for her son to conquer Aufidius 'and tread upon his neck' (I, iii, 48), when at v, vi, 132, it is Aufidius who '*stands on*' Coriolanus.

It is hard to draw the line between those gestures which reinforce the dramatic meaning of a scene and those which assume a wider importance and reverberate through the play. Volumnia's gesture of kneeling to her son carries with it an implication greater than the deed itself, acquired in the context of the play itself. Lear on his knees before his daughter is of this kind too, since the first act showed the significance of obeisance before the King. The gesture now suggests Cordelia's new stature in his eyes, and emphasizes the new wisdom he has acquired during his experience on the heath. Kneeling means little in itself; dramatic context grants it symbolic importance.

An unmistakably symbolic use of kneeling is found in the central scene of *Othello*; it is a gesture so essential to the action that the Quarto retains it as one of its few stage directions.

OTHELLO.　　　　　Now, by yond marble heaven,
　In the due reverence of a sacred vow (*he kneels*)
　I here engage my words.
IAGO.　　　　　　　Do not rise yet. (*Iago kneels*)
　Witness you ever-burning lights above,
　You elements that clip us round about,
　Witness that here Iago doth give up
　The execution of his wit, hands, heart,
　To wronged Othello's service!　　　　　　(III, iii, 462–9)

In the light of the 'devil' and 'damnation' imagery which has surrounded Iago to this point, this might be a pact with Mephistopheles. As they kneel together, we hear,

OTHELLO.　　　　Now art thou my lieutenant.
IAGO. I am your own for ever.　　　　　　(480–1)

Othello has called for blood and revenge, so that his reverence to heaven is blasphemy. When he seems to offer his soul, the Devil accepts it with satisfaction, pretending that he is giving his. The ambiguity of possession in 'I am your own for ever' is pointed. The tradition recorded first by Theobald that Othello should strike his wife across the face on the word 'Devil!' (IV, i, 240) provides the public evidence for the private sacrament of evil: Othello sees her as the Devil because he is now possessed, and the blasphemy is consummated when he smothers her before she can pray (V, ii, 87).

Whenever there is business to be done with the English crown, the gesture accompanying it carries symbolic significance, especially where the subject of the play is the king's succession to the throne or his deposition. So it is in 3 *Henry VI*, I, iv, 95, where Queen Margaret in mockery places a paper crown upon

the head of Richard, Duke of York, before he is beheaded. At
the climax of *Richard III*, Lord Stanley makes ritualistic parade
of the dead king's crown before he places it upon Richmond's
head:

> Lo, here, this long usurpéd royalty
> From the dead temples of this bloody wretch
> Have I plucked off, to grace thy brows withal. (v, v, 4–6)

With similar rites, Cardinal Pandulph crowns King John (*King
John*, v, 1, 2). An unusual example of a regal gesture, one casting
a shadow on the future, occurs in *Richard II*. When Richard
resigns his throne to Bolingbroke, the sacred symbol of majesty
is held between the hands of both king and usurper, who stand
stage-centre for all to see.

> Give me the crown...Here, cousin, seize the crown:
> Here, cousin,
> On this side, my hand, and on that side, thine...
> Now is this golden crown like a deep well
> That owes two buckets... (IV, i, 181–5)

The short line and the broken speech guide the actors in their
performance, and one theatrical gesture cements the scene's
significance.

The most impressive of stage gestures in Shakespeare is one
which is part of the developing fabric of the play and prepared
for the spectator's recognition as thematic. A royalty and a
divinity surrounds Lear in the initial scene of his peremptory
apportionment of lands. At the nadir of the action, when he
finds himself roofless on the heath, into his presence is flung the
lowest of human kind, the mad Bedlamite. Poor Tom had chosen

> To take the basest and most poorest shape
> That ever penury in contempt of man
> Brought near to beast. My face I'll grime with filth,
> Blanket my loins, elf all my hairs in knots,
> And with presented nakedness outface
> The winds and persecutions of the sky.
>
> (*King Lear*, II, iii, 7–12)

This costume and appearance is now a reflection of the King's
thoughts:

Is man no more than this? Consider him well. Thou ow'st the worm
no silk, the beast no hide, the sheep no wool, the cat no perfume. Ha!
Here's three on's are sophisticated: thou art the thing itself. Unaccommodated man is no more but such a poor, bare, forked animal
as thou art.

(III, iv, 103–8)

Lear suddenly sees himself in this appalling vision of bestiality,
and seeks to be as like Edgar as possible. Still in his royal robes,
he strips them off and with them the royalty he has wielded so
thoughtlessly: 'Off, off, you lendings! Come, unbutton here!'
(108–9).[1] In one spectacular gesture he completes his blasphemy
against his divinity as man and king, and prepares the audience
for the final humiliation, the loss of reason.

### MOVEMENT OVER THE PLATFORM

It is a fine distinction between gesture and the actor's movement.
Shakespeare knew that lengthy moves over the platform would
test the actors' power of impersonation, and accordingly he
often decided the actual gait of the player. When Juliet is
anxiously waiting for news of Romeo, she clearly tells us to
expect the Nurse's entrance to be in contrast with her own
impatience.

> But old folks, many feign as they were dead—
> Unwieldy, slow, heavy, and pale as lead.
> (*Enter Nurse*)
> O God, she comes! O honey Nurse, what news?
>
> (*Romeo and Juliet*, II, v, 16–18)

The Nurse makes her long entrance down the platform, while the
girl runs to meet her. Juliet's frenzy seems comic by the time
the old woman arrives at the foot of the platform out of breath:

NURSE. I am aweary, give me leave a while.
    Fie, how my bones ache! What a jaunce have I!
JULIET. I would thou hadst my bones, and I thy news...   (25–7)

---

[1] Is Lear prevented? Shakespeare would not have used these words had he not intended this gesture for the climax of his scene, nor could the Fool or Kent have
restrained the King in the fury of his 'Off, off...'. John Bell's edition of the play,
1773, which represents Garrick's production, explicitly confirms the tradition with
a stage direction, '*Tearing off his cloaths*'.

Within the rhythm of the lines given to Hamlet as he sees Claudius at his prayers, his body is tense and alert. He probably approaches the kneeling figure with abrupt strides:

> Now might I do it pat, now a' is a-praying—
> And now I'll do't, and so a' goes to heaven,
> And so I am revenged.     (*Hamlet*, III, iii, 73-5)

Yet, as soon as he has drawn his sword and it is poised over the silent figure, the stupidity of the act strikes him:

> I his sole son do this same villain send
> To heaven...     (77-8)

The slip of the tongue stops him short with the intake of breath, for the space of the moment indicated by the short line. Then again it is the verse that slows the actor as he retreats into his thoughts, and moves uncertainly away.

A range of suggestion for the actor's posture as he moves is to be found in the lines. Othello's pacing marks the indecision of his mind:

> I think my wife be honest, and think she is not;
> I think that thou art just, and think thou art not...
>     (*Othello*, III, iii, 386-7)

Or Macbeth's rhythmic lines are the index of his slowing, cautious steps toward his victim:   withered Murder,

> Alarumed by his sentinel, the wolf,
> Whose howl's his watch, thus with his stealthy pace,
> With Tarquin's ravishing strides, towards his design
> Moves like a ghost.     (*Macbeth*, II, i, 52-6)

In this word-picture, the player is invited to mime a vision of 'Murder', crouched and bestial, an eye over his shoulder. He warily places one foot before the other in tune with the elongated syllables which guide his silent movement upstage to Duncan's chamber door.

Expository word-painting is not to be divorced from the use of the space on the stage. With economy of word and movement, the soldiers on guard on the battlements in *Hamlet* create the place, the time, the mist and the darkness as they call across the platform to each other. By curt speech they enact their fear and expectancy, and through their tension prepare the spectator for the entrance of the Ghost:

> Who's there?
> Nay, answer me. Stand and unfold yourself.
> Long live the king!
> Barnardo?
> He.
> You come most carefully upon your hour.
> 'Tis now struck twelve, get thee to bed, Francisco.
> For this relief much thanks, 'tis bitter cold,
> And I am sick at heart.
>
> (I, i, 1–9)

This familiar piece of mood-exposition is also inseparably linked with the forty- or fifty-foot movement which Barnardo and Francisco share before they meet centre-stage on the recognition of 'Barnardo?'…'He'. Shakespeare is counting on this distance to provide the actors with time to mime their state to the spectators.

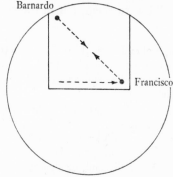

Even in duologue the patterns of gesture and movement are clearly sketched. Thus a somewhat troubled Othello and an impulsive Desdemona perform a dramatic *pas de deux* when she sues for his reconciliation with Cassio:

DESDEMONA.                    Good love, call him back.
OTHELLO. Not now, sweet Desdemon; some other time.
DESDEMONA. But shall't be shortly?

OTHELLO. The sooner, sweet, for you.
DESDEMONA. Shall't be tonight at supper?
OTHELLO. No, not tonight.
DESDEMONA. Tomorrow dinner then?
OTHELLO. I shall not dine at home:
  I meet the captains at the citadel.
DESDEMONA. Why then, tomorrow night; or Tuesday morn...

(Othello, III, iii, 55–61)

This run of questions and answers is accompanied by a visual sequence of rebuffs by the man and pursuits by the wife, until, as Othello tries to walk away, Desdemona finally faces him and traps him where he stands.

Those movements that belong to the lords and nobles who form the background to the protagonists of the history plays must indicate their dignity in their gesture and movement. The norm of their verse is regular, and the structure of their speeches weighty, as if the players must be firmly planted in the earth when they are not in procession across the stage. When, however, a Hal or a Hotspur enters the scene, a Falstaff or a Fluellen, then they bring a life with them, felt in the contrasting vitality of their language:

WORCESTER. He apprehends a world of figures here,
  But not the form of what he should attend.
  Good cousin, give me audience for a while.
HOTSPUR. I cry you mercy.
WORCESTER. Those same noble Scots
  That are your prisoners,—
HOTSPUR. I'll keep them all;
  By God, he shall not have a Scot of them.
  No, if a Scot would save his soul, he shall not.
  I'll keep them, by this hand...

(1 Henry IV, I, iii, 209–16)

In contrast with the stolid Earl of Worcester, Hotspur is impulsive. His angry movement is implicit in the fiery quality of his lines, flinging away, rounding again, gesticulating with his fist, literally standing his ground.

## ENTRANCE ON TO THE PLATFORM

The majority of entrances were made from upstage through one of the two doors. If the actor felt the need, he could perambulate for up to fifty feet, as in a diagonal entrance, or for up to seventy feet, as in an entrance carrying him downstage and across. On the Elizabethan stage, the actor was immediately on display. Shakespeare was aware of the effectiveness of the long downstage entrance, and of the opportunities the journey might lend the actor wishing to create a mood or establish a character. Gloucester and Edgar struggle together down the platform as if 'up' the hill to Dover cliff:

GLOUCESTER. When shall I come to th' top of that same hill?
EDGAR. You do climb up it now. Look how we labour.
GLOUCESTER. Methinks the ground is even.
EDGAR.                                        Horrible steep.
                                    (*King Lear*, IV, vi, 1–3)

The blind man doubts his newly discovered senses; his son is again acting a part, his miming all but comic. In the vein of farce, the entrance of Falstaff puffing and blowing his way up Gadshill is unforgettable:

POINS. Come, shelter, shelter! I have removed Falstaff's horse, and he frets like a gummed velvet.
PRINCE. Stand close.      (*Enter Falstaff*)
FALSTAFF. Poins! Poins, and be hanged! Poins!...The rascal hath removed my horse, and tied him I know not where. If I travel but four foot by the squier further afoot, I shall break my wind...
                                    (*1 Henry IV*, II, ii, 1–13)

Shakespeare here seizes his chance both to keep the 'horse' off the stage and to provide a comic opening to the escapade. Just as tired, but in a different mood, are those who journey through Arden:

ROSALIND. O Jupiter! how weary are my spirits!
TOUCHSTONE. I care not for my spirits, if my legs were not weary...
CELIA. I pray you, bear with me, I cannot go no further...
ROSALIND. Well, this is the forest of Arden!
                                    (*As You Like It*, II, iv, 1–14)

These are unlike the sprightly girls of the first act, and this entrance is so constructed that the audience will feel the change of pace and attitude directly.

Shakespeare seems particularly given to the 'silent' entrance in *Hamlet*. It is traditional for Horatio, Marcellus and Barnardo to enter quietly while the Prince is still engrossed in the private anguish of his first soliloquy, 'O, that this too too sullied flesh...'. When he looks up and sees them (I, ii, 159), he is at first unable to recognize his friend Horatio. Again, happily appropriate is Hamlet's entrance '*reading on a book*':

> QUEEN. But look where sadly the poor wretch comes reading,
> (II, ii, 167–8)

while Polonius sends the King and Queen hurrying away—an enigmatic entrance leading to the enigmatic talk with which Hamlet addresses the foolish Lord Chamberlain. The mad Ophelia's silent reappearance, while her brother Laertes tries in vain to make her recognize him, has the effect of prompting pathos:

> O rose of May,
> Dear maid, kind sister, sweet Ophelia!
> O heavens, is't possible a young maid's wits
> Should be as mortal as an old man's life?...
> (IV, v, 153–6)

She will only sing softly, lost in her solitary world.

The expanse of the platform and its power of embracing several activities simultaneously often made it imperative for Shakespeare to draw the audience's eyes away from one scene of action to another, particularly when a downstage action had to give way to an upstage entrance. This transition he could accomplish swiftly: a sound or a word could do it. To herald an impressive or processional entrance, he might use a 'sennet', an 'alarum' or a 'flourish'. More commonly, a character in the intimate action already on the stage might announce the entrance. Speaking almost as if he were a chorus, a downstage character shifts the spectator's attention, while the posture of the actor leads him to look where he should. A 'Look where he comes' also gave the upstage actor his chance to establish his entrance.

Thus Desdemona and Emilia discuss the recent behaviour of Othello almost as preparing the spectator for what he is to see:

EMILIA.                                    Is he not jealous?
DESDEMONA. Who, he! I think the sun where he was born
 Drew all such humours from him.

Suddenly, attention is directed upstage:

EMILIA.                              Look where he comes!
        (*Enter Othello*)

The spectator judges for himself first: a line allows Othello time to demonstrate his jealous mood as he makes his way towards his wife:

DESDEMONA. I will not leave him now till Cassio
 Be called to him.

Finally she greets him with:

            How is't with you, my lord?
                    (*Othello*, III, iv, 28–33)

The entrance of Ross to report victory over Norway three lines after Duncan's 'Who comes here?' (*Macbeth*, I, ii, 46) is of this kind, since Lennox has time to comment,

    What a haste looks through his eyes! So should he look
    That seems to speak things strange.          (47–8)

And of interest in this connection are the nine rhyming lines given to the Countess of Rousillon for the entrance of Helena in *All's Well That Ends Well*. These allow the heroine to enter dejectedly, but they also invite consideration of the toils of love by comparison with the sympathetic words of the older woman:

    Even so it was with me, when I was young...
    If ever we are nature's, these are ours. This thorn
    Doth to our rose of youth rightly belong.    (I, iii, 125 ff.)

The word 'these' makes little sense in reading, but in performance it is a cue for the Countess to indicate, and Helena to display, her amorous sufferings. The boy actor playing Helena has the difficulties of his part eased as he wanders the length of the platform with downcast eyes.

There is every variety of rapport between a character on stage and a character entering, and, as a result, every variety of irony signalled to the audience. The possibilities are especially useful for comedy. The fun in the farcical duel between Viola and Sir Andrew in *Twelfth Night* is increased because Fabian and Sir Toby prepare each contestant—and the spectator—with an outrageously inappropriate description of the antagonist. As Sir Andrew makes his entrance, Fabian tells Viola that he is 'the most skilful, bloody and fatal opposite that you could possibly have found in any part of Illyria'; and Sir Toby prepares Sir Andrew for Viola with 'Why, man, he's a very devil, I have not seen such a firago' (III, iv, 267 ff.). In the eyes of the spectator, the reluctant entrances of the timid girl in breeches and the effeminate knight delightfully contradict what is spoken.

## ALONE ON THE STAGE

An important moment of solo performance was prepared visually, and soliloquy could be not only the poetic high point of a scene, but a visual climax. When the actor was alone upon his thousand square feet of platform, space itself could speak to the audience. With the impact of the close-up of good cinema, the isolation of the figure had the power to concentrate attention on the individuality of the character and his mind, and on the person of the actor. Moreover, the tradition remained strong for some two hundred years that the character speaking in soliloquy should speak directly to the spectators. In 1779 Mr Puff, the critic-playwright in Sheridan's *The Critic; or a Tragedy Rehearsed*, III, i, was instructing his actor as follows: 'Now, sir, your soliloquy—but speak more to the pit, if you please—the soliloquy always to the pit—that's a rule.' Among modern commentators, Quiller-Couch was in 1918 one of the first to insist that the Elizabethan soliloquy involved a downstage movement. Along 'this horn, or isthmus' of the platform, 'a player who had some specially fine passage to declaim advanced and began, laying his hand to his heart...and, having delivered himself, pressed his hand to his heart again, bowed to the discriminating applause, and retired into the frame of the play'.[1] A somewhat romantic view of the proceeding maybe, but substantially in keeping with the convention of the time. Dissociated from the action, the player could be in intimate and immediate touch with the spectator. His place of dominance was in the centre of the theatre, at the foot of the platform, whence he could command the house.

The development of a soliloquy's sound and meaning often seems to imply that it carried the actor downstage. Thus Banquo makes full use of the platform's depth:

> Thou hast it now, King, Cawdor, Glamis, all,
> As the weird women promised, and I fear
> Thou play'dst most foully for't: yet it was said
> It should not stand in thy posterity,
> But that myself should be the root and father
> Of many kings. If there come truth from them—
> As upon thee, Macbeth, their speeches shine—
> Why, by the verities on thee made good,
> May they not be my oracles as well,
> And set me up in hope? But hush, no more.
>
> (*Macbeth*, III, i, 1–10)

The speech has the effect of extending the spectator's tentative thoughts on Macbeth's conduct, of articulating them, and of preparing the audience for the next murder. Entering by the upstage door, Banquo perhaps sees the throne set ready for the entrance of the new king, and first addresses an imaginary Macbeth upon it. Then, as his thoughts turn upon his private suspicions and his own ambition for the future, one senses that he turns away, moving downstage to the audience, bringing them into closer identity with himself. In this way his intimacy with the audience is directly related to the meaning of what he says. Then, as the sennet is sounded to herald the King and Queen, he seems confident of having secured the spectator's sympathy when he calls for silence as if in some conspiracy: 'But hush, no more.' From the centre of the theatre, he now turns his back upon the audience, and they look upstage with him at the state procession: the action is to pass upstage. This change of

[1] *Shakespeare's Workmanship*, p. 42.

direction stresses the distinction between private truth and public deceit, which is explored as a major theme in the structure of the play. From such an angle, the spectator receives the full implication of the sly questioning by Macbeth which follows, both from Banquo's point of view, as if Macbeth's evil intention were directed against the audience too, and from that of the detached observer, which is the perennial role of the playgoer.

The questions a Shakespearian villain puts to himself and the audience also invite the downstage position. Of this kind are the impertinent confidences of Edmund:

> Why brand they us
> With base? with baseness? bastardy? base, base?
> > (*King Lear*, I, ii, 9–10)

and the barefaced challenge of Iago:

> And what's he then that says I play the villain?
> ...How am I then a villain?
> > (*Othello*, II, iii, 329 and 341)

Of this kind also is Pandarus's naughty address to the ladies in the auditorium:

> And Cupid grant all tongue-tied maidens here
> Bed, chamber, pandar, to provide this gear.
> > (*Troilus and Cressida*, III, ii, 209–10)

There is a joyful impudence in both delivering and receiving such a sentiment by direct address.

An aside from a clown must gain in keenness from a downstage delivery. Speed can be equivocal on the approach of pretty Silvia:

O excellent motion...O exceeding puppet...now will he interpret her. (*The Two Gentlemen of Verona*, II, i, 90–1)

or Launcelot Gobbo can be waggish at the expense of his father as he makes his senile appearance: 'O heavens, this is my true-begotten father...' (*The Merchant of Venice*, II, ii, 32). Launce must address the audience directly for his droll demonstration of his departure from home:

my grandam having no eyes, look you, wept herself blind at my parting: nay, I'll show you the manner of it... (*The Two Gentlemen of Verona*, II, iii, 11–13)

Falstaff is playing to the audience when he gives the account of his escapade in the clothes-basket:

The rogues slighted me into the river with as little remorse as they would have drowned a blind bitch's puppies, fifteen i'th'litter: and you may know by my size, that I have a kind of alacrity in sinking...

*(The Merry Wives of Windsor*, III, v, 8–12)

Why doubt that Falstaff seized with zest all his opportunities in the *Henry IV* plays to set the house in a roar by this kind of confidence?

After the riot of the first Eastcheap tavern scene, it seems that Prince Henry can stand in a wholly new relationship with the audience by the use of the same device. His isolation on the stage deftly breaks the mood of the scene in preparation for the *volte-face* of

I know you all, and will awhile uphold
The unyoked humour of your idleness.

*(1 Henry IV*, I, ii, 187–8)

With the complete visual change Hal can speak his mind, as if there are two spheres of intelligence in the play, determined by the proximity of the audience. Again, the audience knows by Hamlet's proximity in the first court scene that his long silences before Claudius and the court will be broken when he is alone, and they are rewarded by the low-toned, downstage intimacy of his first soliloquy (*Hamlet*, I, ii, 129). The real Hamlet is revealed. Stage positioning makes the link between actor and audience, and in this play it is by many repetitions of the downstage address that the Prince becomes our own.

### PLAYING TO THE AUDIENCE

It is probable that Shakespeare saw his actors as playing to their audience most of the time. In the picture-frame theatre the modern actor is withdrawn into an illusionist's setting, compelled to move from side to side of the stage (the characteristic modern stage direction is '*crosses*'), playing to the other actors rather than to his audience. The Elizabethan actor was at all times vulnerable, and compelled to communicate with the audience, provoking it and provoked by it. This lively tradition of a two-way traffic was part of the actor's art, and its most direct repercussions were felt in Shakespeare's anticipation of his movement.

If we may be allowed a conjecture or two, a single brief episode from the ballroom scene in *Romeo and Juliet* will illustrate his general sense of the actor's movement toward the spectator. The way in which the scene starts is easily overlooked. The servants who are to change a street in Verona into a banqueting hall in Capulet's house in the imagination of the spectator have in fact a more important function, that of changing the mood of the audience. Their lines are few, but calculated for comic business and movement over their own stage:

FIRST SERVINGMAN. Where's Potpan, that he helps not to take away? He shift a trencher! He scrape a trencher!

SECOND SERVINGMAN. When good manners shall lie all in one or two men's hands, and they unwashed too, 'tis a foul thing.

FIRST SERVINGMAN. Away with the joined-stools, remove the court-cupboard, look to the plate—Good thou, save me a piece of march-pane; and, as thou loves me, let the porter let in Susan Grindstone and Nell—Antony and Potpan!

THIRD SERVINGMAN. Ay, boy, ready.

FIRST SERVINGMAN. You are looked for and called for, asked for and sought for, in the great chamber.

FOURTH SERVINGMAN. We cannot be here and there too. Cheerly, boys; be brisk a while, and the longer liver take all.    (I, v, 1-16)

The attack with which Romeo's poetic mood of melancholy is dispelled is apparent. Servingmen with their coarse vernacular are to trot on to the stage at a pace set by the roaring of the First Servingman, who is evidently Capulet's Steward below stairs. The actors emerge from the upstage doors with varying degrees of reluctance and probably pass round the stage perimeter with suitable grimaces at the spectators above their load of stools and plate. The Steward, fat and self-important, as may be deduced, must take his stand imposingly centre-stage in order to supervise the work; naturally, he will be facing upstage, looking toward the doors from which his minions will appear. Already the action is positioned in depth, and a good part of the audience has a view of the man's back. While he bawls his sarcasms, the Second Servingman has reached a place where he can be impertinent to his master behind his back in an effective aside to the spectators:

When good manners shall lie all in one or two men's hands, and they unwashed too, 'tis a foul thing.

As the audience laughs its approval, it is suddenly to see, in this vignette of life below stairs, another side to the character of the Steward. He seizes the Servingman as he passes on his way up to the other door, pulls him back to a place at the edge of the platform where all can hear his rough whisper, and asks for 'a piece of marchpane'. It seems this bully has a sweet tooth.

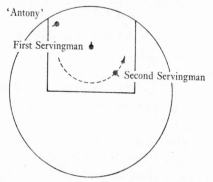

When the servant is again on his way upstage, again he is summoned back: 'as thou loves me' (which may be asking too much, as the Servingman's wry face will show) 'let the porter let in Susan Grindstone and Nell'. At this confidence, we may imagine with what a leer for the spectators the Second Servingman finally proceeds on his way. In the meantime, the Steward has resumed his central control of the stage activity and is already bellowing for Antony and Potpan. It is Antony, we may guess, who makes his hurried appearance as the Third Servingman (a willing helper for once, but rather feeble of limb?), while the Steward rounds on him from his place. Antony is trounced with the tongue, as the rising phrases suggest: 'looked for and called for, asked for and sought for...'. The stage is now busy with sundry servingmen loaded to their chins. Except for one. The Fourth Servingman throws out a cheeky aside from the perimeter as he saunters on: 'We cannot be here and there too. Cheerly, boys...'. This must be the elusive Potpan himself who so riles the Steward. A light response to angry orders seems Potpan's way. This is the man who clears the stage with the cue for exit before the guests enter.

All is done swiftly, peppered with likely asides, and deftly offering the clowns their opportunity to display their comic talents, improvise a quip or two, and bring the spectators into the scene, as the long arm of the platform reaches into the crowded auditorium.

## EXIT

With no black-out switch, no curtain to drop, no door to slam, no convenient wing-piece to slip behind, the actor on the Elizabethan stage had always of himself to make a strong exit. On the open stage he had to remain in sight of the spectators during the long return to the tiring-house. Shakespeare makes provision for such exits.

Two or more players usually reach an agreement to depart, or decide upon the order of their going. The following cues, in great profusion and variety, are all from the first act of *Hamlet*: 'Give you good night', 'Break we our watch up', 'We here dispatch you...', 'Come away', 'So fare you well', 'Most humbly do I take my leave, my lord', 'Come your ways', 'Nay, let's follow him', 'Fare thee well at once' and 'Nay come, let's go together'. However, to cite such tags is to do no justice to the effect of the exits they signal. They provide for the rapid continuity of the scenes, but the quality of the exit lies in its relationship to the mood which the whole scene has engendered. Moreover, the exit occurs at the point when it can clinch the purpose of the scene it caps, and often serves to cast its reflection over the scene to come.

As we might expect, the character making the exit is often given implicit instructions about the form and appearance of his departure. Shakespeare does not allow Shylock to make a vigorously theatrical exit as the villain of the piece. There are to be no flourishes:

> I pray you give me leave to go from hence,
> I am not well, send the deed after me,
> And I will sign it.
>
> (*The Merchant of Venice*, IV, i, 391–3)

This is a quiet, even pathetic, exit, one in keeping with the many-sided man whom Shakespeare has revealed in the play. By contrast, he gives his clowns an exit in keeping with the farce of their performance. He does this for the conclusion of the scene in which the schoolmaster Holofernes decides to present the Nine Worthies as an entertainment for the Princess of France. The schoolmaster and the constable depart to make their preparations:

HOLOFERNES. Via, goodman Dull! thou hast spoken no word all this while.
DULL. Nor understood none neither, sir.
HOLOFERNES. Allons! we will employ thee.
DULL. I'll make one in a dance, or so; or I will play
  On the tabor to the worthies, and let them dance the hay.
HOLOFERNES. Most dull, honest Dull! to our sport: away!

> (*Love's Labour's Lost*, V, i, 144–50)

Constable Dull's notions of a country dance for the Worthies deliciously offsets the pomposity of the schoolmaster's offended dignity. The latter stalks off, while the former must follow with an antic attempt at a dance to demonstrate his idea.

Suggestions for an exit are usually implicit, but there is a case in which Shakespeare insists upon a silent exit of particular effect for the meaning of the play. When in *Coriolanus* a messenger announces that 'the Volces are in arms', a Senator gives an order to the rebellious citizens of Rome: 'Hence to your homes; be gone!' (I, i, 247). Shakespeare is not content with such a cue, and has Caius Marcius suggest instead,

> nay, let them follow.
> The Volces have much corn; take these rats thither
> To gnaw their garners.               (247–9)

At this point is written the stage direction, '*citizens steal away*': it is their cowed silence upon this challenge with which, after their former impulse to riot, Shakespeare points the capriciousness of democratic responsibility in contrast with the noisy display of patrician values by the Senators as they presumably leave by the other door.

At Horatio's 'Break we our watch up' (*Hamlet*, I, i, 168), there are seven more lines before he and the Guard leave. That a cue for exit might occur as much as half a minute before the completion of the move supports the argument that the actors had a distance to walk to the upstage door, and that on occasion Shakespeare took advantage of the ground to be covered. Here Horatio, Marcellus and the Guard are full of doubts, but must come to a decision to tell Hamlet of the mysterious events of the night, and, having agreed, walk quickly off. But a silent exit could carry equal dramatic force. In many performances Cressida walks off promptly upon Diomedes's 'Lady, a word; I'll bring you to your father' (*Troilus and Cressida*, IV, v, 53). In fact there is no '*exeunt*' in either Quarto or Folio at this place, since Ulysses from his downstage position has ten strong lines in which to describe Cressida's characteristic walk:

> Fie, fie, upon her!
> There's language in her eye, her cheek, her lip,
> Nay, her foot speaks; her wanton spirits look out
> At every joint and motive of her body...     (54 ff.)

These lines must be delivered as she is going, and Shakespeare intended the boy actor to have his performance embellished by language which puts a particular stamp on her behaviour. The effect is rewarding only if the spectator is allowed to watch her walk off upstage at the same time as he listens to Ulysses's sarcasms.

# 4

## GROUPING ON THE OPEN STAGE

### PLANNING FOR THREE DIMENSIONS

The Elizabethan open stage stimulated the dramatist's sense of space and spatial relationships. The picture of Shakespeare's work on behalf of the individual actor which emerges from our study is one of opportunities for movement over great distances, creating a kind of splendid Renaissance dance-drama. Gloucester enters with his torch, straining to see Lear upon the heath, Edgar promptly responds with the furious capers of his pretence, and lines later his father is still calling through the imagined rain and mist, 'What are you there? Your names?' (*King Lear*, III, iv, 128). Dispersion of voice and movement helps sustain the impact of the storm. It is now hard to guess with what effect Leontes of *The Winter's Tale* could draw apart and remain critically silent for the gap of 53 ironic lines in I, ii. Where did he stand to observe his wife with Polixenes? What was the nature of his mime? In what relationship was he with the audience? The Elizabethan player would solve such problems from tradition and instinct, using stage space to provoke the nice visual ironies of the scene.

Shakespeare's scenes were written to be acted in depth and staged in three dimensions. Action on a downstage-upstage axis is likely to be planned to distinguish between those characters with whom the audience is most recently acquainted and those with whom it is not. In the *King Lear* scene, the spectator's familiarity with the King and Edgar at the point of Gloucester's entrance makes Gloucester an outsider, and so it proves: he never realizes, as the spectator does, that Lear and Edgar are now not to be separated. Lear will 'keep still with my philosopher', while Gloucester stands aghast, remaining an 'upstage' character in this scene. In *The Winter's Tale*, on the other hand, the audience must find Hermione's charming approach to Polixenes sympathetic, so that the suspicious Leontes remains

81

the upstage observer, until he joins the downstage pair and is in a convenient position to deliver his bitter asides. Yet his presence is important: there is no exit line for him, and the spectator repeatedly sights his louring figure through the equivocal dialogue.

So the depth of the platform helped Shakespeare to distinguish the degree of sympathy a character should share with the audience. It favoured a character when he expeditiously served as chorus or offered a speech of direct confession, or engagingly eavesdropped upon others while inviting the spectator to share his interest. A player's position on the stage added a dimension of meaning to his performance even when he remained silent.

For a simple arrangement of multiple-centred interest neatly combining many of these functions, we might take up again the ballroom scene of *Romeo and Juliet*. After the clownish servants have mimed the preparations for a banquet and withdrawn, old Capulet has his turn to take charge of the stage. In the best of humours, he first welcomes the gentlemen at one door, and then the ladies at the other: the lines are tidily divided so. Then by scurrying between them he contrives to bring the two groups together for the dance:

> She that makes dainty,
> She I'll swear hath corns: am I come near ye now?
>
> (I, v, 20–1)

In his role as elderly host, he offers a heavy joke to each party, and promptly calls upon the musicians to strike up. To augment the comedy, Capulet and his ancient cousin croak together of bygone days. The dance must take place on the central and upper areas of the platform while the two old men perambulate the margins of the stage upon the directive 'Nay sit, nay sit' (31). So their brief music-hall performance dwindles, and the important downstage area is left free.

Now Romeo's voice is heard, and the spectator's attention is attracted to another quarter by Shakespeare's device of arrested movement. Romeo halts a passing servingman:

> What lady's that which doth enrich the hand
> Of yonder knight?                               (42–3)

His tone of voice is new for the scene and the poetry carries the glowing sequence of images which tell of his first sight of Juliet as she dances:

O she doth teach the torches to burn bright... (44 ff.)

This lyrical speech has many marks of direct address to the audience. Romeo must be downstage to be clear of the dancers; he is therefore speaking into the audience's ear. At the same time he must be looking upstage at Juliet as he speaks, looking where the audience is looking. Simultaneously, that is, he can suggest that he has fallen in love, and with words adorn Juliet's

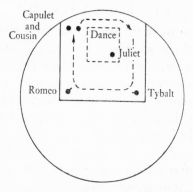

boy actor; Romeo plays both character and chorus. The movement upstage catches the eye, the voice downstage catches the ear, creating an impression of Juliet which is to persist throughout the play.

Suddenly is heard from yet another quarter the stern tones of Tybalt, as it were eavesdropping on the gate-crasher:

This, by his voice, should be a Montague.
Fetch me my rapier, boy. (54–5)

Another arrested movement, and the audience is made quickly aware of the danger lurking behind Romeo's happy discovery of love. Into the sugar-sweet scene of the first meeting is thus deftly introduced the central tension of the play. Yet Tybalt's speech is also an intimate one: he has stalked down the other side of the platform. The director will recognize in his grouping that these two voices, and the two postures, speak for the Montague and the Capulet: Romeo and Tybalt must be set symbolically apart at the foot of the platform.

Even after so short a time, five visual and aural centres of interest have been introduced into the scene, their effects over-lapping and contrasting, their interest at times seductively simultaneous. This is Shakespeare planning his drama for three dimensions, and such scene-patterning is not found when the Elizabethan stage is superseded. Some of the elements in the kind of movement this scene displays will be examined in more detail in this chapter and the next.

### THE DUOLOGUE VISUALIZED

Shakespeare's control of movement over the whole stage is seen in a concentrated way when he is working with two players. His longer duologues are steered not only by the expected differences between two characters in a developing situation, but also by the mimetic pattern of gesture and movement which they share. Two or three motions in duologue are selected from the mature plays as of special interest.

There is no need to assume an inner stage for Brutus's tent in the scene of the quarrel in *Julius Caesar*, IV, ii–iii. Movement flows over the open platform upon the words,     let no man

> Come to our tent till we have done our conference.
>
> (IV, ii, 50–1)

The stage direction for the armies and the generals is simply '*Exeunt*', and Lucilius and Titinius seem to stand guard offstage, leaving Brutus and Cassius to quarrel freely. To have these two passionate leaders seated in a strait-jacket of a setting remotely upstage is destructive. They enforce their drama by movement over the platform.

The pattern of movement has begun from the moment of Cassius's entrance. He storms in:

> Most noble brother, you have done me wrong. (IV, ii, 37)

and Brutus, aware of the eyes of the army watching them, presents him with a 'sober form', perhaps a shoulder turned:

> Cassius, be content,
> Speak your griefs softly. (41-2)

The spectator is thus all the more ready for the explosion of feeling when they are alone: they must stand flanking opposite sides of the platform, impatient for privacy, impatient for the duel. Then Cassius may lead again with

> That you have wronged me doth appear in this...
>
> (IV, iii, 1)

but he is a little taken aback to find Brutus ready with a countering

> —Let me tell you, Cassius, you yourself
> Are much condemned to have an itching palm...
> —I an itching palm! (9-12)

The blood rises on both sides. As Shakespeare's words reach their crisis, Cassius begins to close the physical gap between them:

> Do not presume too much upon my love,
> I may do that I shall be sorry for. (63-4)

Brutus stands his ground, as angry as his friend but with more self-command:

> You have done that you should be sorry for.
> There is no terror, Cassius, in your threats. (65-6)

When Cassius snatches up his dagger,

> There is my dagger,
> And here my naked breast. (99-100)

There must be a sense of real physical threat as they stand face to face. To play this across a table is to eliminate much of the tension implicit in the movement of two men towards each other across forty feet. Only after such impulsive movement can the scene modulate into the suppressed feelings that accompany Brutus's announcement of the death of Portia.

The long probative duologue between Angelo and Isabella in the second act of *Measure for Measure* guides audience response by a more complex stagecraft. It is carefully broken into two scenes (II, ii and II, iv) by the Duke's visit to Juliet in prison, a bridge scene to recall normal human sexuality as well as a device to mark a brief passage of time. Angelo is a changed man after this break, and accordingly the second half of the duologue changes its pattern of movement too. The changes are accentuated by another device which works to striking effect. The first half is acted in the presence of two observers, Lucio and the Provost, as it were respectively representing the forces of anarchy and the law, and they regulate the protagonists and inhibit the action for the purposes of irony and suspense. When Isabella and Angelo meet again, they are alone, and the action grows increasingly overt. The first half ends with a direct confession by Angelo to the spectator, and the second, appropriately, with another by Isabella.

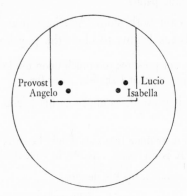

From the beginning, Angelo has asked the Provost to 'stay a little while' (II, ii, 26) and has him at his shoulder as an angel of conscience during Isabella's supplication for her brother's life. Throughout the scene, Angelo is scarcely felt to move, and his curt replies are strangely reserved, spoken almost in a growl. He moves only to turn away in dismissing her, but this, characteristically, is a frank direction for the actor to turn again to point a crucial line:

ISABELLA. Gentle my lord, turn back.
ANGELO. I will bethink me: come again to-morrow.
ISABELLA. Hark how I'll bribe you: good my lord, turn back.
ANGELO. How! bribe me! (144–7)

This one movement of Angelo's marks the idea that has been entering his mind. The situation has been pregnant with sexual overtones, and these are specially engendered by the devil's advocate, Lucio, who speaks at Isabella's shoulder. Because of his insistence, her role is less passive. Again and again she is invited to take the offensive:

> —Give't not o'er so: to him again, entreat him...
> To him, I say. (43-7)
> —You are too cold. (56)
> —Ay, touch him: there's the vein. (70)
> —O, to him, to him, wench: he will relent.
> He's coming: I perceive't. (125-6)
> —Thou'rt i'th'right, girl—more o'that. (130)
> —Go to; 'tis well; away. (157)

Any analysis of the movement and gesture in Isabella's words after her initial reluctance must take into account these provocations of Lucio's: increasingly she corners Angelo by her advance across the platform.

The soliloquy with which Angelo opens II, iv seems a continuation of that with which he closes II, ii. Therefore Isabella finds him alone, once more in his former position downstage on the intimate area of the platform. Shakespeare early provides the remark which starts the new pattern of movement. Angelo has said, 'Your brother cannot live' and Isabella is too promptly resigned: 'Even so...Heaven keep your honour' (34). Whereupon she turns to go, so that Angelo must now be the one to force the answers. He calls after her, 'Yet may he live awhile...', and thereafter he becomes the aggressor:

> Answer to this—
> Might there not be a charity in sin? (60-3)
> Nay, but hear me. (73)
> Were not you then as cruel as the sentence
> That you have slandered so? (109-10)

So the thrust and parry proceeds to the climax of argument with a last dispatching movement, when all ambiguity is finally resolved:

> redeem thy brother
> By yielding up thy body to my will,

> Or else he must not only die the death,
> But thy unkindness shall his death draw out
> To lingring sufferance. (163–7)

The man has cornered the woman; he has spoken out at last and he may now leave; and this he does.

The most absorbing duologue in the canon also follows a pattern of chase-and-be-chased, but with such drive and such wealth of intermediate variations that, though of extraordinary length, it never fades. The duologue between Othello and Iago at the core of the play (*Othello*, III, iii) is subtly manipulated for movement. It too is broken and relieved by a bridge scene, the episode within the scene in which Emilia finds the handkerchief, and again this allows for a significant passage of time and marks a change of mood and movement.

Iago adopts the needle-pricking motions of advance and retreat:

IAGO. Did Michael Cassio,
> When you wooed my lady, know of your love?
OTHELLO. He did, from first to last. Why dost thou ask?
IAGO. But for a satisfaction of my thought;
> No further harm. (94–8)

The stings of Iago's ill-concealed revelations are repeated several times in the first few moments, and a direction is fixed for their complementary gestures and movements, as if Iago after each sally tugs his master with him on a string. The pace increases until Othello seems to be the assailant with lines like,

> Nay, yet there's more in this. (133)
> What dost thou mean? (157)
> I'll know thy thoughts! (164)

When Othello becomes heated, Iago turns and looks him in the eye as he levels his aim more directly:

> —O, beware, my lord, of jealousy;
> It is the green-eyed monster. (167–8)
> —Look to your wife; observe her well with Cassio. (199)
> —She did deceive her father, marrying you. (208)

These shots are on target. Now Othello retreats into his own world of obsessive despair, and his replies are short and subdued:

'O misery!'...'Dost thou say so?'...'And so she did'. The pattern of advance and retreat across the stage is now reversed, and the first round sees Iago leaving the field a complacent victor: 'Leave it to time.'

The second round takes up the fight after time has had its chance in the lapse of 40 lines when Othello is offstage. The new Othello is different in tone, in attitude, in gesture. His entrance shocks us: 'Ha! Ha! false to me?' (335). He turns on all and sundry, driving Iago before him, at one moment lost in a long rhetorical tirade, at another seizing him by the throat, as tradition has it:

> Villain, be sure thou prove my love a whore. (361)

No subtleties of advance and retreat between them now; duologue almost gives place to soliloquy as Othello storms across the platform. Yet Iago is not the man to lose the initiative once gained. He stands his ground and returns to the attack with his ugly imagery of goats and monkeys, and his uglier story of Cassio's dream of Desdemona. The final lash of his tongue brings the Moor to the ferocity of 'O, blood, blood, blood!' (453). Pace accelerates and pitch rises until he is a man destroyed, one who can only drop to his knees for his pact with the Devil. The verbal exchanges have been pointed throughout by a matching dance of movement between the two characters.

#### SPATIAL DISTINCTIONS BETWEEN CHARACTERS

Leaving an actor alone on the platform after a crowded scene is an effect simply arranged, and taking a character aside from his group is particularly meaningful on a stage whose size permitted spatial distinctions. Sometimes a 'Walk with me...' is all that is needed to break up a close group, although it is an inconceivable line for the modern stage. Thus in *Cymbeline*, V, v, 119, such a command serves to allow Belarius and the others to show that they recognize Fidele. Or Prospero's

> A turn or two I'll walk
> To still my beating mind. (*The Tempest*, IV, i, 162–3)

allows him a word with Ariel.

Of a different order of stagecraft is the crowded scene of the
court in the first act of *King Lear*. There is a special problem
here. The elder daughters are identified by their names and their
formal speech immediately, but Cordelia, the one of first significance, must wait until last. Yet it is important for the interest and
irony of the scene to know her feelings, and to recognize the
falseness in the words of her sisters before she addresses the King.
Shakespeare therefore gives her this line:

> What shall Cordelia speak? Love, and be silent.   (I, i, 61)

This is not, however, enough in itself. As one of three women
facing Lear and unfamiliar to the audience, her words may be
lost. Naturally, the line cannot be spoken to the King; it must
involve a movement away. This in turn brings Cordelia outside
the upstage area of the throne and the court, and the sudden view
of her face as she steps away from the symmetry of the courtiers
helps incisively to distinguish her and what she later has to say
from the loquacious Goneril and Regan. The movement toward
the spectators assists, furthermore, the initial impression of her
sincerity, as if her turning away is itself a comment on the
hypocrisy of the others. From the start, the audience is pre-
disposed to sympathize with Cordelia, fully to appreciate the
value of her 'Nothing' and yet still able to enjoy its shock upon
the King. When Shakespeare sets a single character apart from
the group, he immediately defines his image of the scene. Hamlet
or Cordelia is set apart from the court and thereupon compels
criticism of the other figures present.

Since the plays were performed without break, the balancing
of crowd against single figure also works from scene to scene.
In *Romeo and Juliet*, the scene of the death of Mercutio and
Tybalt is towards its end crowded and excited. All Verona seems
to be on the stage: '*Enter Prince, old Montague, Capulet, their
wives and all*'. The Prince pronounces sentence on poor Romeo:

> Let Romeo hence in haste,
> Else, when he is found, that hour is his last.
>
> (III, i, 193–4)

As the stage empties, the one person unaware of events or of her lover's banishment appears: '*Enter Juliet alone*'.

> Gallop apace, you fiery-footed steeds,
> Towards Phoebus' lodging!...          (III, ii, 1–2)

She says this with an impatience the audience knows to be in vain. The effect of the change from the crowd to the individual has the additional value of showing the audience that Juliet faces the world alone.

Like Hamlet and Timon, Coriolanus is constantly isolated from his fellows, although rarely in soliloquy. This has the effect of putting him forward less for sympathy than for censure. Whether fighting the Volces single-handed at the gates of Corioli, or standing self-consciously in the gown of humility before the Roman voices, or tired and 'in mean apparel' before Aufidius's gay banqueting hall, or facing alone the shaming pleas of his womenfolk, or, finally, dressed as a Roman general and surrounded by Volces in their distinctive uniform, Coriolanus is seen as a lonely man, visually always the potential individualist, rebel and traitor.

Contrast between characters can be asserted in vocal tone, pitch and strength; in their appearance by stance, gesture and facial expression; in their costume and its cut and colour; in what they say and the style of their words; and in other less predictable ways, like the quality and presence of the actors. A powerful way of enforcing such contrasts lies in the management of the physical space separating them. The changing distance between players can with all immediacy point the distinctions which other details of characterization may refine.

Such a scene as that of Caesar's processions in *Julius Caesar* may illustrate these qualities of dynamic space.[1] It is a scene in which two groups of players are to interact, those of Caesar's party and those of Brutus's. The first procession is seen objectively, and passes briefly across the upper platform; however, it trails two of the opposite faction: '*Manet* (sic) *Brutus and*

---

[1] Ronald Watkins discusses this and the two succeeding examples in other terms in *On Producing Shakespeare*, pp. 133–4 and 293.

*Cassius'*. Cassius may then commence his seduction of Brutus's mind, closing with the audience when he speaks seditiously of Caesar. Yet soon the procession reappears and Caesar himself has his turn to speak of Cassius, at some length and in privacy with his lieutenant, Antony. The convenient directional lines are given to Cassius:

> As they pass by, pluck Casca by the sleeve…
> Casca will tell us what the matter is.  (I, ii, 179 and 189)

This both gives Brutus and Cassius time to move upstage away from the focal point and allows Caesar and Antony to take their places downstage, perhaps in the alternative corner of the platform, ready for Caesar's sinister lines,

> Let me have men about me that are fat,
> Sleek-headed men, and such as sleep a-nights:
> Yond Cassius has a lean and hungry look;
> He thinks too much: such men are dangerous.  (192–5)

This comment is one which in practice links the two groups visually, directing the contrast between them. So the scene passes once more into the hands of Brutus and Cassius, who now draw Casca secretively down the platform ('You pulled me by the cloak', 215) as Caesar and Antony circle off.

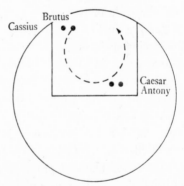

The few words which start Othello on his path to damnation are Iago's 'Ha! I like not that' (*Othello*, III, iii, 35). They are casually dropped in Othello's ear as Desdemona and Cassio move to the door, and they are engineered with care. They are not spoken until six lines have allowed Othello and Iago to get to the foot of the platform, by which time Emilia's warning of their approach and Cassio's insistence that he must take his leave have already directed Cassio's movement toward the other upstage door. As Othello passes down the other side of the platform, he must see his wife's attempt to restrain Cassio: 'Why, stay, and hear me speak' (31). What Iago says confirms what Othello has

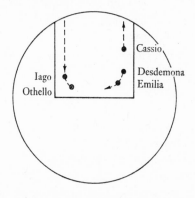

seen, before Desdemona greets him downstage eight lines later with, 'How now, my Lord!' (42). The actors' movement makes the spectator aware of the distance that lends suspicion its force, the diagonal length of the stage.

The scene of Macduff's discovery of the murder of Duncan must seem all confusion, but nice distinctions between reactions to the event are pointed by careful stage planning in depth. The stage is first rapidly filled with all the players upon the ringing of the alarum-bell, but the focus of their attention remains the upstage door which signifies the King's chamber, leaving the downstage area vacant. There Malcolm and Donalbain hold their furtive discussion about their future course of action. This happens at the climactic moment of Lady Macbeth's faint, and Shakespeare considerately sandwiches their debate between Macduff's line, 'Look to the lady' (*Macbeth*, II, iii, 119) and the same line repeated by Banquo (125), so that the spectator's attention reverts to the main action. Malcolm and Donalbain have intruded speeches of intimate honesty,

> Why do we hold our tongues,
> That most may claim this argument for ours?   (119–20)

which balances Macbeth's upstage, public and effusive statement,

> Who can be wise, amazed, temp'rate and furious,
> Loyal and neutral, in a moment?                    (108–9)

This prolixity falls oddly amid the brief, stunned phrases of the others. Words mark the contradiction in the scene, but the physical arrangement of the action makes the irony inescapable. The distance between characters is important for the expression and experience of the drama.

### THE IMPORTANCE OF UPSTAGE AND DOWNSTAGE

What has been called the actor's 'direct address' to the audience, usually with reference to the soliloquy, is but one small part of a whole stage technique which takes into account the actor playing towards or away from his spectators. Soliloquy takes the attention because it is the extreme use of an actor's convention which pervaded the whole play. Writing for the open stage is likely to make for a form of dialogue which, while it is not soliloquy or aside, yet often involves address to the audience.

The 'eloquence of emptiness', our sense of a player alone or apart on the open spaces of the unlocalized stage, permits a direct relationship between actor and spectator, and characters will seem to move out of and back into the scene. It is as if the scene takes the actor upstage from time to time, distancing him like a long-shot in a film, reducing him to a character in a play-within-a-play, while release from the action allows him to become in part a spectator himself, bringing him downstage to be in touch with his audience. It follows that the foot of the platform is sometimes used as neutral ground that is even less localized than the acting area nearer the façade of the tiring-house.

In Lear's first speech before the hovel, he seems to be speaking in part to Kent and the Fool, in part to the storm, in part to himself and in part to the audience:

> Thou think'st 'tis much that this contentious storm
> Invades us to the skin: so 'tis to thee;
> But where the greater malady is fixed,
> The lesser is scarce felt. Thou'dst shun a bear;
> But if thy flight lay toward the roaring sea,
> Thou'dst meet the bear i'th'mouth. When the mind's free,
> The body's delicate; this tempest in my mind
> Doth from my senses take all feeling else
> Save what beats there—filial ingratitude!
> Is it not as this mouth should tear this hand
> For lifting food to't? But I will punish home!...
>
> (*King Lear*, III, iv, 6 ff.)

Even if Lear's clearly defined downstage moves are discounted, it is possible from his words to trace an increasing sense of his address to the audience as the speech evolves. He appears at first to address Kent: 'Thou think'st 'tis much that this contentious storm...', but the climbing voice and his gesture to the open sky on 'this contentious storm' fixes him in an attitude in which he is addressing the audience. 'So 'tis to thee', indeed, embraces his listeners as a whole, on stage and off. 'The greater malady' recalls his present contest with unnatural nature, and is again a gesture to the sky, beyond the immediate world of the platform. On 'the lesser', he drops his voice and his eyes, while his hands fall and touch his clothes and body. The pattern of these first four lines is repeated in the next four. 'The roaring sea' is beyond him, and the bear is met in the mouth by squarely facing the auditorium. The rest of the speech confirms that he has forgotten the presence of Kent and the Fool: it has become soliloquy in all but name. Voice and gesture are matched, but, in addition, the spectators, mankind itself and all the powers of heaven replace Kent and the Fool as Lear's object of attention. 'Indirect address', as it may be called, is therefore used when the poetic drama refreshes and compels its audience by speech which is delivered outside the internal action of the scene and may be subtly woven into the scene itself.

The typical pattern is used in the scene of the baiting of Achilles in *Troilus and Cressida*. Agamemnon, Ulysses, Nestor, Ajax and Menelaus are downstage on the platform already, when Achilles and Patroclus in proud indifference make their entrance upstage. In the conventional way, the dialogue draws attention to their presence. Says Ulysses, 'Achilles stands i'th'entrance of his tent' (III, iii, 38), and promptly offers the Greek leader Agamemnon his plan to humiliate their lethargic ally:

> Please it our general pass strangely by him,
> As if he were forgot. (39–40)

The effect is neat: the spectators are drawn like conspirators into the plot against Achilles, they too savour his overdue mortification and the stage positioning directs whose part they must take. Meanwhile, in the upstage area, the behaviour of Achilles is offered for criticism and condemnation. The distinction between the intimate and the remote presence of the actor has the force of irony; it lends a perspective to the view.

When in *Hamlet* Claudius is discovered by Hamlet at prayer, there seem to be two soliloquies, since neither character speaks to the other or is heard by the other. Yet each offers a different manner of speech, the difference being marked by the actor's proximity to the spectator. Each character is debating with himself, but the spectator does not share Claudius's feelings. He views him objectively, and this response would be promoted by Claudius's disregard of the audience. Hamlet's case is different, since he confirms the spectator's sympathy with him by a comparatively intimate position on the stage.

> Why, this is bait and salary, not revenge... (III, iii, 79 ff.)

is the speech of a man deliberating with himself, but it is also the choric comment of a downstage address, directing the audience to place a valuation upon the proposal to kill the King. When he asks,

> and am I then revenged
> To take him in the purging of his soul,
> When he is fit and seasoned for his passage? (84–6)

this is both the rhetorical question of a chorus and a direct question to the audience. Claudius is therefore remote, pacing upstage and finally falling to his knees; Hamlet is close, having turned away from the crouched figure and come down to us.

The tagged entrance, 'Look where he comes', promptly puts the audience into this special position of participant, and the character who is to enter is objectively distanced. The long temptation of Othello is signposted by such downstage judgments invited from the spectator. After the first attack by Iago, Othello's mind borders on panic as he desperately tries to assess the state of his marriage. He speaks in soliloquy downstage, and invites the audience to study Desdemona as she approaches:

> Look where she comes:
> (*Enter Desdemona and Emilia*)
> If she be false, O, then heaven mocks itself!
> I'll not believe't.         (*Othello*, III, iii, 279–81)

By her tone and her immediate concern for him, we instantly recognize her honesty, and the misconceptions in his mind are ironically accentuated. In his turn, Othello too is scrutinized upon his re-entrance when Iago speaks in soliloquy a moment later:

> (*Enter Othello*)
> Look where he comes! Not poppy, nor mandragora,
> Nor all the drowsy syrups of the world,
> Shall ever medicine thee to that sweet sleep
> Which thou owedst yesterday.         (331–5)

From the startling change in Othello's appearance and the new note in his voice, 'Ha! Ha! false to me?', the spectator knows that Iago is right.

In the case of *Antony and Cleopatra*, Shakespeare starts the impetus of his whole play in this ironic fashion. The argument is opened by the two Roman veterans Demetrius and Philo, who enter and move down the platform with their conversation already under way: 'Nay, but this dotage of our general's...'. After they have furnished the audience with a highly deprecatory if superficial view of Antony's conduct from the choric downstage position, they draw attention to the principals themselves:

97

> Look, where they come:
> Take but good note, and you shall see in him
> The triple pillar of the world transformed
> Into a strumpet's fool. Behold and see.    (I, i, 10–13)

We do indeed behold and see, and are immediately aware of an effective visual and verbal irony. For Antony and Cleopatra play out their first love-scene in the superb terms of

CLEOPATRA. If it be love indeed, tell me how much.
ANTONY. There's beggary in the love that can be reckoned.   (14–15)

We may suspect that while the lovers take their places at the foot of the platform, Demetrius and Philo stand aside, until they speak again at the end of the scene.

### SPEAKING TO THE AUDIENCE

Apart from soliloquies and asides proper, downstage speech in direct and indirect address is an amalgam of confession, chorus and commentary. Sometimes it serves one function rather than another, but it is hard in many cases to distinguish between them. In some scenes Shakespeare actually exploits the dramatic ambiguity which follows upon the close-up position: is the downstage actor going to tell the 'truth' or not? The short judgment of Philo on his general is obviously not that of the playwright; on the other hand, a soliloquy from *Hamlet* is something more than ironic comment. Between the extremes of subjective confession and objective chorus there is room for a great range of speech which can provoke a response from the spectator.

Confessions are recognizable and commonplace. The Earl of Warwick is dragged wounded down the platform by the Prince of Wales to make his dying speech (*3 Henry VI*, v, ii); or Orlando finds himself conveniently close to the audience in order to make the brief tongue-tied assertions of his love for Rosalind (*As You Like It*, I, ii).

In the later plays such addresses to the audience often acquire an ambivalent quality which puts the spectator on his metal. On her arrival at Cyprus, Desdemona is led by Cassio upstage with light steps in keeping with their bantering tone; this leaves Iago free to turn to the audience:

He takes her by the palm. Ay, well said, whisper. With as little web as this will I ensnare as great a fly as Cassio... (*Othello*, II, i, 167 ff.)

This mixture of aside and confession is not needed to reveal Iago's black soul; but it shows how an innocent friendship will lend itself to Iago's plans. Moreover, it reintroduces the sinister note into a scene otherwise pleasant, and serves to cast an ironic blight over the idealized greeting of Desdemona by Othello which follows.

It is worth noticing that Shakespeare adopts a movement pattern which echoes this when Othello, possessed by Iago's spirit, makes his entrance to smother his wife. Before he moves to kiss the sleeping Desdemona on 'I'll smell it on the tree' (V, ii, 15), he has walked *adagio* down to the audience in order partly to confess his mind, partly to invoke 'you chaste stars' (line 2) and partly to argue 'the cause'. The irony is promoted because there upstage she lies in innocent sleep, a steady reminder to the spectator by her presence that she has done nothing to warrant his revenge, and that all he says is dark imagining.

Four times Kent urges Lear to come out of the storm with 'Good my lord, enter' (*King Lear*, III, iv, 1, 4, 5 and 22), and each time this compels the King to assert his indifference by a sequence of avoiding movements which carry him down to the edge of the platform: 'Let me alone' (3), 'Wilt break my heart?' (4), 'Prithee go in thyself, seek thine own ease' (23) and 'Nay, get thee in' (27)—a highly individual method of separating a character from a group. It is at the edge of the platform that he stands in solitary dignity to accost 'this contentious storm', challenging it with 'Pour on; I will endure', crying his remorse to the open skies of the theatre:

> Poor naked wretches, whereso'er you are,
> That bide the pelting of this pitiless storm,
> How shall your houseless heads and unfed sides,
> Your looped and windowed raggedness, defend you
> From such seasons as these? O, I have ta'en
> Too little care of this! (28–33)

This is confession and chorus both, underlining the Christian issues of the play, revealing Lear's new humility and, by his spatial separation from the troubled Kent and the Fool cowering by the upstage door, marking the isolation of the martyr.

An 'epic' form of drama found the presenters named 'Chorus' or 'Prologue' a useful convention as it does in the Brechtian theatre. In *Romeo and Juliet*, such a chorus touches concisely on the themes of death and rebirth, age and youth, civil dissension and fate, themes implicit in the play:

> From forth the fatal loins of these two foes
> A pair of star-crossed lovers take their life;
> Whose misadventured piteous overthrows
> Doth with their death bury their parents' strife.

(I, Prologue, 5–8)

Shakespeare a second time presses the device into service at the beginning of the second act:

> Now old desire doth in his deathbed lie,
> And young affection gapes to be his heir...

(II, Prologue, 1–2)

When this chorus has re-emphasized the theme, he is heard no more, and his work is done thereafter less obtrusively by the Prince. With the one exception of the Chorus in *Henry V*, whose descriptive monologues are an entertainment in themselves, injecting colour into the varied scenes they anticipate, formal choric figures have a thankless task, and it is Shakespeare's more general practice to transmit much of the choric statement through characters working within the action of the play. Hamlet plays chorus for Ophelia in the play scene (*Hamlet*, III, ii) and simultaneously reveals his own tense feelings; this is the method by which Shakespeare imparts a direct impact to a chorus speech, for then the audience, also caught up in the action, lays itself open to other impressions.

It is clear how in much direct choric commentary the downstage position of the commentator may be used by this method to call for criticism of upstage behaviour. One cannot imagine the Doctor and the Gentlewoman upstage within Lady Macbeth's orbit when she enters for her sleep-walking scene. Shakespeare is careful to prepare her entrance with words that both gather suspense and indicate the meaning of what is to be seen. The Doctor's comment,

A great perturbation in nature, to receive at once the benefits of sleep and do the effects of watching!

(Macbeth, V, i, 9–10)

is spoken into the ear of the audience as well as to the Waiting Gentlewoman, and the excitement gains ironically because the sleep-walker is seen by the audience with greater knowledge than the Doctor's. His ejaculations, 'Do you mark that?'... 'Even so?', press the spectator to respond in accord with him, until he clinches the meaning of the scene and stimulates a larger interest with

> Foul whisp'rings are abroad: unnatural deeds
> Do breed unnatural troubles... (70–1)

By the rhythm of his lines, Shakespeare cannot forbear granting this minor character a little gratuitous life, and this serves to emphasize his double function as both *dramatis persona* and 'chorus'.

The choric interpolations of Enobarbus in *Antony and Cleopatra* further the theme and image rather than the plot and action of the play, and for this reason alone are to be played on the intimate downstage regions of the platform. Yet Enobarbus has his own character, though it owes nothing to Plutarch, as firmly delineated as that of any other, but he so plays the impersonal chorus to the play that no small part of its enveloping tone of ironic dialectic is due to his persistent intrusion. When he makes his decision to defect from Antony with 'I will seek/ Some way to leave him' (III, xiii, 200–1), and then in shame to take his own life, 'I will go seek/Some ditch wherein to die' (IV, vi, 37–8), he is speaking truly in soliloquy at the place on the platform appropriate to it. This place is approximately the same as for his choric comments: his twin roles of character and chorus have finally merged, and the stage positioning identifies them.

His death itself passes his last comment on Antony's power to command love and loyalty.

In the mature tragedies, Shakespeare's concern with the deception of appearances increasingly invites use of the oblique commentary, and characters like Horatio, Emilia, Kent, Banquo and Enobarbus serve this function. The role of Enobarbus has become more closely integrated in the play that follows it, *Coriolanus*. The Tribunes of the People, Brutus and Sicinius, share the task of opposing Caius Marcius in Rome, and also serve as commentators on this 'too absolute' man. Shakespeare repeatedly leaves them at the foot of the platform after a lively upstage action, in order that they may express their jaundiced views of the hero. This happens at the end of I, i, II, i, II, ii and II, iii. Coriolanus has fewer moments of isolation even than Antony: he is almost always presented as a public figure; only when he stands alone before Aufidius's gate (IV, v) is he allowed to be downstage with the audience. In this largely public role, it is for us to judge whether he is an enemy of the people or not. Menenius Agrippa would have us see him one way, the Tribunes the other, and neither is wholly wrong. Everyone from Senator to servant gets his chance to pass comment on the hero: he is a man put up for public inspection, and the play is as much a play of dialectic as of tragedy. Coriolanus is typically the upstage figure, all but sinking, in the first half of the play, under his load of choric recrimination.

Something of the same limitation is present in *Timon of Athens*. Timon gets his chance to speak in close soliloquy (IV, i) only after his critics have drawn attention to his apparent simplicity of mind. Shakespeare here employs the anti-illusory stage to the extent of piling comment on comment. A small crowd of satellites first introduces the audience to this gentleman of Athens who gives his wealth away (I, i); in the banquet scene (I, ii), devised to demonstrate Timon's largesse, the playwright interposes yet more commentators. Especially, he creates the churlish philosopher Apemantus who '*comes, dropping after all . . . discontentedly, like himself*'. He is distinguished, that is, from the foppish guests by wearing his everyday dress. While the main table for the banquet must occupy the upstage space, Apemantus is specifically given '*a table by himself*'. This may only be sited close to the spectators, for, as he tells Timon, 'I come to observe, I give thee warning on't' (I, ii, 33). From this position he easily maintains his running commentary upon the flatterers at Timon's table, and upon Timon himself. Not content with this, Shakespeare grants Timon's faithful steward Flavius two or three lengthy asides to warn the audience of his master's short-sightedness:

> 'Tis pity bounty had not eyes behind,
> That man might ne'er be wretched for his mind.    (164–5)

This harping on one theme so deprives the audience of a judgment of its own that few of the ambiguities characteristic of *Antony and Cleopatra* and *Coriolanus* survive the first act.

### THE WAYS OF EAVESDROPPING

A curious convention occurs in a number of Shakespeare's plays, one which serves to illustrate the freedom of Elizabethan stage grouping. This is the convention of eavesdropping. It involves a form of the aside, but it calls for a special pattern of movement. Where actors are to observe others without speaking, there is no problem: as when Claudius and Polonius hide behind an arras in order to observe Hamlet (*Hamlet*, III, i), or when the Duke and the Provost withdraw to overhear Claudio and Isabella (*Measure for Measure*, III, i), an upstage position will serve. What if a 'hidden' character must speak and be heard in the auditorium?

The platform makes it possible for the eavesdropper to do his work from any place on a stage perimeter of some 90 or 100 feet with some part of the audience at his elbow. However, if the spectator was to enjoy the ruse at the expense of the one who was overheard, Shakespeare expected the eavesdropper's position to be downstage. If a stage-pillar was standing available, no doubt this was used for a mock hiding-place; but there was little attempt to create an illusion: tell the audience that a character was in hiding, and in hiding he was.

The effervescent scene of multiple eavesdropping in *Love's Labour's Lost* suggests that a character has only to step aside to be invisible to the others. Each of the young gallants has separately fallen in love and thus broken his celibate vows; nevertheless, he is quite ready to enjoy his colleagues' lapse. First Berowne '*stands aside*' (IV, iii, 19) to overhear the King of Navarre (line 77, 'Like a demigod here sit I in the sky' seems to place him on the balcony or in a tree, but line 148, 'Now step I forth...', hardly suggests the former); then the King himself '*steps aside*' upon the entrance of Longaville; and lastly Longaville overhears Dumain. Each has words to speak from his place of 'hiding', and although the King later declares that he has been 'closely shrouded in this bush' (134), they must all three have been disposed about the edge of the acting area in full view of the spectators. Nor does the distance separating them prevent Berowne from seeming to overhear all the other three, nor the King from overhearing the other two ('I...marked you both', 135). It seems sufficient to say simply 'Now step I forth' in order to pass back into the central action and join the others.

No one has worked out the double eavesdropping scenes of *Much Ado About Nothing* to satisfaction, and this is probably because in our modern imagination we still translate the stage into a realistic garden setting. Shakespeare plants his orchard at the beginning of II, iii, and, upon the approach of the conspirators Don Pedro, Leonato and Claudio, Benedick declares that he 'will hide me in the arbour' (35). If this was the common property arbour, where was it placed? From it Benedick has lengthy asides to speak, and through or round it Claudio too has repeatedly to spy upon him and pass comment. It would be irresponsible to place the arbour upstage where such asides, the best lines in the scene, would be diminished. The spying is the main action, and suggests that centre-stage, at least, was the place for the arbour.

CLAUDIO. O ay, stalk on, stalk on—the fowl sits...(*aloud*)
    I never did think that lady would have loved any man...
BENEDICK. Is't possible? Sits the wind in that corner?    (95–101)

Only if he were centre-stage could the players circle round Benedick to permit such a complicated set of asides to operate. The tricking of Beatrice (III, i) follows immediately, and the same orchard is in the spectator's imagination, and the same arbour remains on the stage. It is Beatrice's turn to hide, and three ladies, Hero, Margaret and Ursula, take the places of the three men in the previous scene. Although Beatrice has nothing to say from her retreat, the movements echo the earlier ones, and the patterning suggests the formality of the game.

In *As You Like It*, the ample platform similarly allows Silvius to act out his lovesick grief to Corin in II, iv, and to Phebe in III, v, at the same time being overheard by Rosalind and company. Yet no one hides and Silvius never shows that he is overlooked. At the funeral of Ophelia (*Hamlet*, v, i), Hamlet and Horatio can 'couch...awhile, and mark' (216), and the Prince can address his asides to the audience without trouble, presumably from another downstage position. The coffin is lowered into the central trap, but convention has it that Hamlet is 'hidden' by the hood of his cloak until he throws it back as he leaps forward.

Did the box-tree from which Sir Toby, Sir Andrew and Fabian eavesdrop upon Malvolio (*Twelfth Night*, II, v) really exist? If it did, the freedom to eavesdrop suggests that it could be planted anywhere. Some modern productions have, indeed, made it as mobile as Birnam Wood. Why doubt that the conspirators played their comedy from the most effective position— downstage—in full view of the audience, so that not a grimace nor a witticism should be missed? Only in this way could the spectator completely share in the joke. Certainly Sir Toby and his men have too much of the dialogue to be tucked away inside an inner stage.

### THE SILENT FIGURE

When a character was both spatially separated from the group and silent into the bargain, he was granted a special strength. The spectator is not allowed to forget him or what his presence implies. In the scene of Richard II's resignation of his crown

(*Richard II*, IV, i) it is as if the King talks himself off the throne while the usurper stands looking on in contempt and silent strength at Richard's diminishing stature. Richard has 132 lines to Bolingbroke's 14 in this scene, and the sinister taciturnity of the latter is pointed by the phrase 'silent king' (line 290) with which Richard addresses him. In another vein, in *Much Ado About Nothing*, Hero has but one line in the scene of her betrothal to Claudio (II, i); she stands apart, and the most that she is allowed to do is to 'stop his mouth with a kiss' (290–1) and whisper into Claudio's ear. This may have been a convenience for the boy actor, but it was a somewhat ready way of depicting feminine modesty in the face of Beatrice's forwardness. It has the unfortunate effect of making Hero a little dull. In *Troilus and Cressida*, every scene between the lovers (III, ii, IV, ii and IV, iv) is sullied by the unwholesome presence of Pandarus. Each 'pretty encounter' has him for overseer, and his cynical comments slowly poison the sweetness: 'Have you not done talking yet?'. . . 'How now, how now! how go maidenheads?'. In the eyes of the audience, it is the hovering figure of Pandarus which has already extinguished the spark of romance in this futile love-affair long before the assignation with Diomedes.

Not until the great tragedies does Shakespeare use a silent presence to complete effect. A silent Ophelia kneels at her orisons during Hamlet's soliloquy, 'To be or not to be' (*Hamlet*, III, i, 56). The presence of her devout innocence, even though she is Polonius's decoy, adds a dimension of meaningful criticism of Hamlet's thoughts of sacrilegious suicide: she is the visible reminder of simplicity as he indulges the complexity of his despair.

The eloquence of silence becomes more explicit in *Othello*. The Emilia who knows the whereabouts of Desdemona's handkerchief holds her tongue throughout the scene in which Othello lashes his wife with angry words for having lost it. Many pages have been expended in argument about this effect. Emilia has only the obvious comment after the Moor has swept out: 'Is not this man jealous?' (III, iv, 103), and to this she adds some bitter remarks about husbands in a general way. Did she fear that she would lose her place in Othello's household if she spoke up? Could she have forgotten about the handkerchief in gross stupidity? Did she go in fear of her husband Iago? Was she merely sceptical about domestic quarrels, having in mind her own life with a 'wayward husband'? The visual effect of her silence resolves the problem. Shakespeare could easily have sent her offstage to avoid awkward questions; the fact is that he wanted her there, in full view, to heighten the tensions in the scene. She stands watching, overcome with astonishment that the Moor could be so uncontrolled, while the audience expects her intervention at any moment; it is denied by the master of stagecraft. At the very end of this play (v, ii), it is Iago's persistent refusal to explain himself in the face of every insult, verbal and physical, which suggests that at the last evil is an enigma beyond our capacity to understand. The Devil himself seems to stand there, looking on at the 'tragic loading' of Desdemona's bed, silent, unflinching and inscrutable.

The forlorn figure of the revolted Enobarbus must stand miserably by to listen to Octavius Caesar as he gives his harsh order:

> Go charge Agrippa
> Plant those that have revolted in the vant,
> That Antony may seem to spend his fury
> Upon himself.      (*Antony and Cleopatra*, IV, vi, 8–11)

This is not a case of Caesar's deliberately ignoring Enobarbus, since his silent presence cannot fail to have ironic repercussions upon the sympathetic spectator.

The artistry of *Coriolanus* is evident in this practice of using the mute figure. In the women's scenes, Volumnia tends to talk to Valeria, while Coriolanus's wife Virgilia remains silent, the embodiment of dumb criticism. Later, the silent approach of the three women and the boy who come to plead that Coriolanus will have a change of heart, tortures both the hero and the spectator, and Coriolanus's own long silence points the moment when he has capitulated. Volumnia's urgent appeal for her son's return ceases with the celebrated stage direction,

'*Holds her by the hand, silent*' (v, iii, 182). This is to lend power to the low-toned words of an unhappy Coriolanus which follow: 'O mother, mother./What have you done?'. The silence and the desolate inflexion of voice, marked by the gesture, tell their story: he knows the fatal consequence of a double betrayal of Romans and Volscians. However, the greater visual irony in this scene is the constant presence of a contemptuous Aufidius upstage among his army, listening for a treacherous response from his new ally as the mother revives old loyalties. In Aufidius, the hatred of an ancient enmity flares up; Coriolanus knows the danger perhaps less than the audience, who are aware of Aufidius's threatening silence. When Coriolanus asks him,

> Were you in my stead, would you have heard
> A mother less? or granted less, Aufidius?　　　(192–3)

the audience does not misunderstand Aufidius's new attitude to Coriolanus, nor does it miss the equivocation in Aufidius's reply in its brevity, 'I was moved withal'. It is a death-sentence. In such a scene, Shakespeare's visual imagination tells him that the character who is dumb can contribute as much as the one who gives utterance.

# 5

## THE FULL STAGE

Following the murder of Duncan or the smothering of Desdemona, both tense, solitary scenes, we can sense Shakespeare's instinct to have his players spill over the stage, increasing the tempo and the movement. Or, as at the end of *As You Like It* and *Twelfth Night*, he will order a crowded stage for a scene of artificial symmetry, the visual pattern acquiring some of the qualities of tableaux. Yet Shakespeare had also to overcome the disadvantage of the confusing impact of a full stage, lest there resulted a destructive blur in lieu of theatrical communication. Planning for a full platform involved the careful deployment of the players.

One method of controlling the action was to fill the stage by a mechanical succession of entrances. The spectator's attention is taken by each new figure and each new voice. In the first scene of *1 Henry VI*, Shakespeare tries out such an effect. The scene begins with the subdued funeral of Henry V, played statuesquely with the regal ceremony befitting Westminster Abbey. It moves in procession to a dead march and is coloured only by cloudy rhetoric in praise of England's soldier king. Suddenly the stage is alerted by a simple expedient: '*Enter a Messenger*', crying,

> Sad tidings bring I to you out of France,
> Of loss, or slaughter and discomfiture...     (I, i, 53 ff.)

And again, '*Enter to them another Messenger*':

> Lords, view these letters full of bad mischance.
> France is revolted from the English quite...     (89 ff.)

And yet again, '*Enter another Messenger*':

> My gracious lords, to add to your laments,
> Wherewith you now bedew King Henry's hearse,
> I must inform you of a dismal fight
> Betwixt the stout Lord Talbot and the French...     (103 ff.)

So, in spite of its prosaic accompaniments, the tempo of the play is accelerated largely by a visual device. The nobles of England thereupon depart, also in sequence, in order to prepare new war against France.

In much the same way the counter-movement in *Richard III* is started by the succession of entrances which announce the danger from Richmond's increasing military strength. Here, however, the sequence is used to more purpose. It forces a reaction from Richard and, following as it does his smooth handling of Queen Elizabeth, thrusts his character into relief. First it is '*Enter Ratcliffe*':

> How now! what news?
> Most mighty sovereign, on the western coast
> Rideth a puissant navy... (IV, iv, 433 ff.)

Then '*Enter Lord Stanley*':

> Stanley, what news with you?
> None good, my liege, to please you with the hearing;
>   ...Richmond is on the seas. (457 ff.)

After which, the pace is in 20 lines built up by the succession of four more Messengers, until the Richard of the over-confident 'There let him sink!' is beside himself, striking a servant with 'Out on you, owls! nothing but songs of death?' (508). He is seen as a man bedevilled by unwelcome news on every side.

In later plays a calculated filling of the stage specifically serves Shakespeare's themes. The renowned opening of *Romeo and Juliet* demonstrates a device for plunging the play, in quasi-realistic terms, into the civil turmoil of the two houses. Some eleven speaking characters are progressively introduced upon the stage, together with an unknown number of others, in order to suggest the unruly streets of Verona. Moreover, the characters as they enter progress in rank, until the Prince himself comes upon the scene. The players represent equally the two sides in the dispute, suggesting that opposite doors are used and used alternately. Before long, the stage seems to seethe with duelling figures, but without confusing the spectator, since the entrances have been controlled, the combatants increasing in significant stature though entering at less frequent intervals. The quarrel of Samson and Gregory, a matter of words, becomes a recognizably serious fight marking the division between the two houses, touched off by such uncompromising language as this from Tybalt:

> What, drawn, and talk of peace? I hate the word,
> As I hate hell, all Montagues, and thee. (I, i, 69–70)

After this attack, the melancholy Romeo may wander on to the stage for a neat contrast.

As in *Richard III*, the succession of entrances is used in *King Lear* to jar upon the nerves of the hero, each entrance a signal for the redoubling of his fury. However, with an improved technique, Shakespeare adds sound and speech to stage movement. The scene is II, iv, in which the King approaches his second daughter Regan in expectation of her hospitality. Having been recently shocked by Goneril's treatment, he is now indignant at finding his loyal Kent in the stocks. Lear's reiterated query, 'Who put my man i'th'stocks?'...'Who stocked my servant?' indicates that his suspicion that he will be treated with equal contempt by Regan is rising to the surface of his consciousness during the action: Kent's silent presence troubles him, and the questions are signals leading the actor to his peak of feeling. He appeals to Regan from the heart, but he is first taken aback by her curt answer, 'Good sir, to th'purpose' (177). He immediately hears the '*tucket within*', and is shaken by learning from Regan that it announces the arrival of the unwelcome Goneril. He is next unsettled by the appearance of Goneril's insolent steward Oswald: this is the third shock in the progression. No sooner has Lear recovered from this, than Goneril herself is seen:

> Who comes here? O heavens
> If you do love old men...! (185–6)

Then, to cap all, Regan greets her sister in friendship:

> O Regan! will you take her by the hand? (190)

He is appalled as the sisters lightly annihilate his dignity. This is the fifth and last in a sequence of blows such as might send him out of his senses. Oswald has no line to speak: his entrance is pure theatre. He is being used as a link in a co-ordinated pattern in which speech, noises off, the entrance and presence of actors and significant gesture are integrated.

## CONTROLLING THE VISUAL IMAGES

From such examples it is arguable that the tempo of a sequence of action on Shakespeare's stage is often as much controlled by visual planning as by verbal. Certainly the sequence of impressions projected to the audience can be violently reorientated by the arrival of characters on the stage.

The scene of Mercutio's death and Romeo's banishment is an early model of scene construction for the full stage determined by arrivals and departures. It develops a shape by filling the platform steadily, but it begins slowly and quietly. Benvolio is walking with Mercutio:

> I pray thee, good Mercutio, let's retire;
> The day is hot, the Capels are abroad.
>
> (*Romeo and Juliet*, III, i, 1–2)

The atmosphere is heavy. Yet within a minute it is '*Enter Tybalt and others*', and the lines take on the sharpness of malice as the enemies face each other. Tybalt has come in search of Romeo, and his hatred finds its particular object when Romeo enters. He may now turn his whole attention upon the man who dared to gate-crash his uncle's house-party.

> Romeo, the love I bear thee can afford
> No better term than this: thou art a villain.          (59–60)

The fiery words stream out, harsh and provocative, and the spectators both on and off the stage hang upon Romeo's reply. When it comes, it comes with the effect of a tense pause in the action. In this moment, the audience realizes that Romeo cannot take up a challenge from his new kinsman, the cousin of the lady he has just married. Slowly his quiet and measured words are enunciated, in direct contrast with Tybalt's, their pace matching our dawning understanding as well as Romeo's thinking:

> Tybalt, the reason that I have to love thee
> Doth much excuse the appertaining rage
> To such a greeting. Villain am I none—
> Therefore farewell; I see thou knowest me not.     (61–4)

He turns his back on Tybalt. Those on stage are stunned, but after the hiatus the impetuous Mercutio can stand it no longer. He draws, and a duel is on, with Romeo vainly trying to stop it while the rival parties encourage their champions. What follows is all of visual excitement, until '*Tybalt under Romeo's arm thrusts Mercutio in; and flies*'. As suddenly again, the stage that was in an uproar falls quiet, while Tybalt flees and Mercutio coughs out his last witticisms, helped away by Benvolio. Romeo is alone, lamenting his lost honour. Now the pace picks up again. Benvolio returns to report Mercutio's death; Tybalt re-appears; and in Romeo's voice is heard an uncharacteristic tone:

> Away to heaven, respective lenity,
> And fire-eyed fury be my conduct now!     (122–3)

The fight is on once more, this time more dangerous and crucial. So Tybalt is slain and Romeo is the one who must flee. Again Shakespeare plays on the pause of horror as the meaning of the deed is gathered up by both Romeo and the audience. 'Stand not amazed', says Benvolio to Romeo, 'Why dost thou stay?'. He runs, and quickly the stage is alive with many angry figures: '*Enter Citizens...Enter Prince, old Montague, Capulet, their Wives, and all.*' The scene closes with Benvolio's account of what has passed and the Prince's sentence upon Romeo.

The stage has been filled, emptied and filled again. Central are the two duels, the two mortal strokes and the two pauses which together signify Romeo's role as fortune's fool. Though the crises are surrounded by the movement of many characters, Shakespeare ensures that the duels are followed by weighty visual 'rests' in the score, the stage held in repose before the next passage of entrance, action and exit. In the final scene in the Capulet tomb, v, iii, Shakespeare plans a parallel sequence. The statuesque and declamatory presentation of Romeo's suicide, Juliet's waking and her response with his dagger provides a scene of climactic pause and a symbolic moment in itself. It too is rapidly followed by the crowding of the stage, with, successively, the Watch, Paris's Page, Balthasar, Friar Lawrence, more of the Watch, the Prince and his train, the Capulets and finally the Montagues. Meanwhile, like a reproach, the dead lie still and silent at the tomb upstage. The private world of human relationships for the first and only time in the play impinges upon the civil struggle, but too late to stop the mortal toll.

In visual terms, the long contest of Hamlet with himself is at the end of the play allowed a sudden, vivid release. The final scene of the court duel between the Prince and Laertes (*Hamlet*, v, ii, 223 ff.) is a sequence of quick tactics and swift retribution as Hamlet fights his last fight with the grim gaiety of relief. By contrast, *King Lear* seems to be about to end with a similar acceleration of visual excitement, prompted and brought to a pitch by Albany's

> Great thing of us forgot!
> Speak, Edmund; where's the king? and where's Cordelia?
>
> (v, iii, 235–6)

and 'Run, run, O run.' (246), and 'Haste thee, for thy life!' (250). The sequence of entrances begins with '*Enter a Gentleman, with a bloody knife*', and this player's feverish appearance and quick calls for help mark a new access of pace. Nor should we forget that at this point the audience, thinking of Lear and Cordelia, does not know whose blood he exhibits, and that his 'O, she's dead!' (223) is still ambiguous and deliberately delayed for our suspense. Nor that when Albany is demanding to know the whereabouts of the King and Cordelia, two bodies are carried in, which we learn afterwards are those of Goneril and Regan. Yet with that momentous direction, '*Enter Lear, with Cordelia in his arms*', the play closes in its quiet, pathetic and questioning key. Set against the sudden action, itself a climax to a sequence of fighting, successive entrances and death, Shakespeare supplies in an aftermath of suffering a moving but reflective end. The play, though raising vital and haunting questions, offers no solutions: in Edgar's words, 'Speak what we feel, not what we ought to say'

(324). An intimate downstage moment is thus reserved for the end of the play, an actor's opportunity and a last pause which grants the audience time to ponder the reality of death which Lear must finally embrace. By its stillness, the full stage can effectively emphasize a meaningful centre of attention—the King in repose with his child.

### CROWDS

Shakespeare taught himself to handle a busy stage by force of experience. What to do with a stage crowded with 'supers' is a special problem, and Shakespeare's treatment of the common people as a crowd in the two Roman plays *Julius Caesar* and *Coriolanus* remains the example in big group movement for later dramatists.

The impersonal, inarticulate crowd of *Julius Caesar* called for close treatment if the stage was not to run riot. From the first scene of this play, the Roman citizens are to take on a defined role, and their mood is indicated at every point:

| | |
|---|---:|
| —Hence! home, you idle creatures, get you home: Is this a holiday? | (1–2) |
| —What dost thou with thy best apparel on? | (8) |
| —Wherefore rejoice? | (36) |
| —They vanish tongue-tied in their guiltiness. | (66) |

Moreover, through the Cobbler, its spokesman, this crowd is given a characteristic voice, although it remains one without particularity. The citizens are intermittently before the audience during three acts, and they are seen to change from this festive gathering to the mob which in III, iii, can tear to pieces Cinna the Poet.

Throughout the scene of Caesar's procession, I, ii, their function in approving Caesar with shouts and applause is clearly indicated. Their service to the drama of the Capitol scene, III, i, is also unmistakable in such lines as these:

CINNA. Liberty! freedom! Tyranny is dead!
Run hence, proclaim, cry it about the streets.
CASSIUS. Some to the common pulpits, and cry out
'Liberty, freedom and enfranchisement!'

BRUTUS. People, and senators, be not affrighted;
   Fly not; stand still; ambition's debt is paid. (78–83)

Here they have become an unthinking animal, and their movement over the platform corresponds; but during the speeches of Brutus and Antony in the Forum, they acquire a human individuality which is carefully prescribed.

At first Shakespeare directs them to be reasonable:

  —I will hear Brutus speak.
  —I will hear Cassius; and compare their reasons,
    When severally we hear them renderéd.
  —The noble Brutus is ascended: silence! (III, ii, 8–11)

A passive group indeed, and one whose voices speak in dignified verse. Further, the citizens have perforce to listen to Brutus's scrupulous arguments. The crowd is impressed by such respectful treatment, but they respond with such a variety of notions that they have certainly not been moved as one man; indeed, their comments suggest that they have not understood a word: 'Give him a statue'…'Let him be Caesar'. Visually, therefore, they are a fragmented group.

This impression is built up in order that Antony's different appeal shall provide a contrast to that of Brutus. Antony judges the temper of the meeting accurately—''Twere best he speak no harm of Brutus here'. He is in a position to work upon the feelings, and as he casts doubt upon Brutus's motives, pausing to shed a tear, hinting at the contents of Caesar's will, disclosing the body itself, the crowd is soon a mob again. It now responds with roars, and as with one voice: 'Revenge! About! Seek! Burn! Fire! Kill! Slay! Let not a traitor live!' (205–6). The increasing tempo of its interpolations suggests that it is no longer standing passively, but intermittently surging forward. It has begun to sway with the wind, and again and again is on the point of stampeding: 'Stay, countrymen'…'Away, then!'…'Yet hear me, countrymen'…'Come, away, away!' With Antony's

    Now let it work. Mischief, thou art afoot,
    Take thou what course thou wilt, (262–3)

the happy citizens of Act 1 have been transformed.

In *Coriolanus*, the crowd has matured, and its visual aspect is rarely that of a mob. The drama of the first half of the play is related to the presence of the Roman citizens, and their individuality as people is more closely drawn. To be sure, the play leads off with attack: the audience is to know that one of its chief issues is to be the community, and the rousing stage direction reads, '*Enter a company of mutinous Citizens, with staves, clubs, and other weapons.*' Yet from the start the deployment of players is under control. The group has its fugleman in the First Citizen, who immediately halts the riotous movement at centre-stage: 'Before we proceed any further, hear me speak' (I, i, 1–2). Before he can incite them to mutiny, and get them on the move again, a Second Citizen swings them round with 'One word, good citizens'. They re-form with a second focal point. Moreover, he compels the First Citizen to argue the case with him, and a divided crowd becomes a thoughtful one. Finally, when the First Citizen's 'To th'Capitol!' brings them once again to the point of action, Shakespeare introduces a more formidable figure. The 'worthy Menenius Agrippa' for a third time halts the citizens in their tracks, and they settle attentively to listen to the fable of the Belly and the Members. This never was to be an unruly mob in this scene; from the beginning their behaviour conveys the idea and strength of thoughtful decision, behaviour against which Caius Marcius's own uncontrolled passion shows badly. His contemptuous bullying of them may send them off subdued and abashed (they '*steal away*'), but the outcome of their new mood remains in doubt.

All this is in preparation for the scene in the Forum in which Coriolanus must win the citizens' voices (II, iii). The group which awaits him there is smaller and more individualized. The new direction is '*Enter seven or eight Citizens*', and they enter in a different temper from that of the first scene. Three do the talking, and this has the air of discussion, although spiced with a little banter to indicate their spirit. The First and Second Citizens of scene i are now gone, and there is no hint of former malice. Furthermore, Shakespeare insists upon their courteous behaviour

as they huddle together in some awe of Coriolanus. He has the
Third Citizen say,

> We are not to stay all together, but to come by him where he stands,
> by ones, by twos, and by threes.                                    (40–3)

Movement is now directed to the position upstage where the
hero appears in his gown of humility. As instructed, they
approach him as it were from the auditorium in small parcels,
but keep their distance and restrain their tongues. However,
Coriolanus's sarcasms are not lost on them, and again they
respond as sentient beings. He, on the other hand, does not
perceive their quiet forbearance in the face of his mockery.

When Coriolanus has gone, it is clear that the wind has changed.
They have observed him more shrewdly than he has observed
them, and they speak their minds at the foot of the platform:

2 CITIZEN.          . . . to my poor unworthy notice,
  He mocked us when he begged our voices.
3 CITIZEN.                              Certainly;
  He flouted us downright.                                            (156–8)

Only one citizen among them sees an excuse for Coriolanus's
behaviour, but the weight of feeling is against him. The Tribunes
recognize their chance to crush their enemy, and within minutes
the men who entered in thoughtful dignity leave the stage for
the first time like a mob. When next they are seen, their movement pattern is that of swarming insects, and the stage direction
significantly uses a new word to describe them: '*Enter a rabble
of Plebeians with the Aediles*' (III, i, 179). There is no mistaking
that 'rabble'. With this new character for the crowd, Coriolanus
has a different problem to deal with, and tactics must be replaced
by strategy.

### ARMIES INTO BATTLE

For the creation of illusionary battle in any theatre, a stage army
must draw heavily upon evocative sights and sounds. Yet it is
the usual case that inadequate theatre equipment and the limited
size of the company prohibit any degree of naturalistic presentation. Sir Philip Sidney and Ben Jonson made scathing comments

on the contemporary Elizabethan tradition, and in 1671 the two-man army was still an object of ridicule in Buckingham's *The Rehearsal*. From Sidney's *Apologie for Poetrie* in 1581:

Two armies fly in, represented with four swords and bucklers, and then what hard heart will not receive it for a pitched field?

From Jonson in 1598:
          with three rusty swords,
     And help of some few foot and half-foot words,
     Fight over York and Lancaster's long jars,
     And in the tiring-house bring wounds to scars.
                    (*Every Man in His Humour*, Prologue, 9–12)

Shakespeare himself in 1599 was conscious of the difficulties:

     And so our scene must to the battle fly:
     Where—O for pity!—we shall much disgrace,
     With four or five most vile and ragged foils,
     Right ill-disposed, in brawl ridiculous,
     The name of Agincourt.    (*Henry V*, IV, Prologue, 48–52)

Although we should not take these jibes literally, the small size of an Elizabethan stage army seems from this evidence to have been a problem, and no amount of drumming and trumpet-blowing will much alter a puny travesty. An audience must indeed mind 'true things by what their mockeries be' if this deficiency is not to trouble it.

Nevertheless, Shakespeare used his stage symbolically. Clarity by such a method was possible even for a scene like *3 Henry VI*, V, i, in which five separate and successive armies, those of King Edward, then the Earl of Oxford, then the Marquess Montague, then the Duke of Somerset, then the Duke of Clarence, each march on '*with drum and colours*', while the Earl of Warwick and the Mayor of Coventry stand '*upon the walls*'—the balcony at least reduced the confusion. Hired hands could be dressed to look like soldiery, and were not required to speak.

However, Shakespeare is careful to suggest that it is offstage that the main body of an army is making its attack or going into retreat. The playwright fields only his protagonists as spokesmen and tokens of the progress of the fight. There is in any case more talking than fighting in a Shakespearian battle, and even Harry Hotspur, 'I that have not well the gift of tongue' (*1 Henry IV*, v, ii, 79), and King Henry, who later protests to Katharine of France that he is a 'plain king' with 'no cunning in protestation' (*Henry V*, v, ii, 146), compete with the trumpets in eloquence. Wedged between the words, the fights themselves are brisk, and the principals do their worst in single combat. Thus the story is told in terms of personal incident enacted by characters already known. The audience is left with martial impressions, and, in communicating these, the spacious stage, undecorated by localizing devices, plays its part.

A few cunning suggestions, then, coupled with symbolic movement over the stage, would delineate the form of battle. The mood and sway of particular encounters could be re-created by entrance, exit and re-entrance, and by marching and counter-marching. In the last act of *Julius Caesar*, the two armies of Brutus and Antony first confront each other across the platform in the persons of their leaders: it is to be 'words before blows' (v, i, 27). Then in sequent entrances, first Brutus in high spirits dresses the stage with his men; then in contrast Cassius enters in trouble. The tempo slows for the pathos of Cassius's death, with its ironic echo in that of Titinius. It slows yet again for Brutus's oration over their bodies. The action quickens as Brutus is next beaten in, only to rush off into the attack once more, leaving the moving incidents of Cato and Lucilius in his wake. For a moment the spectator glimpses a triumphant Antony; then Brutus appears for the last time, now in desperate condition. He too dies by his own hand, and Octavius and Antony thus come upon his body. There is no fighting here: suggestion does it all, and the progress of the battle is pointed simply by the four deaths of Cassius, Titinius, young Cato and Brutus, the last reserved for the climax. In this way entrances themselves supply a rhythm, and the rhythm supplies a meaning. The course of battle reconstructs itself in imagination, but is given particular life by such detail as the over-hasty suicide of Cassius, the ironic return of Titinius, the bravery of Cato and the trickery of Lucilius.

The manipulation of a different kind of battle provides the anticlimactic catastrophe to *Troilus and Cressida*. To be sure, the spectator sees in sequence a duel over the platform by Trojan Troilus and Greek Diomedes, then Trojan Hector, then the Greeks Agamemnon, Ajax and Achilles, then Troilus fighting both Ajax and Diomedes, then Hector with Achilles, then Achilles with his Myrmidons, then Greek Menelaus fighting with Trojan Paris, then the shameful murder of Hector by Achilles, then the Greeks together, then the Trojans together. This is a full picture in stage movement of the switchback of fortune in battle. Yet at the end two contradictory impressions are juxtaposed. Greek Agamemnon's

> Great Troy is ours, and our sharp wars are ended.   (v, ix, 10)

is immediately followed by Trojan Aeneas's

> Stand, ho! yet are we masters of the field.   (v, x, 1)

Shakespeare does not bring the abortive Trojan War to a conclusion: the end is to be one of loss and waste, in keeping with the play as a whole.

The three-day Battle of Actium in *Antony and Cleopatra* demonstrates another technique. The notion of dividing Acts III and IV into twenty-eight self-sufficient scenes has now been scotched by proficient modern performances on an untrammelled stage: the stage, peopled by its symbolic figures, will tell its own story. However, unlike the battles in *Julius Caesar* or *Troilus and Cressida*, the searchlight falls largely upon the central character, and although we glimpse Octavius Caesar, Enobarbus, Cleopatra and the common soldier, chiefly before the eye is Antony himself. The emphasis upon the hero in Act IV has the effect of arranging the sequence of battle scenes into a new pattern. They represent Antony's spirits first up (iv), then down (v/vi), then up again (vii/viii), and then, more prolonged, in sober suspense (ix/xii). The audience's sense of war is thus constructed for the most part by its impressions of one man and one mind. In this act, the brief interpolation of Cleopatra or Caesar exists merely to touch in the external circumstances of Antony's world.

There is a comparison to be made between this sequence and the structure of images that Sergei Eisenstein might have devised for a film. Shakespeare's Battle of Actium is curiously cinematic. Scenes i and ii give the audience a sight of the contenders before the battle: Octavius Caesar cold and confident, Antony compassionate with his weeping servants; the scenes are parallel in time, contrasted in characterization. Scene iii, with the soldiers gripped by the sound of hautboys at night, moves forward in time, although the impressions are atmospheric and symbolic. With scene iv, the night has passed and Antony arms himself in high spirits: the narrative progresses, but in view of the night's omens, the effect is ironic. Scene v exhibits Antony again, but in a sober mood as he learns of Enobarbus's defection: a direct contrast. When scene vi cuts to Caesar's camp, the scene moves parallel in time with what was just seen of Antony, while it accentuates the danger of his position. Scenes vii and viii in rapid sequence hurry the narrative on and suggest a temporary victory for Antony, an impression received with deceptive surprise. Scene ix brings on the second night, made more ominous than the first by the death of Enobarbus. Scenes x and xi again run parallel in time, and they redouble the spectator's suspense as Antony decides for battle at sea and Caesar for attack on land. Antony's peace of mind, and ours, are in the balance until scene xii, which reveals his despair. The scenes are thus edited like film footage for progressive or parallel action, or for contrasting or symbolic action, at times achieving two or three of these effects of montage simultaneously. Antony's mood accordingly fluctuates, like ours, between confidence and desperation as his character is explored under stress.

*Coriolanus* uses battle scenes to another purpose. The long expository review of the situation in Rome and of Caius Marcius's position at home among plebeians, patricians and family (I, i/iii) is suceeded by seven brisk scenes of spirited fighting before Corioli (I, iv/x). The dubious image of the hero as projected by the world of practical politics is now replaced by that of a fearless if foolhardy soldier at his professional best, rallying his men in the face of severe odds, fighting single-handed in the enemy city, seeking out Aufidius for personal combat. Marcius is in his element; the portrait is a challenge to anyone who doubts his nobility. To create this image is Shakespeare's dramatic purpose in these scenes, and to do it he is content to supply a series of varied events—attack, retreat, attack again, looting, rallying, skirmish and duel. In these the agility of the actors, and of the leading player in particular, is taken for granted.

By the time Shakespeare came to write *Cymbeline*, the King's Men were so adept at sweeping on and off the stage in mimic warfare that it seems he left it to them to suggest the narrative of events passing rapidly before the eyes. There is no other excuse for the simplicity of the directions for battle in v, ii. A sentence like '*the battle continues*' may exemplify the dumb show of the period, but it also seems slack work by comparison with the verbally pointed fights of earlier plays.

## TWO-FOLD GROUPING

The naturalistic stage does not easily permit the division of its acting space into separately significant areas. Only in recent years have skeleton and other expressionistic settings seen a return to Elizabethan practice in this respect. Characters in most modern plays enter the stage as if it were a room, and it is implicit in the convention that each character must be aware of the others' presence. The space on the anti-illusionary platform, on the other hand, permitted double, treble and even quadruple grouping without trouble.

It is likely that the more stylized of the early comedies, plays in which the artificiality of plotting and development is pronounced, split the stage in this way. The symmetrical platform, with its twin entrances, is well suited to the comings and goings of the two pairs of twins in *The Comedy of Errors*. The device is at work in the contest of love between Julia and Silvia in *The Two Gentlemen of Verona*, IV, ii, a scene in which Proteus, Thurio and the Musicians serenade the unwilling Silvia on the upper reaches of the platform, while loveless Julia and her host move down to its nether regions to be their unhappy eaves-droppers. In this play the Elizabethan stage helps the twin strands of the plot to separate and entwine.

*Love's Labour's Lost* plays variations upon the technique of double grouping more ambitiously: this time the gentlemen are set against the ladies. When the King of Navarre and his friends are visited by the Princess of France and her ladies, the King's oath of abstinence insists that the two groups shall keep their distance. Thereafter Shakespeare executes pretty manoeuvres with the opposing parties, while the Princess's ancient attendant Lord Boyet plays the go-between. The love games begin when the platform becomes the King's park, and the park a dancing-ring. With Boyet as a sprightly messenger, the two groups are linked in this stylization of courtship:

ROSALINE. Know what they would!
BOYET. What would you with the princess?
BEROWNE. Nothing but peace, and gentle visitation.
ROSALINE. What would they, say they?
BOYET. Nothing but peace, and gentle visitation.
ROSALINE. Why, that they have—and bid them so be gone.
BOYET. She says you have it, and you may be gone.

(v, ii, 178–83)

and so it continues. The visual effect is as amusing as it is charming, and lightly catches the spirit of young love-play as if genially dissected for inspection. Thereafter the two groups come together, but only to break up into four pairs, each gentleman with a lady on his arm. The game is played out, and the King's separation of man and maid is thwarted when nature takes a hand. The young people are matched by individual and personal feeling, and thus is theory sent packing.

With another kind of sophistication in the third act of *As You Like It*, Rosalind, Celia, Corin and the audience watch 'a pageant truly played' (III, iv, 49)—by the scornful Phebe who rejects her true love Silvius. The division on the stage marks a division in sensibility, since Rosalind watches with mounting irritation the conventional manners of mistress and lover.

Human feelings in the pastoral mode have for Phebe become toys, and Rosalind's realistic heart tells her that this is life-destroying. She captures the audience's sympathy when she breaks the grouping, introduces the touch of nature and turns fiercely on the cruel Phebe:

> Who might be your mother,
> That you insult, exult, and all at once,
> Over the wretched?
>
> (III, v, 35–7)

Unluckily she makes the situation worse, since not surprisingly Phebe now turns her attention upon this attractively fiery young Ganymede. When pastoral Phebe pursues realistic Rosalind, the pattern of grouping is altered once more.

*Twelfth Night* sports a double-action scene as cleverly contrived as it is delightful. This is the sequence of the mock duel between Sir Andrew and Viola as Cesario, III, iv. There is nothing quite like it in Elizabethan drama, and the fulfilment of the conception depends on the duality possible on the stage. Womanish timidity is to confront comic cowardice, with Fabian prompting the girlish Cesario and Sir Toby prompting the effeminate Sir Andrew from opposite quarters. The words that strike fear into the hearts of Viola and Sir Andrew have more effect than their weapons, but more pertinent to the farce of the action is the space between the players, telescoped and expanded by advance and retreat from and to the extremities of the platform. The Folio text handicaps the sequence with the uncalled-for exit and entrance of Fabian and Viola, but when Toby tries to terrify Andrew, it is clear from his line, 'He will not be pacified: Fabian can scarce hold him yonder' (282–3), that the comic irony also arises because Viola can be seen by the spectator. She is struggling, not to get to grips with her adversary, but to escape him. In the triple pattern of duologues which follows, often set about with editorial additions of '*aside*' ...'*aside*', Toby has space to talk to Viola and Fabian to Andrew, and still there is room for an exchange between Toby and Fabian. The stage is alive with puppet movement as the conspirators manipulate their victims. When by a quick movement Toby switches his attention to Andrew (and presumably this is echoed by Fabian's corresponding movement to Viola), he uses the same phrase, 'There's no remedy', to the effeminate man that he had used to the mock man. In the laughable test of their manhood, Sir Toby equates them.

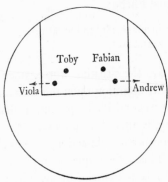

The tragedies and histories are not without scenes of double grouping, but these lack the symmetry of the comedies. A notable instance is in *King Lear*, III, iv, the scene '*before a hovel*'. In this the spectator sees a deliberate regrouping of the players, whose arrangement supplies a visual suggestion to underscore the meaning of the words. The regrouping takes place upon the approach of Gloucester, who has come to bring the King to a farmhouse 'where both fire and food is ready' (153). In the exchange that follows, Gloucester's persistence compels Lear to part company with the sane group of Gloucester, Kent and the Fool, and to link arms with Edgar the sham madman.

LEAR. First let me talk with this philosopher.
    What is the cause of thunder?
KENT. Good my lord, take his offer; go into th'house.
LEAR. I'll talk a word with this same learned Theban.
    What is your study? (154–8)

In some irritation Lear has turned his shoulder to those most concerned about his safety, as is indicated when Kent returns to Gloucester with 'Importune him once more to go, my lord' (161). Gloucester tries yet again, 'I do beseech your Grace' (171), only to receive for his trouble a caustic snarl:

> O, cry you mercy, sir.
> Noble philosopher, your company.
>
> (172–3)

The Elizabethan spectator is shocked to see a king in his divinity in company with a beggar apparently possessed of the Devil. However, Lear has walked apart from the 'sophisticated', but perplexed, group of his friends in order to discover his identity.

## GROUPING, THREE- AND FOUR-FOLD

Shakespeare's was a stage, therefore, which encouraged scenes of multiple-centred interest, although the interest was not truly a dramatic split—the contrasting or echoing of groups linked them. The audience feels the pleasure of gaining an omniscient perspective through the grouping. In modern drama such multiple ironies are to be found only in Chekhov's family scenes and in Brecht's divided and alienated stage.

*A Midsummer Night's Dream* provides an instance of this kind of stagecraft. The diverse groups of which this play is made up, the fairies, the lovers and the clowns, finally come together in its scenes of resolution, III, ii, and IV, i, which are continuous. Puck hastens to do Oberon's bidding and to set to rights the muddle he has caused among the lovers. He first leads Lysander and Demetrius a separate dance about the acting space, and then has them lie down in opposite quarters to sleep. When Helena and Hermia return one after the other, and then most conveniently fall asleep beside their true loves, Puck departs satisfied that 'Jack shall have his Jill' (III, ii, 461). The lovers occupy the neutral corners of the stage, and the next entrance, that of Titania and Bottom, follows immediately. These two ignore, as if unaware of, the little heaps of lovers, nor do they see Oberon who has also entered '*behind them*' as a jubilant observer. The Fairy Queen and the Weaver play their grotesque love scene until they too fall asleep, and Oberon and Puck advance to survey the amorous carnage of 'this night's accidents'. Bodies are now strewn about several parts of the arena, and all the lovers are caught within the same magic. For the Elizabethans it would have been nonsense to hide any part of this elaborate comic pattern behind a tree or a brush, as is often done today, or to push it into an inner stage.

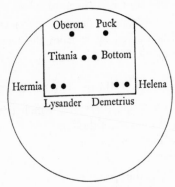

The diagram uses the form of the public theatre, since the play served both this and the private house for which it was probably first written

The Gadshill robbery of *1 Henry IV*, II, ii offered another chance to practise triple grouping. Although we cannot be certain where on the platform the various groups disposed themselves, its intimate nature suggests that when first the Prince and Poins 'stand close' (3), they are downstage near the body of the groundlings, close to the theatre's axial point in order that the spectators may physically anticipate their pleasure in spying on Falstaff.[1] For a prime piece of farcical business, the gross man himself must lie down, probably at the opposite corner of the stage:

PRINCE. Peace, ye fat-guts! lie down, lay thine ear close to the ground and list if thou canst hear the tread of travellers.
FALSTAFF. Have you any levers to lift me up again, being down?
(30–4)

Falstaff is by now as nervous as a kitten, and when Gadshill, Bardolph and Peto creep in with a sinister 'Stand!', this is a farcical prelude to the joke. The whispering and the mimed

[1] A notion advanced by Ronald Watkins in his lively account of the stagecraft in *On Producing Shakespeare*, p. 137. In other instances his grouping attempts to accommodate John Cranford Adams's 'study' and 'chamber', the conjectural inner stages behind the platform and balcony.

groping in the dark add relish to their suspense of waiting. The Prince and Poins resume their 'hiding-place', watching the four thieves waiting for the four travellers. In this way the spectator enjoys a double place of vantage through the technique of triple

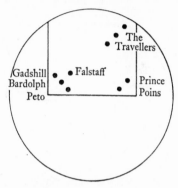

grouping: in imagination he jumps both with Falstaff when he sets upon the travellers, and with the Prince when he sets upon Falstaff.

*Troilus and Cressida*, too, has a triple scene of visual originality. In V, ii, Troilus and Ulysses, who eavesdrop upon Diomedes flirting with Cressida, are themselves the objects of eavesdropping by the cynic Thersites. Every criticism of Cressida that Thersites makes is a criticism of Troilus's romantic idealism as a lover: while Cressida's flirtation is staged for her former lover's dissection, he too suffers such clinical examination.

DIOMEDES.                                    How now, my charge!
CRESSIDA. Now, my sweet guardian! Hark, a word with you.
TROILUS. Yea, so familiar!
ULYSSES. She will sing any man at first sight.
THERSITES. And any man may sing her, if he can take her clef; she's
    noted.                                              (7–12)

This time none of the three groups is at the centre of the action— the drama lies in the ironies set up by the relationships between them, relationships which are here emphasized by spatial distinctions. The audience is made to feel the nearness of Troilus relative to Cressida, probably on the balcony, and the greater nearness of Thersites relative to Troilus: Thersites's speech is direct address, but only he has this privileged link with the audience. Such a three-dimensional scene of double perspective could only have been conceived for the Elizabethan platform.

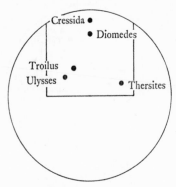

The play scene in *Hamlet*, III, ii is more complicated than the play-within-the-play in *A Midsummer Night's Dream*, V, i. The latter uses the full stage, but it is a scene of two simple groups, the players and their stage audience, however scattered they may have been. The burlesque of Pyramus and Thisbe casts its comment on the lovers, and the lovers in turn try their wit at the expense of the play—the grouping has no further ironic function.

The difficulties of staging Hamlet's 'Murder of Gonzago' presented no problems on the platform at Shakespeare's disposal. Indeed, the involved ironic structure of this scene might not have been conceived if the Globe stage had not prompted it. There are, at the minimum, three centres of interest, each seen by the audience and seen to be seen by each other. These essential groups are the King and Queen, Hamlet and Ophelia, and the Player King and Queen; the courtiers themselves, with Horatio, probably make up a fourth. The richness of the scene is only to be discovered by arranging these groups so that each can contribute its separate impression to the spectator, and yet at the same time reflect upon the others. The Elizabethan spectator saw all the groups interacting: Elizabethan sight-lines allowed him to see the mouse-trap play, the consequent agitation of Claudius and the response of the court to both of these; but, above all, it compelled him to get the sense of watching the whole action with Hamlet himself. This is a scene of tension only if the spectator can watch the watcher being watched.

In the first few lines Shakespeare is careful to indicate how the grouping shall be observed. Hamlet is present on the stage

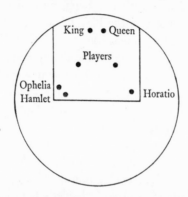

when the court enters, and he first sends Horatio to 'get a place'. Horatio has the function of a second Hamlet, since his eyes are Hamlet's eyes also. Horatio's place is therefore opposite Hamlet's eventual position, where between them they can bracket the King. Hamlet now has a casual word with each important spectator in turn: the King, Polonius and the Queen. As he speaks, he guides each player to his or her place. His own position he has also decided upon:

QUEEN. Come hither, my dear Hamlet, sit by me.
HAMLET. No, good mother, here's metal more attractive.     (6–8)

With this he leads Ophelia downstage to a place facing his mother, and sits at the girl's feet the better to watch the throne. Hamlet can see both Claudius and Gertrude, but he spends more time watching Gertrude than Claudius; this is apparent from remarks like 'Look you how cheerfully my mother looks' (124 5) and, upon Ophelia's comment on the brevity of the dumb show, 'As woman's love' (152). When the Player Queen's discourse on widowhood sails close to the wind, he says of his mother in alarm, 'If she should break it now!' (223), and, as it proceeds, he teases Gertrude with 'Madam, how like you this play?' (228). Such remarks, with those to Ophelia, constantly remind the audience of his presence and his vigilance.

Yet in the end his attention is fastened upon the King himself. The swift dumb show serves both to advance and to extend the silent contest of wits with the King, and, since the audience now knows the content of the Players' scene, it also allows it to watch Claudius with complete attention during their subsequent mouthings; thus the speeches of the Player King and Queen are prolonged in order to prolong a tension already felt. If the King and Queen are on the thrones upstage and Hamlet and Horatio at the foot of the platform, the Players will play their scene 'in the round', centre-stage.

Before the play is done, Hamlet has in heat shown his feelings. His voice rings across the theatre to his uncle: 'poison in jest' ...'the mouse-trap'...'begin, murderer'...'a'poisons him i' th'garden for's estate', and it is Hamlet's taunting which helps to take the attention of the watching courtiers. These courtiers, meanwhile, have a double duty, wherever they may be distributed about the circle. Their eyes will first be upon the Player King and Queen, but as they hear Hamlet's pointed comments and the wild tone of his voice, as they become aware of the play's criticism of the royal house of Denmark, in ones and twos they switch their attention to Claudius and his queen. Murmurs and gestures between the courtiers will attract the audience's attention to the role they are playing, and to the fact that the true action on the stage is not the Murder of Gonzago but the murder of King Hamlet. It is this concentration of public notice, hastened by the play and urged on by the Prince, that finally brings Claudius to his feet and the scene to a climax with his exasperated cry, 'Give me some light—away!' (269).

## THE SHAKESPEARIAN SPECTACULAR

An account of the full stage would be incomplete without reference to the processions, pageants, masques and shows with which Shakespeare repeatedly pleased his audience. The luxury of open space encouraged the players in their creation of theatrical spectacle. The dignity of a procession passing slowly round the stage with spreading cloaks and splendid trains needs room for its full display. Caesar's early processions in *Julius Caesar*, I, ii are part of the process of building up the sense of his importance; against this background, the night-time manoeuvres of the conspirators look sordid. Thus even the spectacular may be put to good dramatic use. In *Troilus and Cressida*, I, ii, the parade of the Trojan heroes, so often imagined offstage in modern productions, is placed early as an ironic way of introducing Troilus to Cressida, and her to us; meanwhile, Pandarus's commentary reduces the heroes to life-size in preparation for the tone of the play.

A formal procession was a conventional way of bringing a play to a ceremonial close, and this is true of most of the histories and some of the tragedies: to their processions *Hamlet* adds '*a peal of ordnance are shot off*', *Macbeth* a chorus of 'Hails' and a flourish or two, and *King Lear* has '*a dead march*' played. Justifiable occasions for procession occurred in the history plays, and none was more magnificent than that which depicted the coronation of the King in *Henry VIII*, IV, i. Holinshed supplied Shakespeare with elaborate details for the spectacle, and at least eighteen players were needed to fulfil its requirements. The glorious 'Order of the Coronation' details the music, the properties, the costumes, the colours and the symbols, and even the dressing of the Queen's hair '*richly adorned with pearls*'. It was as part of this ostentation that in 1613 the King's Men set off the chambers which burned their Globe to the ground.

Pageantry on this scale had not been equalled before in a public theatre, but scenes which called for a strong element of ceremony appeared in every kind of play. Both the convention and the taste for it were persistent. Again, the history plays especially lent themselves to it, even to the extent of burlesquing the ceremony itself in *Richard III*, III, vii, where Richard enters '*aloft, between two bishops*' to receive the Lord Mayor of London, 'two props of virtue for a Christian prince' (96). The comedies in their fantasy are also lavish with display. *Love's Labour's Lost*, with its affected young men and their conceits, is brought to a suitable close (V, ii) when the gentlemen are dressed 'like Muscovites or Russians' (121) and the ladies in their turn are masked (158). The ceremonial of the three fairy-tale casket-scenes in *The Merchant of Venice*, II, vii, II, ix and III, ii, may have matched the rhetoric of the foreign princes' speeches with suitably exotic splendour.

The last plays are rich in visions, shows and masques. Pericles has at least four (II, Chorus; II, ii; III, Chorus; and IV, iv). In *Cymbeline*, V, iv, the apparitions which come to Posthumus in gaol, with the descent of Jupiter '*in thunder, and lightning, sitting upon an eagle*', serve to hasten the resolution of a complicated story; while the moving scene of reconciliation which closes *The Winter's Tale*, V, iii, has a special quality, resolving the plot in terms of warm human feeling.

This scene, designed to provide graduations of Hermione's return to life, is planned with elaborate care. Before the assembled characters of the central story, Leontes is shown the statue of his queen by Paulina, who acts as mistress of the ceremony: 'Behold, and say 'tis well'. The audience is to see Hermione, who must stand upstage behind a curtain on a pedestal, through Leontes's eyes. At first he looks at the vision in rigid silence, amazed at the living likeness. Says Paulina,

> I like your silence, it the more shows off
> Your wonder...                              (V, iii, 21–2)

Perdita, too, is overcome, and she kneels before her mother and makes as if to kiss her hand, almost confounding Paulina's prepared effect.                    O, patience;
> The statue is but newly fixed; the colour's
> Not dry.                                          (46–8)

Intent upon stirring feeling in Leontes, she twice teases him by moving to close the curtain:

LEONTES.                 Do not draw the curtain.
PAULINA. No longer shall you gaze on't, lest your fancy
    May think anon it moves.
LEONTES.               Let be, let be!              (59–61)

Leontes is the next to make as if to kiss the image:

PAULINA.              Good my lord, forbear:
    The ruddiness upon her lip is wet;
    You'll mar it if you kiss it; stain your own
    With oily painting...Shall I draw the curtain?
LEONTES. No! not these twenty years.          (80–4)

Finally, the climactic moment comes. Paulina announces that she will make the statue move if 'all stand still':

                       Music; awake her: strike!
    'Tis time; descend; be stone no more; approach;
    Strike all that look upon with marvel; come;
    I'll fill your grave up; stir; nay, come away;
    Bequeath to death your numbness, for from him
    Dear life redeems you! You perceive, she stirs.    (98–103)

So Hermione comes down from her pedestal, and nature and art unite in the human sphere. This coming to life is prolonged with intensity for almost five minutes, extending to more than 80 lines, a slow miracle exactly traced by the author for a mood of ritual and magic. Especially remarkable is the way in which Paulina hints at the life in the statue little by little before the consummation, so that if the audience does not believe in the cold stone, she at least compels it to share Leontes's experience with him.

The precisely placed theatrical gestures reach their peak of meaning when Hermione, still silent, embraces her husband.

POLIXENES.          She embraces him!
CAMILLO. She hangs about his neck—
    If she pertain to life, let her speak too.       (111–13)

So she clings to him for the space of some twelve lines, until Paulina's 'Turn, good lady,/Our Perdita is found'. This is her first action on coming to life and stepping from the pedestal, and in it is felt the sixteen years' endurance of the memory of her rejection and humiliation. In one silent gesture must be felt the happiness of bringing to an end the long torment of waiting and hoping. Spectacle, characterization and theme are fused in these last moments.

Both the show in *Cymbeline* and that in *The Winter's Tale* are supported with '*solemn music*', like the grand entrance of Antiochus's daughter in *Pericles*, I, i, and the heavenly vision which comes to the dying Queen Katharine in *Henry VIII*, IV, ii. The masque as such appears in Perdita's pastoral dance of shepherds and satyrs in *The Winter's Tale*, IV, iv, to establish the play's new spirit of youth and natural generosity. It is also a relevant device to introduce the audience to the luxurious society of *Timon of Athens*, I, ii, in which the lavish banquet is appropriately accompanied by Cupid's masque of dancing Amazons, the better to contrast the loneliness and despair of Timon's end.

In order persistently to conjure up the atmosphere of *The Tempest's* magic island, Shakespeare almost throughout the play thinks in terms of the supernatural display characteristic of the court masque. He seems to call on Prospero to act as his presenter, with Ariel as his agent, and the magician works his spell in five spectacular gestures, so that the formal and symbolic qualities of the masque emphasize the structurally important episodes in the action. These are, in turn, the enthralment of Ferdinand (I, ii), the bewitching of the conspirators Antonio and Sebastian (II, i), the vanishing banquet which Prospero arranges from his position 'on the top' to charm his enemies (III, iii), the masque of Iris, Ceres and Juno with which he celebrates the betrothal of Miranda and Ferdinand (IV, i), and lastly, after Caliban, Trinculo and Stephano have been hunted by '*divers spirits, in shape of dogs and hounds*', the curtain-discovery of Miranda and Ferdinand '*playing at chess*', by which the younger generation symbolically reconcile the enmities of the older (V, i).

The square movements of Elizabethan dances were especially suited to the Elizabethan platform. As in the scene in *Love's*

*Labour's Lost* in which the gentlemen assume possession of their ladies, v, ii, the balletic quality of the dialogue and action dictates the elegance of the style in *Much Ado About Nothing*, II, i, where four masked couples circle in conversation round the stage, each in turn heard by the audience, dovetailing drama with dance. In *As You Like It*, Shakespeare writes the patterned dialogue of both a balletic and a vocal quartet. Only a dull production would have the players sitting motionless during these lines:

PHEBE. Good shepherd, tell this youth what 'tis to love.
SILVIUS. It is to be all made of sighs and tears,
   And so am I for Phebe.
PHEBE. And I for Ganymede.
ORLANDO. And I for Rosalind.
ROSALIND. And I for no woman.
SILVIUS. It is to be all made of faith and service,
   And so am I for Phebe, etc.       (v, ii, 79 ff.)

Here is evidence that Shakespeare has designed the movement of a circular dance. He repeats the stanza form three times, and then adds two more variant patterns; the speakers are perfectly balanced by number and by sex; the lines themselves insist upon a recognizable beat, although one not finally repetitive in mood or pace; and they carry the formal gestures of stylized mime.

*All's Well That Ends Well* demonstrates an exceptional rhyming experiment. In the scene in which Helena chooses a husband, rhyme, used in direct contrast with the prose asides of Lafeu, actually controls the formal movement, grouping and tone of the scene. This scene is the one most true to the play's folk-tale origins, which Shakespeare would feel the old-fashioned air of rhyme suited best, as he did in the Players' scene in *Hamlet*. With a rhyme the King of France sends Helena on her tour of the platform, decorated as it is with presentable officers and gentlemen of the court:

               Make choice and see,
   Who shuns thy love shuns all his love in me. (II, iii, 75–6)

As to a musical accompaniment, she goes her rounds with a couplet and a curtsy for each:

HELENA.                 Sir, will you hear my suit?
I LORD. And grant it.
HELENA.          Thanks, sir—all the rest is mute.     (79–80)

So she comes to confront the man of her choice, Bertram:

HELENA. I dare not say I take you, but I give
    Me and my service, ever whilst I live,
    Into your guiding power...This is the man.
KING. Why then, young Bertram, take her, she's thy wife.
BERTRAM. My wife, my liege? I shall beseech your highness,
    In such a business give me leave to use
    The help of mine own eyes.         (105–11)

Suddenly the rhyme has stopped and the gaiety is arrested. With 'This is the man', a shocked silence falls upon the company and reality returns in a rush as Bertram rejects her. The couplets are resumed by the King only when he assumes the impersonal role of a gnomic chorus. At his best, Shakespeare uses stage spectacle to a dramatic end as calculated as any achieved by words alone.

# III

# SHAKESPEARE'S AURAL CRAFT

# 6

## SPEAKING THE SPEECH

### VOCAL TONES

In *Romeo and Juliet*, with all its rhetorical devices and formal patterning of the verse, Shakespeare is already practising a verse line which can reproduce the pace of Juliet's physically felt fright and hesitation when she is about to drain Friar Lawrence's vial:

> How if, when I am laid into the tomb,
> I wake before the time that Romeo
> Come to redeem me? There's a fearful point!
> Shall I not then be stifled in the vault,
> To whose foul mouth no healthsome air breathes in,
> And there die strangled ere my Romeo comes? (IV, iii, 30–5)

The thought of waking in the tomb at first hurries her tongue, until she catches her breath at the prospect, with a pause on 'There's a fearful point!'. As her imagination works, the breathlessly long syllables of 'To whose foul mouth no healthsome air breathes in' re-create the horror in her mind. When Macduff learns of the slaughter of his family with

> Did you say all? O, hell-kite! All?
> (*Macbeth*, IV, iii, 217)

the loss of two syllables is replaced by the actor's slow, stunned speech and the swelling of his gesture caught up with the long, low call of the spondees: 'O—hell—kite—all!'. The jealous passion of Leontes is expressed in such lines as

> Is whispering nothing?
> Is leaning cheek to cheek? is meeting noses?
> Kissing with inside lip? stopping the career
> Of laughter with a sigh?...
> (*The Winter's Tale*, I, ii, 284–7)

Any prosodic scansion of the feverishness of this verse is histrionically inadequate.

As Shakespeare passes from the early to the late plays there is increasing evidence that he was controlling the actor's voice by rules of his own making, and that he was aware of the instrument which must speak his lines. The actor's voice was for him an agent whose variety and flexibility was a constant resource in communicating the tune of a speech, and thereby its feeling. Sound and rhythm guide the actor toward the sense intended. In this skill there is an observable development: early Shakespearian verse tends to exhibit the requisite feelings, ordering them like a loud-speaker message, an external announcement of intention; the mature Shakespeare reproduces the changes and movements of a character's mind, like a private confidence. The first is dramatized feeling; the second is drama itself, the shifts of tone implicitly embodying the feeling. 'Ah!' *not* ' I bleed'.

Complementary to this is Shakespeare's art of building one sound upon another. Granville-Barker wrote of Shakespeare's 'moulding of verse and prose into such variety of expressive form that it is a wonder any unity of effect is kept at all—yet it is...Witness such a seemingly haphazard mixture of verse, prose and snatches of song as we find in the scenes between Lear, Kent, Gloucester, the Fool and Poor Tom. Yet the dramatic vitality of these scenes lies largely in this variety and balance of orchestration.'[1] It is orchestration of voice and sound which creates a scene's aural image in the mind of the audience, and Shakespeare's variety of styles and shades of language provided a new discipline for the actors and another signpost for the audience. In practice, language and its sound became a manner of stagecraft.

Open to the sky, the public playhouse could accommodate the actor's wildest cries; intimate in the extreme, it allowed the actor to drop his voice to a murmur and still be heard. For Shakespeare, this quality permitted emphatic contrasts within a play—the public scenes for Prince Hal, King Claudius and Macbeth are in aural opposition to their scenes of privacy. Scenes can thus be effectively juxtaposed: the violent scene of the attack on Roderigo and Cassio is set between those in Desdemona's hushed chamber (*Othello*, IV, iii/v, i/v, ii), or

[1] *Prefaces to Shakespeare, First Series*, p. 156.

busy scenes in the Capulet household are contrasted with those in which Juliet pathetically displays her feelings (*Romeo and Juliet*, IV, ii/iii/iv). Tonal variety permitted major contrasts within a speech. In the disjointed speech of Lear which indicates the breaking of his spirit, Shakespeare uses tonal contrast within the line to re-create the oscillation of his mind:

> But I will punish home!
> No, I will weep no more. *In such a night*
> *To shut me out?* Pour on; I will endure.
> *In such a night as this? O Regan, Goneril!*
> *Your old kind father whose frank heart gave all!*
> O, that way madness lies; let me shun that!
> No more of that.                    (*King Lear*, III, iv, 16–22)

In these lines the italicized words continue his rage at 'this contentious storm' *forte*, while the rest are spoken *piano* as he senses the danger in his loss of control.

However, the recognition of vocal inflexion is one of the more elusive of Shakespearian studies. Sometimes a marked change of intonation is pointed by the use of parentheses. The tone of Lucio's interview with Isabella the novice is made characteristically irreverent by this device:

> Hail, virgin (if you be) as those cheek-roses
> Proclaim you are no less.
>                    (*Measure for Measure*, I, iv, 16–17)

Here Shakespeare interpolates a throw-away phrase to force our laughter, as when Justice Silence announces the incongruous entrance of burly, red-nosed Bardolph with Falstaff's diminutive page:

> Here come two of Sir John Falstaff's men (as I think).
>                    (*2 Henry IV*, III, ii, 55–6)

The Folio insists upon the innuendo on 'men' by placing 'as I think' in parentheses.

In such cases it must always be the conjunction of sense with sound which guides the actor home. This snatch of Leontes in the early stages of his jealousy demonstrates the use of parentheses working together with verbal devices:

> many a man there is (even at this present,
> Now, while I speak this) holds his wife by th'arm,
> That little thinks she has been sluiced in's absence,
> And his pond fished by his next neighbour (by
> Sir Smile, his neighbour).   (*The Winter's Tale*, I, ii, 192–6)

The Folio text is again precise in punctuating for speech: the first parentheses abruptly cutting into the line of thought, its broken, staccato fling at the audience a little shrill, its triple repetition, 'even at this present'...'now'...'while I speak this', forcing a rising pitch by its urgency. Following upon this, the ugly jocularity embodies a sarcastic imagery which prompts the exact quality of feeling, jaundiced, defensive; while the sibilants, often stressing sexual bitterness elsewhere in Shakespeare ('sluiced in's absence'...'fished'...'Sir Smile') accumulate in a progression of increasing vocal emphasis. The repetition of 'neighbour' doubles the insinuation, and the second parenthetical phrase points the anger in the voice and suggests a quick turn upon the spectators, while the running-on accelerates the expression of emotion.

A system of punctuation, or of syllabic values, cannot notate precisely the range of tunes in a poet's auditory imagination, although it is possible to recognize some of the distinctions intended. The norm of speech in a scene, from which vocal tones expand, may be prompted simply by an event, and the actor will build from there:

ATTENDANT. News, my good lord, from Rome.
ANTONY.                                         Grates me! the sum.
CLEOPATRA. Nay, hear them, Antony:
   Fulvia perchance is angry...

> (*Antony and Cleopatra*, I, i, 18–20)

These are three contrasting tones, readily perceptible because they are distinctly set against each other. Circumstance supplies the variety: the Attendant formal and a little hesitant in the order of his words, but fixing the norm of tone for the sequence; Antony over his shoulder in sharp irritation; Cleopatra sarcastic in the mock reasonableness of her 'nay' and 'perchance'. This variety in vocal colouring is no surface embellishment, but the life-blood of the drama.

When Edgar stands with his blind father on the pretended edge of Dover cliff, Shakespeare is displaying his actor's gifts in a virtuoso piece. Edgar is required to change his tones absolutely within the scene, and to speak in two voices both different from his own, one before the imaginary fall and one after. First is heard the Edgar who must create the cliff:

> ...The murmuring surge
> That on th'unnumb'réd idle pebble chafes,
> Cannot be heard so high. I'll look no more,
> Lest my brain turn, and the deficient sight
> Topple down headlong.     (*King Lear*, IV, vi, 20–4)

As if to anticipate a new vocal function, Gloucester had twice before (lines 7 and 10) remarked Poor Tom's more articulate speech. Now the detail of birds the size of beetles, of the minuteness of the men working below, and even the reproduction, with its touch of irony, of the inaudible sounds of the beach, paints a particular picture for the blind man in terms unlike the scattered and tangential phrases of the mad beggar. The speaking is rounded and emotive, urgent and persuasive, even when Edgar is not conjuring an image: 'Lest my brain turn, topple down headlong'. However, when Edgar addresses the audience in his own voice:

> And yet I know not how conceit may rob
> The treasury of life when life itself
> Yields to the theft.     (42–4)

he speaks to confirm his pretence; the tones are firmer, the thought reasonable and controlled by its regular iambics and balanced rhythm, breaking tidily at the caesura, 'life/when'. Yet one more note of the actor in Edgar is heard in this scene before he pulls his father to his feet:

> Hadst thou been aught but gossamer, feathers, air,
> (So many fathoms down precipitating),
> Thou'dst shivered like an egg: but thou dost breathe,
> Hast heavy substance, bleed'st not, speak'st, art sound. (49–52)

Wonder catches at the words and clips the phrases, the parentheses mark the tone of astonishment as the mind flies up to the height of the cliff, until a homely image, 'shivered like an egg', brings us back to the unhappy figure of Gloucester on his knees. The irony of these ingenious vocal changes is all the greater because the spectator sees that Edgar has not necessarily changed, not moved from the spot on which he stands. Thus we may enjoy the error of Gloucester's attempted suicide, and still indulge the drastic cure for despair Edgar has invented for his father—a curious mixture of the ludicrous with the terrible in a scene which might have been written for the theatre of the absurd.

## USES OF TONE AND RHYTHM

The mysteries of timbre and modulation continue to awe us. Our interest here, however, has less to do with Shakespeare's technical control of the voice than with the range of dramatic uses to which he puts it. A recurrent function of tonal qualities in the verse is the creation of the mood which must pervade a scene. King Henry IV opens his play in immediately recognizable tones, which serve both to point his character and to establish the early spirit of the court:

> So shaken as we are, so wan with care,
> Find we a time for frighted peace to pant,
> And breathe short-winded accents of new broils
> To be commenced in stronds afar remote...
>
> (*1 Henry IV*, i, i, i ff.)

To suggest the King's failing powers, what more natural than that Shakespeare should choose shaken and short-winded accents for his speech? The tone is bloodless, the consonants breathy, the rhythm sluggish. It is the voice of a sick man, which is also calculated to transport its audience at once into a sick land. By contrast, King John is a man of doubtful will and intelligence, but he promptly suggests the boldness and strength of his court by such speech as this to the French ambassador:

Here have we war for war and blood for blood,
Controlment for control: so answer France...
Be thou as lightning in the eyes of France;
For ere thou canst report I will be there,
The thunder of my cannon shall be heard...

(*King John*, I, i, 19 ff.)

The tones are curt and masculine, and the images vivid, fierce
and to the point. They start the performance with the crack of a
whip.

Although the meaning of the lines must always be the actor's
primary guide, in this way the opening of a scene has its character
signalled also by a particular quality of sound. The bitter mood
of the interminable Trojan War is touched in by the first dis-
pirited cadences of Troilus's voice:

Call here my varlet: I'll unarm again:
Why should I war without the walls of Troy
That find such cruel battle here within?

(*Troilus and Cressida*, I, i, 1–3)

Here is heard the mood of the hero and the spirit behind the
play's theme. Meanwhile the mocking trumpets remind him and
us of the unwelcome presence of war outside the gates of Troy.
The blasts of an alarum were part of an aural language as adjust-
able as the taped effects of today, and three times in this first
scene an alarum is sounded like a reprimand in the reluctant
ears of Troilus, each time inviting his jaundiced view of the war.
The trumpet pejorative speaks to him almost as a sarcastic
player would, as when Aeneas serves his challenge on the Greeks:

Trumpet, blow loud,
Send thy brass voice through all these lazy tents.

(I, iii, 256–7)

The tone of speech and the function of character are inseparable, for Shakespeare is also capturing in sound and rhythm the
dance of an individual mind. The falling tunes of the Troilus
who opens his play have quite changed key after he has seen his
enigmatic Cressida in the embrace of Diomedes:

> This she? No; this is Diomed's Cressida.
> If beauty have a soul, this is not she;
> If souls guide vows, if vows be sanctimonies,
> If sanctimony be the gods' delight,
> If there be rule in unity itself,
> This is not she...                                    (v, ii, 137 ff.)

The angular rhythm of the first line exactly catches the clumsy, stunned posture of a Troilus taken aback by the need to re-orientate his ideas. A switchback rhythm replaces it in the second line, but this time 'If beauty have a soul' has become the cry of a young animal in pain. His voice rises to a formalized tune as it takes on the rhetorical pattern of 'if...if...if', and at the same time it climbs the scale of vowels through 'souls...vows ...sanctimonies...delight...unity itself'. Upon the final shrill note, Troilus returns to his starting point, the shocked refusal of 'This is not she'.

Dramatic poetry of this order is like a finely ribbed frame: sound and rhythm support the actor in his effort to re-create the character's mood, and help to shape his performance as it grows.

### REPETITION AND PACE

Imagery will often suggest the pace at which Shakespeare wants his words delivered and invite the actor to echo the picture in sound:

> like to the Pontic sea,
> Whose icy current and compulsive course
> Ne'er feels retiring ebb, but keeps due on
> To the Propontic and the Hellespont...
>                                          (*Othello*, III, iii, 455 ff.)

In these lines Othello goes on to refer to the 'violent pace' of his thoughts. In another mood, there can be no rushing the limping syllables of Macbeth's distracted 'To-morrow, and to-morrow, and to-morrow...' (*Macbeth*, V, v, 19 ff.) which creeps 'in this petty pace'. But for the most part the actor has to listen for prosodic clues—the running-on of lines and the tripping of short syllables, or the end-stopping of a line with hard caesuras and stronger vowel sounds—in conjunction with the emotional impulse behind the speech. There is, however, a particular Shakespearian mannerism which is helpful for vocal interpretation: his trick of repetition.

The reiteration of a word or phrase can make a simple rhetorical effect, like repeatedly hitting the same note. This may suggest a mind under stress, or remind the audience of a theme playing through the scene, but it always signals the pace and pitch of speech. The rhetorical repetitions scattered through *Richard II* show how Shakespeare discovers and employs a neat ladder for an ascending voice. Accelerating pace as well as a changing timbre of voice may be heard in this (until the last two lines):

> I'll give my jewels for a set of beads:
> My gorgeous palace for a hermitage:
> My gay apparel for an almsman's gown:
> My figured goblets for a dish of wood:
> My sceptre for a palmer's walking-staff:
> My subjects for a pair of carvéd saints,
> And my large kingdom for a little grave,
> A little little grave...          (III, iii, 147–54)

As Richard reviews the symbols of his office in progression, his thoughts grow reckless, until the expansive gesture on 'my large kingdom', balanced by the 'little grave', induces a shudder of self-pity, and pace and pitch drop away.

A theatrical device is transcended by psychological insight when Shylock's urge for revenge plucks again and again at his thoughts:

ANTONIO.                    Hear me yet, good Shylock.
SHYLOCK. I'll have my bond, speak not against my bond,
   I have sworn an oath that I will have my bond.

And again,                              (*The Merchant of Venice*, III, iii, 3–5)

ANTONIO. I pray thee, hear me speak.
SHYLOCK. I'll have my bond—I will not hear thee speak.
   I'll have my bond, and therefore speak no more.          (11–13)

The almost comic hammering of the phrase reproduces the drumming in his head, but it also insists that the voice modulate its pace to echo the character's increasing charge of feeling.

So Hamlet's first soliloquy, I, ii, has its pattern of feeling broadly shaped by a chiming and climbing reference to time: 'But two months dead'...'and yet within a month'...'a little month'...'within a month'...'O most wicked speed'. The recurring emphasis is here composed as music might be, and the actor will pursue the reiteration through the scale of irony, as Antony does his caustic phrase 'honourable men' in *Julius Caesar*, III, ii. The creative success of Hamlet's speech is rhythmical. The words exercise an absolute management of the voice, the tonelessness and rhythmical regularity of the first lines, the flat speech and falling accents accurately capturing the lassitude of the character's disgust with life. A ripple in the rhythm is heard when Hamlet dwells on the thought of his own death, and immediately afterwards a wince of bitter feeling in the repeated 'fie...fie' and in the 'un*weed*ed garden/That grows to *seed*'. The disturbance in the rhythm is felt more strongly when the Prince's thoughts flicker over the hasty re-marriage of his mother,

> That it should come to this,
> But two months dead, nay not so much, not two.

Like a sensitive needle, the beat and repetition of the words measure the hidden pressures of the mind. Only when once more he thinks with affection of his father do the words gather a sweeter lilt,

> so loving to my mother,
> That he might not beteem the winds of heaven
> Visit her face too roughly,

as if he senses his father caressing his queen with his breath, and at the same time from the grave having the power to soothe his son. But these variations are governed by the general shape imposed on the speech by the reiterations of the notion of time, and the practical needs of Hamlet's actor are married with a convincing psychological realism. Is this art or artifice? If the rhetoric of Henry V's 'ceremony...general ceremony...thou idol ceremony...thrice gorgeous ceremony' (*Henry V*, IV, i) was tautophony, Hamlet's reiterative phrasing has become compulsive stressing. Spontaneity informs theatrical technique and in Shakespeare's hands an aural device becomes symptomatic of a diseased mind, as on Othello's tongue the trivial 'handkerchief', repeated and repeated, directs his voice in pitch and intensity, and itself acquires the force of all his doubts about his wife's chastity.

## 'FOR EVERY PASSION SOMETHING'

Mountjoy declares that 'our voice is imperial' (*Henry V*, III, vi, 121–2); Coriolanus talks of his 'throat of war' (*Coriolanus*, III, ii, 112)—but these were soldiers' parts, and the speaking of their lines hardly needs this sort of gloss. Falstaff reports that he lost his voice 'with hallooing and singing of anthems' (*2 Henry IV*, I, ii, 185–6)—a character joke as much as an aural direction for cracked tones. As for the boy players, they might comfortably speak 'between the change of man and boy/With a reed-voice' (*The Merchant of Venice*, III, iv, 66–7), as Portia promises to do when she turns advocate; and the audience listening to *Twelfth Night* accepts that the boy's 'small pipe'

> Is as the maiden's organ, shrill and sound—
> And all is semblative a woman's part.        (I, iv, 32–4)

as Orsino persuades Viola when she goes courting Olivia. Difficulties in vocal illusion could be happily excused by the game of changing sex. To determine feeling, however, the efficient instrument was the poetry.

Speech from the foot of the platform encouraged lower tones, which in turn permitted a special subtlety in intonation and pace. The confidential exchanges of lovers would be marked by this tone: 'Speak low if you speak love' Hero is advised in *Much Ado About Nothing*, II, i, 88. After Cordelia and Octavia, Brutus's Portia most simply exemplifies the gentle tone felt through the verse. She approaches her husband quietly after the conspirators have left, with 'Brutus, my lord!' (*Julius Caesar*, II, i, 233), and her voice is not enough to rouse the sleeping Lucius. Then she speaks of soft domestic matters:

> You've ungently, Brutus,
> Stole from my bed: and yesternight at supper
> You suddenly arose and walked about,
> Musing and sighing, with your arms across... (237–40)

This is husband-and-wife intimacy, the particular references to everyday detail lacking flamboyance and remaining firm in their colloquial rhythms. The speech takes for granted the relationship between the two, and only incidentally reveals Portia's love and understanding. Thus she says that she has left him,

> Fearing to strengthen that impatience
> Which seemed too much enkindled, and withal
> Hoping it was but an effect of humour,
> Which sometime hath his hour with every man.
> ...Dear my lord,
> Make me acquainted with your cause of grief. (248–56)

The strength of these lines lies in their quiet regularity, their even tone, their soft assurance.

Not only the women are granted the low tone. As his drama requires, Shakespeare provides speech which cannot be satisfactorily rendered other than in a hushed voice. Ross, with his news of the murder of Macduff's family, tells us how he will *not* speak:

> I have words
> That would be howled out in the desert air,
> Where hearing should not latch them.
> (*Macbeth*, IV, iii, 193–5)

Shakespeare as of instinct refuses his actor licence to tear a passion to tatters. As Hamlet advises the Players, 'In the very torrent, tempest, and as I may say whirlwind of your passion, you must acquire and beget a temperance that may give it smoothness' (*Hamlet*, III, ii, 5–8).

To identify Shakespeare's tones in this way is as endless as dividing the shades of colour in the rainbow. Flat and even tones themselves admit a wide variety. Regularity of tone and rhythm establishes Othello's integrity in the eyes of the audience when he addresses the Duke and Senators of Venice:

> Most potent, grave, and reverend signiors,
> My very noble and approved good masters,
> That I have ta'en away this old man's daughter,
> It is most true; true, I have married her...
>
> (Othello, I, iii, 76 ff.)

Simplicity of diction at once lowers and strengthens the tone and rivets the attention as the speech unfolds. Yet an equally level voice is heard in Claudius as he humours his nephew:

> 'Tis sweet and commendable in your nature, Hamlet,
> To give these mourning duties to your father,
> But you must know your father lost a father,
> That father lost, lost his...      (Hamlet, I, ii, 87 ff.)

Each within its context projects a different image, built of the contrast with other voices heard or not heard—Iago's coarse prose or Hamlet's silence. Lines like these qualify as primary examples of good dramatic poetry because they are right for their task.

At the other end of the scale is another recognizable group of louder tones. Raised voices in comedy are usually indicated—Bottom's roars, or the noisy Gower on the eve of Agincourt:

> GOWER. Captain Fluellen!
> FLUELLEN. So! in the name of Jesu Christ, speak fewer.
>
> (Henry V, IV, i, 64 ff.)

Fluellen checks his companion in arms, but it is this doughty warrior who rattles on. A merry Pandarus embarrasses Cressida with his cries of admiration for the passing Troilus:

> PANDARUS. 'Tis Troilus! there's a man, niece!
>   Hem! Brave Troilus! the prince of chivalry!
> CRESSIDA. Peace, for shame, peace!
>
> (Troilus and Cressida, I, ii, 228 ff.)

Staccato phrasing helps the actor's confident delivery.

In the tragedies the poetry directs the pitch of the voice, often again with broken phrasing. Thus when Richard II descends from the battlements of Flint Castle, both movement and voice are made to mark the hysterical climax to the scene:

> In the base court? Base court, where kings grow base,
> To come at traitors' calls, and do them grace.
> In the base court? Come down? Down court! down king!
> For night-owls shriek where mounting larks should sing.
> (Richard II, III, iii, 180–3)

A comment from Northumberland confirms the manner of Richard's speech:

> Sorrow and grief of heart
> Makes him speak fondly like a frantic man.     (184–5)

For Othello at his wits' end over the handkerchief, these tones are repeated:

> Is't lost? Is't gone? speak, is it out o'th'way?
> (Othello, III, iv, 83)

So, too, he confronts his weeping wife:

> and she can weep, sir, weep;
> And she's obedient, as you say, obedient,
> Very obedient. Proceed you in your tears.     (IV, i, 255–7)

The repetitive stabbing at the point of pain, the curt queries or jerky utterance, the tendency to move through a scale of piercing vowels, mark the vein of hysteria in the words. What was once dismay heard in the enigmatic balance of meanings, like Juliet's

> My only love sprung from my only hate!
> Too early seen unknown, and known too late!
> (Romeo and Juliet, I, v, 138–9)

when she finds that she loves a Montague, is now dismay heard in the confusion of the tones of the voice.

Shakespeare's final secret for a lively stage speech is simplicity. If his stage allowed speed of utterance, his verse form invited the rhythm, if not the idiom, of natural speech. He came to use it to the benefit of his characterization, since it released character from the constriction of being a verbal concept. He used it to the benefit of dramatic form, since within a scene he could shift mood and tone to start a new impulse in the auditorium. When Juliet, newly married to Romeo, is told by an irate father that she must marry the County Paris, she responds with the suitably balanced rhetoric of a commonplace sentiment:

My husband is on earth, my faith in heaven...
(*Romeo and Juliet*, III, v, 205)

The Nurse's matter-of-fact reply offers a counter-stroke which undercuts the sentiment and yet points Juliet's loyalty, asserting a quality of less idealized life and remaining true to the rich, coarse grain of her character, as she speaks of Paris:

> O, he's a lovely gentleman!
> Romeo's a dishclout to him. An eagle, madam,
> Hath not so green, so quick, so fair an eye
> As Paris hath. Beshrew my very heart...        (218-21)

The verse leaps from the tongue to suggest her surge of feeling, and the form accommodates the complete transition without dislocation. Between the one speech and the other is Shakespeare's span of realized characterization in the scene, a breadth which the actors must straddle and the spectator measure.

The simple line warms a character to life—the touch of the vernacular, the unadorned idiom, which goes to the heart of the character. Cordelia's 'Nothing, my lord' (*King Lear*, I, i, 86) shines a clear light after the mouthings of her sisters. Helena, repeatedly questioned by the Countess about her regard for Bertram, is at last revealed as the passionate creature she is by the simple effect of straight talking:

> Then, I confess,
> Here on my knee, before high heaven and you,
> That before you, and next unto high heaven,
> I love your son. (*All's Well That Ends Well*, I, iii, 188-91)

After the stammering, she speaks these last four honest words, and having said them, her pent-up feelings are released. The brief view of the wronged Juliet in *Measure for Measure* is enriched by her artless replies to the Duke:

DUKE. So then it seems your most offenceful act
   Was mutually committed?
JULIET.               Mutually.        (II, iii, 26-7)

And when Rosalind hears of Orlando's encounter with the lioness, all her wit is suddenly reduced to 'I would I were at home' (*As You Like It*, IV, iii, 160). She faints, and speech and gesture promptly remind us of her sincerity.

155

Shakespeare places with care plain words in a tense context, as when Desdemona is approached by Othello, ugly with his suspicions about her virtue:

OTHELLO. How do you, Desdemona?
DESDEMONA.                               Well, my good lord.
OTHELLO. Give me your hand: this hand is moist, my lady.
                                        (*Othello*, III, iv, 35–6)

This is a manner of understatement where what is unspoken is more powerful than the words which submerge it. The gulf between the speech and the thought is filled by the audience. Thus Lear is as vivid to us when he lapses into guileless words after the stress of the storm as when he was roaring on the heath:

Make no noise, make no noise; draw the curtains. So, so; we'll go to supper i'th'morning.                        (*King Lear*, III, vi, 82–3)

When he wakes to see Cordelia, simplicity of speech acquires, with its small particularities, a special force and beauty:

LEAR. Methinks I should know you, and know this man,
    Yet I am doubtful: for I am mainly ignorant
    What place this is; and all the skill I have
    Remembers not these garments, nor I know not
    Where I did lodge last night. Do not laugh at me,
    For (as I am a man) I think this lady
    To be my child Cordelia.
CORDELIA.                    And so I am: I am!       (IV, vii, 64–70)

The vibrant 'subtext' of feeling in this exchange takes its strength, even its gently falling tones, from its placing in the sweep of the play. Shakespeare again finds a natural evocative speech for Cleopatra in her final role as a mother clasping the asp to her breast:
                                        Peace, peace!
        Dost thou not see my baby at my breast,
        That sucks the nurse asleep?
                            (*Antony and Cleopatra*, V, ii, 307–9)

The grandeur is distilled from the strange humour of the image, the momentous occasion and the plain language. Against these, the subtext gives the delivery of such lines *sotto voce* its theatrical force.

# Speaking the Speech

## THE VARIATION OF SHAKESPEARE'S SPEECH

The Elizabethan playwright was free to range between the extremes of patterned verse and naturalistic prose. This freedom was a freedom for the actor. The forms of speech permitted him to address his audience intimately or distantly, to throw out a quick aside, or to build a vocal effect akin to operatic aria; they would animate him like a puppet or like a sentient creature. If light and shade is essential to creative drama, we think first of the chiaroscuro of speech.

At one extreme, Shakespeare's drama approximates to opera and its language to song. On occasion he introduces verse which projects an impression of character or situation in a symbolic mode. As a vocal device, stichomythia, for example, introduces tension into an exchange of dialogue. To be sure, the balance of line, phrase and word suits Richard of Gloucester's wit, both when he woos the Lady Anne,

ANNE. I would I knew thy heart.
GLOUCESTER. 'Tis figured in my tongue.
ANNE. I fear me both are false.
GLOUCESTER. Then never was man true...

*(Richard III*, I, ii, 192 ff.)

and when he demands of Queen Elizabeth her daughter's hand:

QUEEN ELIZABETH. Shall I be tempted of the devil thus?
KING RICHARD. Ay, if the devil tempt you to do good.
QUEEN ELIZABETH. Shall I forget myself to be myself?
KING RICHARD. Ay, if yourself's remembrance wrong yourself.
QUEEN ELIZABETH. Yet thou didst kill my children.
KING RICHARD. But in your daughter's womb I bury them.

(IV, iv, 419–24)

His terse lines seem to master the Queen with words; intelligence manoeuvres its forces in a battle of passionless sex. Yet the stichomythia also serves to formalize the two wooing scenes, while the repetition of the second emphasizes their difference: Anne is subdued, but Elizabeth evades—she hopes to marry her daughter to Richmond. The play has a ritualistic shape of rise, fall and retribution, and patterned speech makes statuesque its critical moments. However, when this figure is found in the later Shakespeare, it is used to grant a posturing character a note of mockery:

QUEEN. Hamlet, thou hast thy father much offended.
HAMLET. Mother, you have my father much offended.
QUEEN. Come, come, you answer with an idle tongue.
HAMLET. Go, go, you question with a wicked tongue.
(Hamlet, III, iv, 9–12)

Gertrude is in no mood to banter, and she gets the worse of these ripostes. Hamlet's formality here is that of the torturer laying out his instruments, and Shakespeare simply calls on patterned verse when a particular dramatic end warrants it.

Lines take on formal characteristics when delivered by a character in a ritualistic role. Solemnity descends on the scene when the Prince of Verona stops the street-fight:

> Rebellious subjects, enemies to peace,
> Profaners of this neighbour-stainéd steel...
> (Romeo and Juliet, I, i, 80 ff.)

The same grandiloquence closes the tragedy. A ritualistic authority is also heard in the tone of the Ghost in *Hamlet*, contrasted with the false ceremony of Claudius's voice and intimating to the spectator his authenticity. It is heard in the voice of King Duncan:

> I have begun to plant thee, and will labour
> To make thee full of growing... (*Macbeth*, I, iv, 28 ff.)

It is heard in the early Lear, and is followed by the slow collapse of the verbal formality, tracing the King's loss of authority in his realm and in his mind. Shakespeare teaches our ears that Richard II or Lear have slipped their responsibility as kings, and measures their fall by the strength or weakness of their rhetoric.

The change between verse and prose always marks a change in theatrical mood: a rise or fall in the level of the spectator's imaginative apprehension, a break in the continuity of feeling and a shift in the manner of characterization. Modulating from one style to another must always call up an ironic state of receptivity in the auditorium. Thus Shakespeare was quick to break the decorum of prose for unworthy characters and verse for their betters, and Prince Hal and Hamlet vary their style of address because the author is at pains to show these men in two lights: Hal projects his popular tavern image alongside that of his necessary symbolism as the soldier king; Hamlet is a man of attitudes, an actor to others and sometimes to himself. By contrast, the so-called actor-king Richard II lacks Hamlet's variety of masks, and his speech is less flexible.

The history plays provide an insight into Shakespeare's handling of this technique over the years. The earliest histories are almost exclusively in verse—even Richard's Gardeners speak it where Hamlet's Gravediggers do not. Then, as if the playwright were congratulating himself upon his success in moulding Juliet's Nurse and Quince's company with prose, he sets up half the scenes in the *Henry IV* plays in the same way. Prose and verse divide the Falstaff scenes from those of the nobles, and govern the balance of the plays' structure. The frivolity of the prose cutting across the gravity of the verse is immediately apparent to the ear, accentuating the contrast in the action between scenes of honour and of happy dishonour. Falstaff parodies sentiments about kingship, duty in wartime, and personal courage and honour, extending the play's vision by broadening its moral spectrum. His is the voice of more prosaic man, and his prosaic view of the world showed Shakespeare the way to solve the structural problem created by the more human qualities in the character of the Prince.

Artificial comedy offered Shakespeare a special opportunity for experiment in verse and prose. The romantic leads could have their verse, and yet share the prose comedy of the clowns. Clowns like the Dromios, and Speed and Launce, are used to keep the plays earthbound, and the tenor of their scenes makes the giddy lovers seem giddier still. No scene more incongruously counterpoints verse and prose to a comic end than the love scene in *A Midsummer Night's Dream* between the Queen of the

Fairies, who speaks in lilting verse, and Bottom the weaver, who speaks the plainest of prose.

TITANIA. What, wilt thou hear some music, my sweet love?
BOTTOM. I have a reasonable good ear in music. Let's have the tongs and the bones.
TITANIA. Or, say, sweet love, what thou desir'st to eat.
BOTTOM. Truly a peck of provender. I could munch your good dry oats. Methinks I have a great desire to a bottle of hay. Good hay, sweet hay, hath no fellow...                      (IV, i, 27 ff.)

Bottom's confidence seems fit for all occasions, and he even rises in our esteem, with his bluntness suiting his egotism and his homely asinine tastes.

In a comedy of romance and wit like *Much Ado About Nothing*, the romantic lovers Claudio and Hero speak verse when they are impassioned. Thus after ten minutes of conversational prose, Claudio declares his love in verse (I, i, 272 ff.). Hero, his idealized betrothed, speaks verse until she is caught in the comic plot against Beatrice, when she tends to speak prose with the rest. Like the broad prose for the officers Dogberry and Verges, all this might be expected. What language, however, was to be expected for the sophisticated comedy of Benedick and Beatrice? They speak a little verse in the last two acts when the play's romantic mood draws them into its magnetic field, but for the rest their mercurial repartee is not asked to suffer this imposition. The melodious verse of their prototypes in *Love's Labour's Lost*, Berowne and Rosaline, had, it seems, hamstrung their wit. The toss of a word between Benedick and Beatrice, its catching and its rebound, demand the slippery turns of the colloquial. It may have been that they were first introduced to leaven the comedy, but they steal attention from the romance because their badinage has a living accent almost absent from the rest. Shakespeare in these years judges each case for prose empirically.

*As You Like It* shifts from prose to verse as soon as love colours the scene (I, ii, 208); thereafter Rosalind tends to speak verse in her initial love-lorn mood, and when playing mentor to the pastoral lovers Phebe and Silvius. But she speaks prose with

Touchstone, or when teasing Orlando: that is, in her anti-romantic role the spirit of the playing is lighter and less obsessed, and the intermixture of the lyrical and prosaic matches her duality as heroine and self-critic. This technique is reflected in *Troilus and Cressida*, where Cressida shares prose with Pandarus but verse with Troilus, suggesting her dual role as a realistic girl and an idealized mistress. In *Twelfth Night*, the scenes without Sir Toby circulate in an aura of poetry, but in the central scene, III, iv, the technique is put to the test. Here the Malvolio and Viola plots are pursued together, and the mood passes successively from Olivia's 'mad' poetic anguish to the witty taunting of 'mad' Malvolio in prose; then it passes to Olivia's verse and again back to prose for the farce of the duel, finally rising to verse for the resurgence of the romantic plotting as Antonio the sea-captain re-enters to save 'Sebastian'. The manner of this unusual scene, which varies mood, pace and style of acting throughout, is guided by variations in language.

Having early learned through Juliet's Nurse with what effect the vernacular could prepare a tragic scene for an emotional statement, Shakespeare repeatedly stresses a tonal distinction with a verbal contrast. Why in *Julius Caesar* does the Casca of of I, ii, speak prose, but in I, iii, verse? The question is resolved by the tenor of the respective scenes. The first Casca is cynically reporting Caesar's refusal of the crown, while the second Casca is creating the prodigious atmosphere of tempest and omen—in a form of direct address which is designed to transport the audience to Caesar's Rome at a time of fatal history. However, Shakespeare's most successful linguistic experiment in this play is to grant Antony an emotive poetry for his Forum speech and to limit Brutus's effort to a spiritless prose (III, ii).

In the mature tragedies, the range of creative experiment becomes richly unpredictable. Hamlet's prose in the nunnery scene seems to assault Ophelia in her orisons coming after the detached prelude of 'To be, or not to be' (*Hamlet*, III, i). After the poetic presentation of his noble Moor, Shakespeare contrives to drop our level of apprehension by the interpolation of harsh prose in *Othello*, I, iii. This is given to Iago, whose cynicism saps the joy from the marriage made in heaven. When Desdemona is re-introduced in Cyprus, Iago's prose aside again taints the image of her beauty (II, i), and after the warm greeting of his wife by Othello, again Iago's words descend like a blight. And when Othello has been brought to obscenities, Iago's gross prose is heard on his lips too. Like Hamlet and Ophelia in their madness before, Lear slides into prose as his mind dissolves and he echoes the language of Edgar (*King Lear*, III, iv, 101). Yet the contrasts of language in this play by no means bow to convention. After the florid speeches of false allegiance from Goneril and Regan, their drop into prose at I, i, 281, promptly shows the spectator their other face, an extension of the Iago manner. In the first encounter between the new Goneril and her father, the Fool's skittish prose is used to spike her haughty verse (I, iv)—a gadfly manner which every audience enjoys; but Shakespeare does not hesitate to use the same device to prick Lear's egotism too.

His most subtle shifts of tone, however, are felt when he learns to slip at will from rhetorical into more 'natural' speech within the iambic form. Already in *The Merchant of Venice* verse suitable for fairy-tale courtship is juxtaposed with verse suitable to the more realistic theme of the bond. This stratagem also transmutes a thin-blooded Portia into richer life. Thus Shakespeare sustains the tinsel enchantment of the casket scene against a background of music, until the moment comes when the lovers must face reality. Salerio gives Bassanio the letter with its news of Antonio's losses, and Portia comments,

> There are some shrewd contents in yon same paper,
> That steals the colour from Bassanio's cheek.  (III, ii, 244-5)

Strict metrical form is abandoned with Portia's startled aside, the catch in the breathing on that stressed 'shrewd' pointing another quality of interest to follow in the play.

In *Macbeth*, Shakespeare is found alternating rhetoric and conversation between two characters, at once suggesting differences between their states of mind and manipulating the tension in the audience. In the scene of Duncan's murder, Lady Macbeth is all impatience—looking for practical action like the spectator himself. Macbeth's thoughts, however, stray into realms she cannot envisage, as he looks at his red hands and the meaning of the crime appals him. Their difference in sensibility is marked by the abrupt contrast in the verse:

LADY MACBETH. A foolish thought, to say a sorry sight.
MACBETH. There's one did laugh in's sleep, and one cried 'Murder!'

(II, ii, 21–2)

moving into the incantatory poetry of

> Methought I heard a voice cry 'Sleep no more'.
> Macbeth does murder sleep—the innocent sleep,
> Sleep that knits up the ravelled sleave of care...    (35–7)

The alternation of the two styles that follows does not offend the ear, since both are drawn from the same mould, and the excessive contrast in speech puts Macbeth's mode into aural perspective for our objective judgment. But such variations of tone are better seen within a single speech.

## THE SETTING AND THE SOLO SPEECH

The Elizabethan actor, like any other, enjoyed his moments in the limelight, and Shakespeare, writing for a particular company, satisfies the demand. Alone on the stage or not, the actor has his virtuoso piece. There are in *Macbeth*, besides the great soliloquies of the principal, Lady Macbeth's sleep-walking scene, Banquo's soliloquy to the throne, Duncan's 'My plenteous joys', the Porter at the gate, Macduff on losing his family and Malcolm's finale. These speeches do not represent a low point of attention; rather, they bring in their train an activity of the mind, for they gather together crowding impressions. Shakespeare therefore prepares the ground for such moments that they may strike home, and he uses a variety of means to mark their importance.

In the lines before Macbeth's 'Is this a dagger which I see

before me...?' (II, i, 33 ff.), the duologue with Banquo is emotionally charged in its sinister double-talk. This preamble diligently sets the stage for the evocation of evil. A torch introduces Banquo's 'How goes the night, boy?'—

FLEANCE. The moon is down; I have not heard the clock.
BANQUO.                    ...There's husbandry in heaven,
  Their candles are all out...
  A heavy summons lies like lead upon me,
  And yet I would not sleep. Merciful powers,
  Restrain in me the cursèd thoughts that nature
  Gives way to in repose!                                   (1–9)

Another torch approaches, and Banquo is able to tell Macbeth that Duncan is, unlike himself, sleeping well 'shut up/In measureless content'. He then reminds us of the Witches, and although Macbeth says 'I think not of them', we know this to be untrue, and it is confirmed by his hasty response. What the weird women represent is impressed again upon the mind of both character and spectator. By the time Macbeth sees his illusory dagger and removes all further restraint upon his thoughts, the atmosphere is sufficiently 'heat-oppressed' for every member of the audience to re-create the same vision. Macbeth's other major speeches are equally well placed.

Building towards the mood of the major speech becomes common practice. Thus in *Antony and Cleopatra*, Enobarbus's dying speech, 'Be witness to me, O thou blessed moon' (IV, ix, 7 ff.) is prepared by a thickening of the atmosphere and a mood of defeat, which the enemy sentries create before Enobarbus speaks: 'They say we shall embattle/By th'second hour i'th'morn'. This pattern is not uncommon, but in this play the principals have their solo pieces set up by a variety of methods. Antony's soliloquy, 'O sun, thy uprise shall I see no more' (IV, xii, 18 ff.), is prepared by contrast, since it follows the swift passage of opposing armies across the stage, IV, x–xii, and comes at a point of rest after the visual clashes. Cleopatra speaks her lines, 'Give me my robe, put on my crown' (V, ii, 279 ff.), after jocular repartee with the Clown, a grotesque figure of death who brings her the basket with its mortal contents, the speech prepared by that daring stroke of incongruity.

The ground for Hamlet's soliloquies is prepared almost to a pattern, and one which is unique to this play. In *Hamlet*, I, ii, 129 ff., Shakespeare empties the stage of a crowded court, bringing the silent figure of the Prince to slow life in a mood of disillusion; for the second act soliloquy, II, ii, 553 ff., he empties it of the lively company of actors. The set-piece 'To be, or not to be' (III, i, 56 ff.), a speech in even more desperate a mood, is prepared by tragic incongruity, being overheard by Claudius and Polonius who, like us, expect a confession of love, and get instead a meditation on death. It is the contrast between the irresolute Prince and the warrior Fortinbras with a marching army bent upon a clear purpose that sets in perspective the soliloquy, 'How all occasions do inform against me' (IV, iv, 32 ff.). For each of Hamlet's major speeches Shakespeare contrives to show him as a solitary figure rejecting the external world.

These examples may suggest that the big speech, with the actor confronting his audience, was a way of directing their response and creating a particular impact, not as oratory but as theatre. The soliloquy was always spoken to the audience and was never a mumbling into beard or bosom in a simulation of naturalistic thinking, as if the spectator were not there. Thus the attempt to catalogue the soliloquies into genres—as expository, meditative, emotive, sententious, and so on—tells us little about their theatrical impact.

A breakdown of the functions of the soliloquy more useful for theatrical analysis and performance might be into four categories, three of which need further qualification:

1. For the *character* speaking: to define him, strengthen his reality, reveal his secrets and review his motives. In many cases this function is negligible. The self-revelation of an Angelo is theatrically different from that of, say, Falstaff, who tells us little that we do not know about him already and whose soliloquizing chiefly allows him to play to the audience in the frank tradition of the clown.

2. For the *theme* of the play: to propound or point the moral significance of an action already witnessed. Nevertheless, Shakespeare rarely speaks in his own voice, and such a soliloquy is usually meant to affect the audience as would an open-ended discussion. Thus the apparent finality of Isabella's decision at *Measure for Measure*, II, iv, 184,

> Then Isabel live chaste, and brother die;
> "More than our brother is our chastity...."

does not resolve, but accentuates, the hard choice between life and honour forced on the spectator's attention.

3. For the *player's* performance: to give him the chance to share an emotion with the spectator, and touch off his feelings. This, too, needs qualification. Hamlet may establish through his soliloquies an empathetic link with the spectator which is not granted to any other tragic hero. Yet what kind and degree of feeling is shared with characters like Macbeth, Othello or Coriolanus who are designed in part to antagonize our sympathies? To understand the play is to know the limits of this sharing.

4. For the *audience* in relation to the progress of the action: to quicken tension and, since the play is a cumulative art moving in time, to accent the impressions preceding it and anticipate those to come. This, the loosest of the four categories, is the only certain one.

That certain plays like *Hamlet* and *Macbeth* which are 'introspective' in character have for that reason a larger number of soliloquies than usual is a misleading notion. It is not possible to think of these plays without their action. Hamlet and Macbeth are introspective characters because they are secret men battling with themselves, and they must speak to the spectator in soliloquy or not at all. Yet a play of the jealous mind like *Othello* grants its hero few true soliloquies—these are given to Iago. Iago is allowed to speak alone on the stage because in this way he may present a vile face to the audience and a smooth one to his master; but Othello is not a secret man, and speaks his mind; between them their forms of speech help to demonstrate the play's theme of honesty and dishonesty. The error springs from the wish to see soliloquy as the glory of Elizabethan conventions. It is but one species among the variety of speeches addressed to the audience. *King Lear*, *Antony and Cleopatra* and *Coriolanus* do not lack soliloquies because they are less plays of 'meditation', but because their author wishes to offer external views on their dialectical themes through speeches distributed among more than one character.

The development in the theatrical virtues of the soliloquies is rapid. Even the coarse-grained expository speech of the Duke of York at the end of the first scene in *2 Henry VI* shows signs of that life which is characteristic of later soliloquies. It has its element of intimacy:

> And, when I spy advantage, claim the crown,
> For that's the golden mark I seek to hit... (I, i, 240–1)

Moreover, Shakespeare raises its affective temperature with logical patterning, 'Nor...Nor...Nor', and caps the crescendo with emotive imagery,

> Then will I raise aloft the milk-white rose,
> With whose sweet smell the air shall be perfumed...
>
> (252 ff.)

Such devices are designed to help the actor exert pressure on the audience within the frame of direct address.

When Shakespeare writes the big speeches for Richard of Gloucester, the passion of his harangue matches the monstrous ideas he conceives:

> Then, since this earth affords no joy to me,
> But to command, to check, to o'erbear such
> As are of better person than myself,
> I'll make my heaven to dream upon the crown,
> And, whiles I live, t'account this world but hell...
>
> (*3 Henry VI*, III, ii, 165 ff.)

The speech rises to a pitch of rhetoric, and exotic embellishments are brought into service:

> I'll drown more sailors than the mermaid shall;
> I'll slay more gazers than the basilisk... (186 ff.)

The audience, one imagines, hisses this melodramatic creature with the zest of the Victorian playgoer. The speeches given to Gloucester in *Richard III* are less lurid and more subtly sophisticated, and the irresistible first soliloquy is shot through with a witty spite which any audience enjoys sharing. We mock with him at the portrait of the warrior who

> capers nimbly in a lady's chamber
> To the lascivious pleasing of a lute... (I, i, 12–13)

and who struts before the 'wanton ambling nymph'; while his open display of his feelings and his awareness of his own deformities begin curiously to endear him to us. Richard is not a character communing with himself; no accidental disclosure of a personal secret lies in the text: the speech is an unashamed address to the audience. Richard manipulates us with confidence, and yet remains a villain.

If flourishes and figures suit the flamboyant Richard II, the speeches in *Richard II* generally lack the life of those in the mature tragedies; while John of Gaunt's panegyric on England (II, i) lives as oratory, the business of dying, which was later to stimulate fully dramatic poetry, was still the cue for lexical tightrope-walking. It is in *King John* that the laws of the formal speech undergo a radical change in the mouth of the Bastard. Here Shakespeare's sense of character has power to govern the familiar devices: the fire of the speaker is realized in the warmth of the speech,

> Well, whiles I am a beggar, I will rail,
> And say there is no sin but to be rich... (II, i, 593–4)

and the verbal balances in this discourse on 'tickling commodity' suit the quality of the man. The same life is felt elsewhere in this play: for example, the slow lilt and falling rhythms in these lines of the Dauphin's on the fate of Prince Arthur and the grief of his mother Constance,

> There's nothing in this world can make me joy:
> Life is as tedious as a twice-told tale
> Vexing the dull ear of a drowsy man. (III, iv, 107–9)

unite mood and sentiment in the drama of the scene. The idiom of such speech, tuned to the mind of the speaker, begins to turn the stage-bound puppet into the being whose presence reaches beyond the limits of the stage.

In *Julius Caesar*, Mark Antony's address to his master's body will exemplify Shakespeare's new craftsmanship for the actor. The speech at once creates the energy of a man suffused with grief and points the theme of the play. It comes as the climax to the scene of the assassination, resolving the ambiguities of Antony's manner in the presence of the conspirators and confirming for the audience the fears expressed by Cassius. Thus it has the weight of the situation upon it, and yet remains personal to Antony and his actor. It is instrumental in guiding the audience in its search for a single-minded response to events: when this speech has been delivered, the audience knows which side it is on, and, while remaining familiar with Brutus's condition, it may now regard him with a more sceptical eye. The speech reads,

> O, pardon me, thou bleeding piece of earth,
> That I am meek and gentle with these butchers!
> Thou art the ruins of the noblest man
> That ever livéd in the tide of times.
> Woe to the hands that shed this costly blood!
> Over thy wounds now do I prophesy
> (Which like dumb mouths do ope their ruby lips
> To beg the voice and utterance of my tongue),
> A curse shall light upon the lives of men;
> Domestic fury and fierce civil strife
> Shall cumber all the parts of Italy;
> Blood and destruction shall be so in use,
> And dreadful objects so familiar,
> That mothers shall but smile when they behold
> Their infants quartered with the hands of war;
> All pity choked with custom of fell deeds:
> And Caesar's spirit ranging for revenge,
> With Até by his side come hot from hell,
> Shall in these confines with a monarch's voice
> Cry 'Havoc', and let slip the dogs of war;
> That this foul deed shall smell above the earth
> With carrion men, groaning for burial.     (III, i, 255–76)

Imagery is no longer loose ornamentation: rather, metaphor is worked into the fabric of the thought to a point where it becomes that fabric. A principle more important than the players' re-enactment of the death of Caesar is at work. The blood from Caesar's wounds becomes the blood of earth itself, as if Caesar's spirit embraced all nature, while the image preserves the simpler notion of the assassins as butchers. Nothing is obtrusively conceited here. The fall of the Roman Empire, the premature crumbling of its tradition and solidity is implicit in 'ruins', and the idea of the surge of history itself is taken up again in 'the tide of times'. So much for the initial statement of the speech.

The lines begin in a personal way—this is Caesar's lieutenant mourning, apologizing for himself as a man in an impossible situation—but before long he is speaking impersonally and prophetically. After an initial impulse of direct sympathy, the audience is caught up and made to feel Caesar's symbolic role. Even then, this is done with steady reference to the particular situation: Antony more than once returns to the blood, which remains visible throughout; the poetry gives the wounds themselves a reality; the choking of pity reflects his particular impulse toward Até and revenge; and his thoughts revert to the actuality of the dead Caesar, 'this foul deed' and the immediate problem of burial. Nevertheless, the over-riding sense is of the importance of the murder for the world in general. The images acquire monstrous proportions, with terrifying pictures of mothers smiling at their infants quartered, and of Caesar partnered by Até 'hot from hell' like a huge hunter 'ranging for revenge' and bearing down upon mankind with the dogs of war.

The shaping of these images overwhelms the audience by a careful husbandry of vocal effects. The first few lines are restrained and with descending tones. Then three times an inverted iambic marks a vocal gesticulation which lifts the voice: 'Woe to the hand...!', 'Blood and destruction...' and 'Cry "Havoc", and let slip...'. These are three crises which accentuate the timbre of the speaking, preludes to the three momentous images which make up the speech. From this the lines rise—'fierce civil strife...all the parts of Italy...be so in use...objects so familiar...'—until the last two drop away. The progressive lengthening of the spoken paragraphs is striking—a run of five relentless lines after 'Blood and destruction ...' and of six racing ones to the end of the speech. In meaning and sound, it is shaped for player and spectator, and is irreducible dramatic poetry. G. Wilson Knight pictures the shape of a Shakespearian soliloquy thus: 'The normal procedure is to start quietly, perhaps colloquially, and then, smoothly taking off like an aeroplane, to become poetically airborne, and finally return to earth'.[1] So with Antony we return to the body of Caesar, now weighty with meaning and feeling, 'groaning for burial'.

[1] *Shakespearian Production*, p. 278.

# 7

# THE ORCHESTRATION OF SPEECH

## CONTRASTING PATTERNS OF SOUND

In the ear of the audience at a play, voices form a continuum of sound and meaning, whether made up of two voices or twenty, in contrast or in concert. The flow will undergo variations in tune and speed, and be broken by silence and physical action, but the verse dramatist especially will be aware of the rhythms and patterns of the stream of speech from the first act to the last, and be concerned for its total orchestration. Excess of realism in modern Shakespearian production tends to destroy this aural shaping of the plays. Speech rather than invented business, the rise and fall of tone in a scene, the pace of playing, with its variations, and the total sound pattern of the play should have an unshakable place in the creative experience.

At the roots of Shakespeare's aural art lie the contrasts in his verse. The characterization of Hamlet turns upon the variety of moods heard, his special qualities suggested by surprising transitions from one tone to another—from 'O, what a rogue and peasant slave am I!' (*Hamlet*, II, ii, 553), for example, to 'To be, or not to be' (III, i, 56) two or three minutes later. Or, when Shakespeare wants his audience to mark a shift in the structure of a whole play, he sketches a Lear with a voice like a storm— 'Blow, winds, and crack your cheeks!' (*King Lear*, III, ii, 1 ff.)— and pits against it the muted simplicity of 'We two alone will sing like birds i'th'cage' (V, iii, 9 ff.), after the reconciliation with Cordelia. In such an instance, the tone of the poetry can outline the development of the play's theme and structure. The wild Lear of the storm and the calm Lear of the prison are two aspects of the struggle against the facts of mortality.

An idea in a play may echo and reverberate. When it is sounded again in another tone or on another tongue, the resulting ironies point to the values underlying the drama. The visual joke of the fights between Hotspur and Prince Hal and its farcical counterpart between Douglas and Falstaff is capped by Hal's twin epitaphs upon the dying Hotspur and upon Falstaff shamming death nearby (*1 Henry IV*, v, iv, 87 ff.). In *Measure for Measure*, Shakespeare juxtaposes the grotesque preparations for the execution of the drunken Barnardine with the realistic terror of Claudio, and further matches the Duke's cool reasons why man should 'be absolute for death' (III, i, 5 ff.) with the mortal fears of Claudio. When Shakespeare employs this facility for parallel and contrast, he anticipates that the active imagination of the audience will supply meaningful links between one speech and another.

As the appearance of a single figure is more striking if it follows a full stage, so in the orchestration of sound useful contrast is felt when one voice follows a medley. The virtue for drama, although not by modern standards for consistency of character, of Prince Hal's first soliloquy (*1 Henry IV*, I, ii, 187 ff.) is its startling antipathy with the spirit of his preceding scene with Falstaff and Poins. The bantering prose is idiomatic and witty, swift and lightly touched, the ball passing quickly from one speaker to the next. It so firmly establishes a temper for the scene that Hal's formal verse in direct address falls with the shock of anti-climax. The audience is led to believe one thing about the Prince, and is then shown another: the technique makes its necessary point about the Janus-faced Prince, but this does not mean that it can be accounted a pleasing effect.

In another vein, the audience gains a sense of Macbeth's isolation of mind, and even has an illusion of his ability as an impostor, because of the variety of other voices which precede his. His speech aside,

> Two truths are told,
> As happy prologues to the swelling act
> Of the imperial theme...          (*Macbeth*, I, iii, 127 ff.)

discloses the secret paths he must walk, after the frank dialogue between Ross, Angus and Banquo, and his hesitant surmises are in another order of poetry:

> This supernatural soliciting
> Cannot be ill; cannot be good.          (130–1)

The formal and public scene of Macbeth's coronation, dominated
by the new king's voice mouthing the even tones of its hypocrisies,

> We hear our bloody cousins are bestowed
> In England and in Ireland, not confessing
> Their cruel parricide, filling their hearers
> With strange invention.                    (III, i, 29–32)

is capped by the new and urgent rhythms of furtive soliloquy:

> To be thus is nothing,
> But to be safely thus: our fears in Banquo
> Stick deep.                                (47–9)

Again, during the crowded banquet scene, III, iv, Macbeth's
starting at Banquo's ghost is enhanced by a poetry of vivid
private imaginings at odds with his assumed role of genial host.
By such tonal contrasts, Macbeth the man of borrowed robes
also hits the ear as a double-tongued, if deeply troubled, villain,
and the statement of the play emerges in part through our aural
apprehension of duplicity.

The life of the drama depends in some measure upon the
playwright's ability to modulate sound and rhythm to distinguish
one aspect of a developing situation from another, and this can
be as quickening as the switch between prose and verse. In
particular, Shakespeare's experiments in shifting the tone are at
their most provocative when he splices the tragic with the comic.
Yet he saw no need for a gentle verbal modulation into comic
counterpoint. In *Romeo and Juliet*, the audience willingly joins
him in the risk of near-farcical volte-face and revels in it. At
every appearance of Juliet's Nurse, the drama leaps into another
key, but without destroying its own romantic fabric. The youth
and idealism of Juliet gain in richness by being spiked by the
experience of an ageing comic confidante. The relationship
between Romeo and his cynical friend Mercutio does not repeat
this effect, Mercutio's scintillating language leaving Romeo's
somewhat anaemic: the ages of the two men are too close. The
experiment with Juliet's Nurse was an audacious success, and
the effect is heard again when *Hamlet*'s Gravediggers sustain
the theme of mortality threading the play, prepare the ground

for the bitterness of the struggle with Laertes, and yet add that typically Shakespearian edge of comic objectivity.

The tragicomic tones heard in the poetry of *The Winter's Tale* are bound up with the flexibility of the play's moods; in particular the tragic tendencies of the first two acts force upon Shakespeare the major problem of redressing the balance in the last three. In II, iii, when Leontes's jealousy is at its peak ('Nor night, nor day, no rest...'), Paulina's needling sarcasm,

> I'll not call you tyrant;
> But this most cruel usage of your queen
> (Not able to produce more accusation
> Than your own weak-hinged fancy) something savours
> Of tyranny...                                 (II, iii, 116–20)

starts the shift to comedy by its simple normality. The Clowns who find Perdita complete the reversal in III, iii, although even here the prose edges nervously between a farcical vernacular and emotive description:

> I would you did but see how it chafes, how it rages, how it takes up the shore! but that's not to the point...O, the most piteous cry of the poor souls!...                                 (III, iii, 86–8)

By the fourth act, the presence of Autolycus has decisively lightened the atmosphere, and the sheep-shearing feast, IV, iv, blends with ease the Arcadian romanticism of Florizel's poetry with the realistic Englishness of the old Shepherd, Perdita's homely pastoralism and healthy freshness embracing the two. The quasi-tragic and the comic move comfortably alongside each other in the scene's balanced sequence of tones.

### DUOLOGUE AND DUET

Two characters, two voices; but to the playwright wishing to sustain a lively stage this is not the straightforward piece of orchestration it might seem. Shakespeare always has in view a developing aural pattern in an exchange.

Shakespearian duologue deals in discords, and even an effect of harmony needs its preparatory discord, an Iago preceding a Desdemona. The lyrical harmony of Romeo and Juliet's tones in the balcony scene owes some of its sweetness to the preparatory work of Mercutio's ribald verse:

> Cry but 'Ay me!', pronounce but 'love' and 'dove';
> Speak to my gossip Venus one fair word...
>
> (*Romeo and Juliet*, II, i, 10–11)

Shakespeare even gives him the line, 'Appear thou in the likeness of a sigh' (8), knowing that this will be Romeo's first intimation of Juliet's presence with her 'Ay me!' (II, ii, 25). Yet the audience does not dissolve in laughter at the echo: Mercutio has sapped it of its mockery of young love, and the succeeding harmony of tones proceeds from its genuine warmth. However, as practical theatre, this idyllic duet could not have sustained its length without the hidden edge of Mercutio's worldly tones and our knowledge of the disagreement of the worldly parents.

The abdication scene in *Richard II* offers a normal pattern of duologue. King Richard's prolonged flourishes of rhetorical imagery are answered with short brutality by the practical Bolingbroke:

> I thought you had been willing to resign.    (IV, I, 190)

is the usurper's riposte to Richard's elaborate figure of the two buckets dancing in the air, and when the King flies off into yet another lexical flounce with

> Your cares set up do not pluck my cares down.
> My care is loss of care, by old care done,
> Your care is gain of care, by new care won:
> The cares I give, I have, though given away,
> They tend the crown, yet still with me they stay.    (195–9)

Bolingbroke's hard, prosaic answer comes again like a slap in the face:

> Are you contented to resign the crown?    (200)

The antagonism of the two personalities is stressed by the contrast in speech mannerism, not unlike the cutting reply of Regan to her father's pleading, 'Good sir, to th'purpose' (*King Lear*, II, iv, 176).

*Hamlet* shows a mastery of the dramatic uses of passing up or down the rhetorical scale: it is a play of contrasted voices designed to guide the audience's sympathies. The mellifluous lines of the smiling Claudius, replete with balanced figures, are those of the logician. Why should the Prince continue to mourn his father?

> fie, 'tis a fault to heaven,
> A fault against the dead, a fault to nature,
> To reason most absurd... (I, ii, 101–3)

The Claudius tone accentuates the warmth of Hamlet's subsequent soliloquy, and the difference between those who 'seem' and those who are true is thus sounded. The notion is re-introduced in Hamlet's mock-mad lines to Polonius, II, ii, and again, in yet another key, in the contrast between his crazed abuse of Ophelia and her genuine fear and grief:

HAMLET. ...I say we will have no more marriages—those that are married already, all but one, shall live, the rest shall keep as they are: to a nunnery, go. (*Exit*)
OPHELIA. O, what a noble mind is here o'erthrown!...

(III, i, 150 ff.)

It is a calculated effect that Claudius's double-dealing with Laertes to bring about the death of Hamlet should be succeeded by Gertrude's feeling account of the drowning of Ophelia, the false and the true again marked out in aural forms. If there is a secondary image of the manoeuvres of pretence received from this play, it is projected by such linguistic virtuosity. Each contradiction of voice is an aural signal intended to put the audience on its mettle.

In tragic and quasi-tragic scenes, a central duologue comes under the verse control of re-created feeling. In *Measure for Measure*, the alert Angelo picks his words with nervous care, leading on the blinkered Isabella by his ambiguities:

ANGELO.                       Answer to this—
 I (now the voice of the recorded law)
 Pronounce a sentence on your brother's life:
 Might there not be a charity in sin,
 To save this brother's life?
ISABELLA.                       Please you to do't,
 I'll take it as a peril to my soul,
 It is no sin at all, but charity. (II, iv, 60–6)

The rhythm rushes Isabella blindly into the logical trap. Or Iachimo shrewdly teases and provokes his disarmed victim: separated from her husband, Imogen asks whether he is 'disposed to mirth'.

IACHIMO. Exceeding pleasant; none a stranger there
  So merry and so gamesome: he is called
  The Briton reveller.
IMOGEN.               When he was here
  He did incline to sadness, and oft-times
  Not knowing why.
IACHIMO.           I never saw him sad.

                           (*Cymbeline*, I, vi, 57–62)

This is the villain's short answer as he observes the girl's growing alarm.

The characters of the prose duologues in the comedies are usually contrasted in their sex, but otherwise they share the given mood; this is true even of Beatrice and Benedick. Therefore it is not inappropriate to think of such exchanges as duets. These display a special skill in verbal manipulation based upon the idiom of colloquial speech which can accommodate its own range of tone and tempo. A musical pattern is framed by the derision of Beatrice, who scarcely parries her lover's advances before she cuts them down:

BEATRICE. Against my will I am sent to bid you come in to dinner.
BENEDICK. Fair Beatrice, I thank you for your pains.
BEATRICE. I took no more pains for those thanks than you take pains
  to thank me. If it had been painful, I would not have come.
BENEDICK. You take pleasure then in the message.
BEATRICE. Yea, just so much as you may take upon a knife's point,
  and choke a daw withal.   (*Much Ado About Nothing*, II, iii, 241–9)

The sway of thrust and retreat guides the tune of the repartee, although it is hard to consider it apart from the interplay between misogynist and misanthropist as each shifts ground, a situation which is provocative in itself.

Situation helps the exchanges between Rosalind and Orlando too—a girl in a man's role and forced to woo without revealing her sex. In *As You Like It*, the Rosalind-Orlando chase is not only contrasted with the bloodless amours of Silvius and Phebe and Touchstone and Audrey; it is also at variance with accepted behaviour, since Rosalind's borrowed breeches grant her a freedom of speech she would not otherwise have.

ROSALIND. Come, woo me, woo me; for now I am in a holiday humour, and like enough to consent... What would you say to me now, an I were your very very Rosalind?

ORLANDO. I would kiss before I spoke.

ROSALIND. Nay, you were better speak first, and when you were gravelled for lack of matter, you might take occasion to kiss: very good orators, when they are out, they will spit, and for lovers, lacking (God warr'nt us!) matter, the cleanliest shift is to kiss.

ORLANDO. How if the kiss be denied?

ROSALIND. Then she puts you to entreaty and there begins new matter.

$\qquad$ (*As You Like It*, IV, i, 65–78)

These lovers may of course only talk of kissing in lieu of practice. Here is a love scene lifted into an operatic convention, and the notion of physical contact is no more substantial than in Celia's mock marriage ceremony a few minutes later. Yet the scene retains its strength of feeling. Rosalind has Orlando quite at a disadvantage—he may be enjoying the mockery, but not with half the edge of poignancy felt by a Ganymede who knows she is really Rosalind. Thus the interchange is very much one way, falling into a regular pattern, with Rosalind leading and Orlando trailing. This is unfortunate for the actor playing the lover, but it happily throws special attention upon the heroine and the ticklish position in which she finds herself. The scene proceeds with the lightness and distancing of a play-actor play-acting a part and yet being herself. So the phrases lift ('I am in a holiday humour') and fall ('an I were your very very Rosalind?'), and before the dangerous reality of Orlando's sentiment intrudes they lift again ('Nay, you were better speak first') only to fall again ('the cleanliest shift is to kiss'). The dance of her words gracefully embraces and repels the loved one.

## PACE

The speed of speech resides in the written lines, and if it is arbitrarily imposed by the actor it is meaningless. As an actor himself, Shakespeare adopted it as a rule that, if the actors were to speak quickly, he must himself supply a lively language.

The breaking of the verse line into short phrases distributed between two or more speakers is usually a signal for a rapid pace, the actors speaking hard on their cues and the dialogue tossed smartly between them. Thus Macbeth and his Lady after the murder of Duncan:

LADY MACBETH. Did you not speak?
MACBETH.                    When?
LADY MACBETH.                      Now.
MACBETH.                              As I descended?
LADY MACBETH. Ay.
MACBETH.          Hark!          (*Macbeth*, II, ii, 16–18)

and the unfinished last line marks the tension of a pause as they listen together. These are the Murderers as they wait alert to pounce upon Banquo and Fleance:

2 MURDERER.          A light, a light!
3 MURDERER.                    'Tis he.
1 MURDERER. Stand to't.
BANQUO. It will be rain to-night.
1 MURDERER.              Let it come down.
(III, iii, 14–15)

and again the unfinished third line suggests the suspense as actors and spectators alike hold their breath. So Cleopatra hunts anxiously for Antony:

CLEOPATRA. Saw you my lord?
ENOBARBUS. No, lady.
CLEOPATRA. Was he not here?
CHARMIAN. No, madam.
CLEOPATRA. He was disposed to mirth, but on the sudden
    A Roman thought hath struck him. Enobarbus!
ENOBARBUS. Madam?
CLEOPATRA. Seek him, and bring him hither.
(*Antony and Cleopatra*, I, ii, 79–86)

The curt lines suddenly reveal Cleopatra's fear as an ordinary woman that her lover might lose interest in her. She has entered in haste, troubled because Antony has left her side. By short lines Shakespeare distributes her agitation to those about her as she flashes at each of them. They pick up her pace until an unexpected, regular line slows her thought and suggests that she has turned away. Yet her quicksilver mind is alight with another idea: she flings back at Enobarbus, and further clipped words reassert her urgency.

Complete pentameters which Shakespeare wants spoken rapidly are also recognizable, when brief phrasing can equally raise the rate of delivery. After the report of Fulvia's death, Cleopatra makes her entrance with an emotionally charged attack:

> See where he is, who's with him, what he does:
> I did not send you: if you find him sad,
> Say I am dancing; if in mirth, report
> That I am sudden sick. Quick, and return.    (I, iii, 2–5)

Prosaic monosyllables, run-on lines, the quick sequence of orders, whip the speech along. Yet the rhythm in such lines is not submerged, and it can reassert itself as required. The speeches of Leontes at the height of his jealousy afford fine examples of the blank verse line flexed for pace:

> Dost think I am so muddy, so unsettled,
> To appoint myself in this vexation, sully
> The purity and whiteness of my sheets
> (Which to preserve is sleep, which being spotted
> Is goads, thorns, nettles, tails of wasps),
> Give scandal to the blood o'th'prince my son
> (Who I do think is mine, and love as mine),
> Without ripe moving to't? Would I do this?
> Could man so blench?    (*The Winter's Tale*, I, ii, 325–33)

This cataract of words, marked by its rising phrases and run-on lines, periphrases and elliptical sentence-structure, demonstrates Shakespeare's verse line at its most serviceable for rapid pace and the suggestion of less controlled feeling.

## CRESCENDO

The wealth of imagery in Claudio's speech on death in *Measure for Measure* may blind the reader to its careful shaping in pace. It makes a slow and agonized start,

> Ay, but to die, and go we know not where,
> To lie in cold obstruction, and to rot...    (III, i, 117 ff.)

but a degree of hysteria in the thought increases the pace of the speech, which rushes to its crisis with the breathless lines,

> To be imprisoned in the viewless winds
> And blown with restless violence round about
> The pendent world...                          (123–5)

until a longer paragraph brings it to a sobbing close. Shakespeare often guides his speaker with a crescendo, whether by patterned language, as when Rosalind tells Orlando of his brother Oliver's love for 'Aliena':

for your brother and my sister no sooner met but they looked; no sooner looked but they loved; no sooner loved but they sighed...

> (*As You Like It*, V, ii, 31 ff.)

or by repetitions to simulate a climax of violent thought, as in Leontes's shrill speech:

> Is this nothing?
> Why then the world, and all that's in't, is nothing,
> The covering sky is nothing, Bohemia nothing,
> My wife is nothing, nor nothing have these nothings,
> If this be nothing.                   (*The Winter's Tale*, I, ii, 292–6)

Nor does dialogue between two or more characters proceed at a steady pace without risking loss of attention. If the audience is to catch the excitement when Hamlet faces the implications of seeing his father's ghost, the preparatory cross-questioning of his friends must increase its pace in a crescendo:

HAMLET. Armed, say you?
ALL. Armed, my lord.
HAMLET. From top to toe?
ALL.                              My lord, from head to foot.
HAMLET. Then saw you not his face.
HORATIO. O yes, my lord, he wore his beaver up.

At this, the Prince's sudden challenge to Horatio—'Then saw you not his face'—is logically answered, and it suggests a momentary pause before he pursues a new line of thinking and the pace accelerates again:

HAMLET. What, looked he frowningly?
HORATIO. A countenance more in sorrow than in anger.
HAMLET. Pale, or red?
HORATIO. Nay, very pale... (*Hamlet*, I, ii, 226 ff.)

Only the reflective 'I would I had been there' breaks the run before the clinching decision, 'I will watch to-night' (242), and after this Hamlet halts the sequence by the firm lines of verse with which he orders the men to meet him.

Hamlet's interview with his mother, III, iv, does not turn on the usual give and take of words between two characters, but upon the drive in the lines given to the Prince, who dominates the scene. He attacks her with words, and words are his weapons. The duologue has a slow and sinister beginning, 'Now, mother, what's the matter?' (III, iv, 8), and proceeds like a diabolical game, until Hamlet's voice takes on a sharper, commanding edge and the Queen cries for help. The killing of Polonius increases the heat and pace of the speaking, and Hamlet's words finally soar with his fierce emotion:

> Such an act
> That blurs the grace and blush of modesty,
> Calls virtue hypocrite, takes off the rose
> From the fair forehead of an innocent love
> And sets a blister there, makes marriage vows
> As false as dicers' oaths, O such a deed... (40 ff.)

He belabours her with violent, poisonous images, lashing her with peremptory orders, exclamations and questions as in his anger he returns to the thoughts that plague him. Repetition urges on the actor's speech, as in 'Have you eyes?...ha! have you eyes?', 'waits upon the judgment, and what judgment...?', 'sense sure you have...but sure that sense/Is apoplexed' and

> Eyes without feeling, feeling without sight,
> Ears without hands or eyes, smelling sans all... (78-9)

until the voice is finally a hiss between clenched teeth as Hamlet accuses his mother of living 'In the rank sweat of an enseaméd bed/Stewed in corruption'. At the peak of passion, Shakespeare produces his *coup de théâtre*, the re-appearance of the Ghost.

The scene of the smothering of Desdemona, rhythmically contrasted with the street-fight, climbs from its slow ritualistic beginning in the brooding of the Moor, and moves through the increasingly frenzied appeals of Desdemona:

DESDEMONA. O, banish me, my lord, but kill me not!
OTHELLO. Down, strumpet!
DESDEMONA. Kill me tomorrow; let me live tonight!
OTHELLO. Nay, if you strive—
DESDEMONA. But half an hour!
OTHELLO.                    Being done, there is no pause.
DESDEMONA. But while I say one prayer!
OTHELLO.                    It is too late.
                                            (*Othello*, v, ii, 82–7)

At this point of frenzy the stage falls quiet and Desdemona's struggles cease; then through the silence the calls of Emilia wake the dazed man to a realization of what he has done. The slow corruption of Othello's mind is one of cunning modulations within the general framework of sound, from the blissful if ironic

> Excellent wretch! Perdition catch my soul
> But I do love thee...                         (III, iii, 91–2)

through the hesitant ambiguities of 'honest' and 'think' and 'seem', to the bitter self-communing of

> Farewell the tranquil mind! farewell content!...    (350 ff.)

and on to the raging of 'Blood, blood, blood!' (453) and the racing Pontic sea (455). A slow, drawn-out climb is graduated by the rhetoric of the verse to the irretrievable

> Damn her, lewd minx! O, damn her! damn her!    (477)

for an overwhelming crisis in the action.

There is in *King Lear* a similar careful gradation of steps through a scene, and the squalls of the King's mood are directed by many regulated moments of crescendo. Outstanding in this is the familiar scene with Regan, II, iv, where repeated phrases

are planted as signposts for the actor's pitch of emotion to match
the action on the stage. When Lear seeks out Regan, he finds
Kent sitting in the stocks; immediately he refuses to believe that
she and Cornwall could have intended such an insult. The duologue with Kent marks a first quick accession of feeling, and the
submerged element of the ridiculous in the form it takes hints
at the onset of his loss of complacency:

LEAR. What's he that hath so much thy place mistook
　　To set thee here?
KENT.　　　　　　It is both he and she,
　　Your son and daughter.
LEAR. No.
KENT. Yes.
LEAR. No, I say.
KENT. I say yea.
LEAR. No, no, they would not.
KENT. Yes, yes, they have.
LEAR. By Jupiter, I swear no!
KENT. By Juno, I swear ay!　　　　　　　　　　　　(11–21)

With Lear's 'Hysterica passio! Down, thou climbing sorrow'
(55), Shakespeare deliberately takes his central character off,
gives the stage to the Fool and effectively reduces the emotional
pressure. When Lear returns to learn that Regan and Cornwall
will not speak with him, the pressure climbs again: 'My rising
heart! But down!' (117). Thereafter the King's passions rise
with his responses to Regan's expostulations with him over her
sister Goneril. It is then that the troubling evidence of Kent's
degrading punishment begins to seize his mind:

> Who put my man i'th'stocks?　　　　　　(178)
> Who stocked my servant?　　　　　　　　(184)
> How came my man i'th'stocks?　　　　　(194)
> You? Did you?　　　　　　　　　　　　(196)

These questions, interpolated during the business of Regan's
humiliating reception of Goneril, are further signposts leading
the actor to his peak of feeling. The reiterated 'Return to her?'
(203, 207 and 211) continues the exertion of pressure. The sisters
with alternate thrusts then lightly annihilate his dignity:

| | |
|---|---|
| What! fifty followers? | (233) |
| ...but five and twenty. | (244) |
| What need you five and twenty, ten, or five? | (257) |
| What need one? | (259) |

These echoes increase the pace until Lear's exasperated cry, 'O reason not the need!' (260), abruptly halts in its racing career this destruction of his hopes and values. He stumbles off, a defeated man: 'O Fool, I shall go mad!' (282). By such incontrovertible means, almost a theatrical mannerism in this scene, Shakespeare regulates the pace and pitch of the action which must lead Lear and his audience into the storm itself.

### VARIATION OF TEMPO

It is implicit in what has been said that the meaningful quickening or slowing of pace in a scene is always relative to a norm: a sequence will seem fast by contrast with a slow one, and vice versa. A few lines from the handkerchief scene in *Othello* suggest Shakespeare's control and ordering of tempo:

OTHELLO. I have a salt and sorry rheum offends me;
  Lend me thy handkerchief.
DESDEMONA. Here, my lord.
OTHELLO. That which I gave you.
DESDEMONA. I have it not about me.
OTHELLO. Not?
DESDEMONA. No, indeed, my lord.
OTHELLO. That's a fault. That handkerchief
  Did an Egyptian to my mother give;
  She was a charmer, and could almost read
  The thoughts of people...         (III, iv, 51 ff.)

The short lines signal a rising pitch and quickening pace. With Othello in the immediacy of his anger and Desdemona in her thoughtless innocence, the lines hurry on to the prick of reproof, 'That's a fault.' The short line marks a change, and the Moor passes into a slower, almost sinister, primitive mood and looks hard at his wife on 'read/The thoughts of people'. Accentuated by this new tone and speed, the handkerchief assumes a mythological quality in its exotic imagery, until the loss of it seems sacrilegious. The handkerchief becomes for him the symbol of her adultery, of a sin against race and blood, and the audience's sense of this is built up by the incantatory tone with which Othello now endows his lines. This happens only after the changing tempo of the sequence has made Desdemona catch her breath ('Is't possible?'), gripped the attention of the audience and penetrated their imagination. By the raising and lowering of tension and through the consequent sharpening of the senses, the audience is helped to recognize an important stage moment.

The romantic comedies are delicately varied in pace. Appia's notion of drama as a picture composed in time suits the gossamer of these creations more than it does the coarser texture of comic life in the later history plays. In *As You Like It*, the lingering movement of the first exchange between Rosalind and Orlando after the violence of the wrestling match is in a lighter mood which is galvanized at once by Le Beau, who strides in to spur the action:

> Good sir, I do in friendship counsel you
> To leave this place... (I, ii, 249 ff.)

In a style of comparative leisure, Rosalind then discusses her fluttering heart, until, repeating the pattern, Duke Frederick banishes her:

> Mistress, dispatch you with your safest haste
> And get you from our court. (I, iii, 41–2)

and the girls hurriedly leave the court. The languor of the exiled Duke in Arden, II, i, checks the pace once more, until, back at the court, Frederick starts the pursuit of his daughter and Orlando departs in danger with old Adam, II, ii–iii, their haste contrasting with the life in the forest. Here Rosalind, Celia and Touchstone now arrive exhausted, and their mood of lassitude characterizes the pace until Orlando enters with drawn sword to demand food, II, vii. In another leap back to the palace, Frederick urges on the hue and cry,

> Not see him since? Sir, sir, that cannot be... (III, i, 1 ff.)

and then we are returned to the moon-struck Orlando pinning his verses to the trees. Thereafter the intricacies of the love-chase replace the antithesis of court and forest as a pace setter. When in particular Rosalind finds that her lover has put her name on every tree, her happy eagerness starts the new movement post-haste:

Alas the day, what shall I do with my doublet and hose? What did he when thou saw'st him? What said he? How looked he? Wherein went he? What makes he here? Did he ask for me? Where remains he? How parted he with thee? and when shalt thou see him again? Answer me in one word.                                    (III, ii, 217–22)

During the passage of the subsequent scenes between the lovers, a calculated slackening in pace points the elements of frustration and fear which inform the action.

The scene of Desdemona's 'willow song', *Othello*, IV, iii, is sandwiched between the two harsh scenes of Iago's plotting and the killing, and it is not only heard to be a gentle scene of feminine tones set among fierce masculine ones, but also a scene of markedly slower pace after the rush of the previous action. The new pace is dictated by the elegiac mood of the song itself, and by the intensely feminine, even languid, detail of Desdemona's undressing and the preparation of the sheets. It is as if Shakespeare must re-create the degraded bride as a woman of flesh and blood, and not another of the Moor's myths, before she dies, so that the evil of Iago's remoter machinations shall be felt in human terms. The tension of imminent disaster remains, and even Desdemona senses that her preparations for bed follow a ritual of self-sacrifice: her wedding sheets are to be her shroud, her fidelity of love proved in her death. The song itself is introduced by the painful little story of the maid Barbara who 'died singing it', and for Desdemona as for the audience it assumes a quality of ominous inevitability, so that the details of the scene are coloured by its ironic correspondence with Desdemona's own case. In the absence of actual weeping, its 'salt tears' supply what Desdemona's passive dignity refuses: she will die in love, trust and resignation. She sings it informally, breaking the lines naturally as Emilia unpins her, or as she forgets a phrase here and there, or as she tells Emilia to hurry, or as she, and we, listen for her husband's step outside. The detail of the business which accompanies it is small, particular and touchingly domestic, and this is happily balanced against our sense of ritual in the scene. A bride again, the Desdemona who sings herself to her death-bed is all grace and submission. This is Shakespeare using song for its functional contribution to the play: any decorative purpose is minimal. The controlled pace of the singing and the business is the uneasy rest in the music before the dénouement of the action.

### A NOTE ON PAUSE AND SILENCE

Silence can be eloquence in a verse play provided it is prepared by its theatrical context in such a way as to school the audience to recognize its implication. The dramatic value of the scene governs the value of the pause within its flow of speech.

When Shakespeare writes an instruction for a pause into his lines, there is no gainsaying its importance. The Fiends who appear to Joan la Pucelle punctuate her appeal to them by their silent refusals of help:

> Help me this once, that France may get the field.
> (*They walk, and speak not*).
> O, hold me not with silence over-long!
> (*1 Henry VI*, v, iii, 12–13)

and afterwards, '*They hang their heads*' and '*They shake their heads*'. When she offers the Devil first her body and then her soul, the audience must wait in suspense.

When the Prince of Arragon unlocks the wrong casket, his amazement is reflected in Portia's line,

> Too long a pause for that which you find there.
> (*The Merchant of Venice*, ii, ix, 53)

In this instance, Shakespeare manages to direct the player and retain some dramatic interest in the statement. Portia's requital of Shylock's cruel conditions in his bargain with Antonio is presented with a renowned clarity of effect when she says,

> Why doth the Jew pause? take thy forfeiture.  (IV, i, 331)

This is the climactic moment in Shakespeare's most powerful trial scene—and the crushing pause saps Shylock's whole strength and pride. After this, the spectator once more sees in the Jew an animal at bay.

Both Brutus and Antony punctuate their speeches in the Forum with a stated pause: 'I pause for a reply' (*Julius Caesar*, III, ii, 33–4) from Brutus, and from Antony,

> Bear with me;
> My heart is in the coffin there with Caesar,
> And I must pause till it come back to me.    (106–8)

Brutus's pause is that of the orator who waits for an answer but expects none; he is entirely confident, and he takes up the thread of his discourse oblivious of the irony in his situation, which both his stage and his theatre audience perceive, but which he does not. This is a pause without suspense, although it neatly points the character. The case is different with Mark Antony, who speaks the first 35 lines of his address with delicacy, feeling his way, uncertain of his hearers. His pause is a test of the strength of his position, fortified by a show of emotion; it is appreciated as such by us, while it holds the crowd of citizens in suspense. It allows the Citizens to try their own feelings among one another, and they find that they agree. Antony may now proceed with a confidence he has earned and shrewdly pull out the rest of the stops.

The celebrated instance of meaningful silence is Macduff's, upon hearing at last from Ross that his wife and children have been murdered by Macbeth's killers. In another author we might expect the situation to prompt a gross, rhetorical and 'theatrical' response. Shakespeare uses Malcolm to indicate the restraint in Macduff's performance and the hiatus in the flow of speech with those poignant lines,

> What, man! ne'er pull your hat upon your brows;
> Give sorrow words: the grief that does not speak
> Whispers the o'er-fraught heart and bids it break.
> (*Macbeth*, IV, iii, 208–10)

Macduff's silence, and the gesture with it, are explained in these lines as a natural symptom of intense grief—the actor's work is motivated in the manner of the naturalistic theatre—but the audience, too, has time to digest the meaning of the atrocity and what may follow from it. Such moderation here also increases the impact of the impassioned outburst which eventually comes.

Other crucial pauses may be assumed from supporting evidence, although they may not be indicated in so many words. Claudius's long reproof of his nephew Hamlet for his continued mourning for his father must end upon the strongest of pauses. He waits for the Prince's reply, and it does not come. Such a silence here, with its satisfying theatrical irony enforced by the space between the two players, gives the audience a tantalizing hint about the initial relationship between them. However, the mute Hamlet is pressed into speech by the intervention of his mother, although even now his response is ambiguous in the extreme, and tantamount to saying nothing:

I shall in all my best obey you, madam.

(*Hamlet*, I, ii, 120)

The King's half-sarcastic response to this equivocal reply, ''Tis a loving and a fair reply', caps our first impression of the feeling between uncle and nephew, and justifies the pause.

Throughout his career, Shakespeare practised this theatrical device, and time and again secures a minor *coup de théâtre*. Beatrice's unexpected demand of Benedick to 'Kill Claudio' (*Much Ado About Nothing*, IV, i, 288) must elicit such a pause that the frivolous tenor of their romance is radically altered and the structure of the comedy redirected. The stupefaction of Othello after he has smothered Desdemona in *Othello*, V, ii, or the stunned silence of Macbeth following the appearance of the Witches, marked by 19 lines from Ross and Banquo, in *Macbeth*, I, iii, 89–107, or Macbeth's numbness at Seton's 'The queen, my lord, is dead' (V, v, 16), or Coriolanus's initial embarrassment before Aufidius's gate in *Coriolanus*, IV, v, are of a kind. The import for player and spectator of each event is stamped by silence, orchestrated within its scene.

Such moments are likely to be lost on the reader. He should always ask himself why Shakespeare arranges for a character's entrance when he has little or nothing to say. 'To be, or not to be' is not the same when read as when Hamlet is seen speaking it with the pitifully ardent Ophelia praying behind him. Volumnia's pleading with Coriolanus induces a more complex tension than the words alone allow when the scowling presence of Aufidius is seen upstage overlooking the figures of the mother and the son.

# IV

# CONCLUSIONS

## 8

# TOTAL THEATRE

### EYE AND EAR INSEPARABLE

At one time the word 'Shakespearian' was taken in much the
same way as the word 'Dickensian': it described a work full of
life and variety, warmth of feeling and wealth of character. Both
of these generous epithets were accredited terms in the late
nineteenth century, and both gained currency with the begin-
nings of a literary criticism of the novel. Today 'Shakespearian'
best identifies a particular kind of theatre experience, one which
attempts the total involvement of an audience.

Recently the notion of 'total theatre' has been in vogue, and
abused by an over-literal reading of Antonin Artaud's theories in
*The Theatre and Its Double*. Artaud's was an early reaction against
the naturalistic movement which swept Europe in the first
decades of this century; in his attempt to discredit a too literary
drama, one in which speech had become overrated as an agency
of theatrical communication, he demanded that the spectacular
elements of drama—the décor, the lighting, the miming of the
actor—should convey more. He thought it wise to modify his
view of what constituted total theatre, and this is expressed in
a later letter in 1932: 'I am adding another language to the
spoken language, and I am trying to restore to the language of
speech its old magic, its essential spellbinding power, for its
mysterious possibilities have been forgotten'.[1] He was arguing
a philosophy of theatre parallel to that put forward by Edward
Gordon Craig in a 'dialogue' in 1905. In this, Craig insisted
that 'the Art of the Theatre is neither acting nor the play,
it is not scene nor dance, but it consists of all the elements of
which these things are composed: action, which is the very
spirit of acting; words, which are the body of the play; line and
colour, which are the very heart of the scene; rhythm, which is
the very essence of dance'.[2]

[1] *Op. cit.* trans. Richards, p. 111.　　[2] *The Art of the Theatre*, p. 138.

The modern playgoer now looks to Shakespeare for primary examples of a drama which uses every appeal to eye and ear, except those of modern scenic and lighting art—and even these find full opportunities for imaginative expression in a drama which operates at some remove from naturalism. Shakespeare had the talent to exploit a ripe and evolving theatre in its own terms, and in discovering that what he had to say and the way in which the audience received it had to go together like flesh and blood, he chanced upon an imperishable stagecraft, although the bulk of the study of Shakespeare's achievement has been literary. Yet any estimate of his value as a dramatist must take into account how he gains an audience's full participation—at the least, by provoking their visual imagination and invoking their sense of rhythm. The contrasts and emphases of his visual effects—in form and movement, mime and gestic expression— are as powerful an agent as the aural skills of his craft. The existence of these in such abundance throughout his plays suggests that he rarely forgot his audience. For stage contrasts are created only on the assumption that an audience will deduce meaning from them.

Total theatre implies a total assault upon the spectator's mind and senses. Othello and Iago are black and white to increase our sensitivity to their qualities of good and evil. For the Elizabethan audience the Moor was black, not a romantic chocolate colour, and the audience must share some of the primitive feelings of a white community against a Negro who steals one of their women. Teasing the sympathies, Shakespeare proposes an outrageous view of his black hero in *Othello*, I, i, and before the end of the act shows its doubtful integrity. This view is Iago's, the black-hearted white devil, and Shakespeare perversely characterizes Othello as 'far more fair than black' (I, iii, 290, the Duke of Venice). The visual stress which falls upon a black Othello and a white Desdemona every time they are together makes a paradox of their idealized love-match, and thereby draws the strongest attention to it. 'I saw Othello's visage in his mind' (I, iii, 252), declares Desdemona, and the spectator is made aware of his own

prejudices. Like Jean Genet with *Les Nègres*, Shakespeare masks
a black actor in white to exact a black justice. The techniques
outlined in this book are practised in order to do one thing above
all—to prompt the audience's imagination, engage its fullest
attention and provoke an inevitable evaluating experience.

Therefore the division between visual and aural elements is,
in the nature of theatre, an arbitrary one. Ideal theatre, as
Elizabethan drama at its best proves, is a synthesis. What is
heard directs, and yet seems to echo, what is seen. The mocking
verbal parody by Richard of Gloucester of Christian devotion
(*Richard III*, III, vii) is reinforced by his misshapen appearance
'*between two bishops*'. The verbal distinctiveness of the sonnet
with which Romeo and Juliet greet each other at Capulet's ball
(*Romeo and Juliet*, I, v) sets them physically as well as spiritually
apart from the irascible Tybalt and the destruction he represents.
As King Harry's bright armour is cloaked and his form made
severe before the camp fires of Agincourt (*Henry V*, IV, i), so his
thoughts grow frank. These stage effects are conceived as a unity.

Speech and movement are so interrelated that the vocal pattern
matches the visual one: Macbeth furtive with his wife, Cleopatra
furious with her lover, Lear childlike before his new-found
daughter:

> I will not swear these are my hands: let's see;
> I feel this pin prick. Would I were assured
> Of my condition!       (*King Lear*, IV, vii, 55–7)

Such lines are as if enacted by Shakespeare in his mind as they
are written, and the actor cannot forbear to articulate them with
his gesture as he speaks them. They tell him what to do and what
to feel; they suggest the quavering of the voice, the raising of
the hands before the eyes, the fumbling for the pin, and the
prick of it, and the relapse into doubt. Moreover, this living scene
is fully supported by our hearing the Doctor's music and seeing
Lear in 'fresh garments'. The healing music represents a new
harmony after the discordant thunder of the storm, and Lear has
changed his costume for the third time, for now he is neither in
the formal regalia of his monarchy nor in the rags of his madness:

a dress of new simplicity covers him. He wakes to be kissed and touched by his daughter, seeing 'fair daylight'; and for the spectator as for the King the wild night of the heath scenes has passed. Such effects, aural, visual and verbal, actually control the shape and meaning of the play. At such keen moments, the focus of all technique is the actor, the verse accurately animating mind and tongue and limb, creating an impression of theatrical transparency possible only to a playwright who can govern all our senses simultaneously.

At certain rare moments—Shylock foiled at the last by Portia, Coriolanus standing silently before his mother—Shakespeare knows when the words have done their work. Even on so poetic a stage as his, he does not neglect the impressions of the eye— even when he is writing most lyrically. Romeo and Juliet's sonnet outlines a complete pattern of gestures for the lovers as they speak. Nor does he forget what the eye must see when it contradicts what the ear must hear. Othello and Desdemona in their newly wedded happiness pass lightly upstage while Iago's obscenities fall on our ears:

She is sport for Jove...And, I'll warrant her, full of game...What an eye she has! methinks it sounds a parley to provocation...

(Othello, ii, iii, 16 ff.)

Both mind and senses of the spectator are engaged as he measures one set of impressions against another; the irony of the contrast is a challenge he cannot resist.

## THE ACTOR'S CONTRIBUTION

The assertion throughout this book that Shakespeare's signals to the actors are rich and precise, that he knows exactly what he wants, seems, however, to suggest that he was a dramatist who allowed his players no freedom. But the Elizabethan actor was no more an automaton than the actor of today; moreover, Shakespeare was himself actor enough to know that the player needs a degree of liberty to make his own expressive contribution; nor would Shakespeare's colleagues have been so pleased with his work if his control had been too inflexible, if he had emasculated them. I believe that his feeling for the life of the theatre, the success of a performance and the satisfaction of the actors follows from his understanding of the need for 'improvisation', the prompting of a *controlled freedom* for the actor. His text defines the limits of control, which the actor recognizes before he assumes the granted freedom. Otherwise, why do performances differ from production to production, each one often equally acceptable in its difference? It is right that this should be so: the stereotyping of productions of Racine or Molière in Paris could never provide the pattern for a tradition in Shakespearian production.

There is obvious evidence of improvisation in the frequent opportunities for clowning, by which Shakespeare seems to encourage the actor's personal skills at setting the house in a roar. When Feste must torment Malvolio in his prison, Shakespeare gives his clown the rare chance to play two parts:

Maintain no words with him, good fellow.—Who, I, sir? not I, sir. God buy you, good Sir Topas.—Marry, amen.—I will, sir, I will.

> (*Twelfth Night*, IV, ii, 100–2)

Feste will delight in Sir Topas's parsonical weight of voice in 'Maintain no words with him, good fellow' and in the change to the cheeky innocence of the flippant monosyllables spoken in his own voice; he will leap from posture to posture as he pulls his beard on and off; and who knows whether the original Feste stopped his clowning at that? So it is for a host of minor comic characters, but probably no less for some major ones too. If the soliloquies of Hamlet are quite firmly controlled, Falstaff's addresses to the audience in prose are much less so, and it is for the actor to time and tune his tones and pace to the laughter of the particular audience he faces.

It is evident, too, that brilliant stage moments, although carefully prepared by the dramatist, are finally left to the actors to exploit. The duel between Viola and Sir Andrew, with all its likely comic business, is marked in the text by the simplest of cues, '*They draw*' (*Twelfth Night*, III, iv, 309). The attacking entrance of King Duncan at the opening of *Macbeth* carries only a hint of its stage force in the dry words, '*meeting a bleeding Captain*' (I, ii). The entrance of Juliet's Nurse to Mercutio's line 'A sail, a sail!' (*Romeo and Juliet*, II, iv, 98) must prompt a comic performance from the Nurse like a proud ship at sea with all its streamers flying, and she must ironically add the gesture of a fine mistress herself when she disdainfully calls for her fan from Peter.

The vocal control of the auditorium and the visual management of the platform indicated in the preceding chapters suggest only Shakespeare's broad guide-lines for voice and movement. There is also room for the creative art of the actor: good dialogue feeds and enlarges the actor and does not starve and diminish him. Shakespeare loosens and tightens his control over his players as a good horseman uses the reins. So when Edgar leads his blind father towards Dover Cliff, the actors are allowed a considerable freedom for improvisation as they make their grotesque entrance downstage, but when the emotion of the scene must be squarely evoked, Edgar's cliff speech,                     how fearful

And dizzy 'tis to cast one's eyes so low!...

(*King Lear*, IV, vi, 11 ff.)

tightens the grip on the actor and the audience as we are to sense the horror of the situation and the pain of the projected suicide. Or when Lear's finely directed prayer before the hovel has created a vivid impression of the wretchedness of poverty, then Shakespeare allows Poor Tom the freedom of the stage with his racing and raving—the player brings to life, albeit ironically, the very image of Lear's thinking (*King Lear*, III, iv, 45). It is Shakespeare's habit to build upon the actor's living contribution to the scene, and to allow the actor to build upon his own keen suggestions.

The practice is no different in comedy. When Viola as Cesario must woo the Lady Olivia in Orsino's name, and suffer the pangs of knowing that her success in winning Olivia will also mean her failure to win Orsino for herself, Viola is allowed every liberty to mock the formal speeches of love. 'Most radiant, exquisite, and unmatchable beauty!', she declaims in verse, perhaps after a little clearing of the throat, but she stops short with,

I pray you, tell me if this be the lady of the house, for I never saw her. I would be loath to cast away my speech; for besides that it is excellently well penned, I have taken great pains to con it.

(Twelfth Night, I, v, 171–5)

Here the switch of tone is almost an invitation to improvise. When, however, her true feelings as a woman in love rise to the surface with the 'willow cabin' speech (lines 272–9), Shakespeare provides her with a poem perfectly controlled in tone and pitch. Or, in reverse, an Olivia who poetically bemoans her distraction in love,

> I am as mad as he,
> If sad and merry madness equal be. (III, iv, 14–15)

must seem as surprised as we are by Malvolio's own wildly improvised demonstration of madness in love: 'Sweet lady, ho, ho!'

In his best scenes Shakespeare balances this opportunity for improvisation in a gratifying counterpoint with a more rigidly shaped text, and it is this conjunction of freedom and responsibility which gives an audience its sense of total theatre. As Desdemona improvises her undressing for death, she must sing Barbara's song of forlorn love, which exactly recounts her situation with the Moor (*Othello*, IV, iii)—the real girl unpins as in life, while the ritual victim in a poetic drama is presented through her song. Or as Isabella pleads her brother's cause before judge Angelo (*Measure for Measure*, II, ii), Lucio's loose commentary on the sidelines, 'You are too cold...You are too cold', helps the spectator see the sexual implications in an encounter between two people dedicated to celibacy, and thus the scene is alive with the vitality of improvised theatre.

The interaction of the verbal and the histrionic in total theatre is of an ironic kind in which actor works with actor and both stimulate the spectator to a total response. Ulysses's comments on Cressida's exit,

> There's language in her eye, her cheek, her lip,
> Nay, her foot speaks; her wanton spirits look out
> At every joint and motive of her body...

(Troilus and Cressida, IV, v, 55 ff.)

are more than a submerged direction for the manner of her ambling upstage: the comment also reveals to us Ulysses's own sexual proclivities, ones already seen in his degrading marshalling of the Greek generals for their kisses. Iago's downstage comment on the warm greeting between Cassio and Desdemona, 'With as little a web as this will I ensnare as great a fly as Cassio' (*Othello*, II, i, 168), employs a vividly simple image which shows Cassio a man of little worth in Iago's eyes, but which at the same time poisonously makes Iago a spider in ours; add to this the distance on the stage between the players as the aside is spoken, and we receive a spatial image of Iago's plotting done cerebrally from afar. What is heard is within Shakespeare's control; what is seen is all the actors'. The language control is set against the improvisation of the actor's grimace and the stage's space, resulting in a moment of great dramatic compulsion.

So a lyrical balcony is prepared for the reality of Juliet's performance, or the formal repartee of love from Silvius and Phebe is the poetic foil for a livelier Rosalind, or the practical thinking and behaviour of Lady Macbeth is set against the hypnotic poetry from her husband in his throes of conscience, or a romantic world of fairies provides the background for the prosaic clowning of Bottom. In recognizing this quality in Shakespeare's stagecraft, we not only acknowledge Shakespeare's ability to engage all the senses, as well as the intelligence, of the spectator, but also his readiness to keep the actors at the centre of his play, allowing their full contribution both as interpreters and improvisers. This is why actors love him and audiences find each new performance rewarding.

### BUILDING THE ACTION

Shakespeare's final concern is to appeal to the creative faculty of the audience, and his gestic and tonal language for the actor is also image-building for the spectator. What impels the actor to a display of feeling or to a comic attitude also determines the quality of the audience's participation, and the author contrives a progressive seduction of the imagination by regulated steps.

Such a sequence, for example, is the approach of King Duncan to the castle at Inverness (*Macbeth*, I, vi), and its familiarity in performance will help to make the point quickly. As a unit of action it is entirely dominated by the previous one, in which Lady Macbeth heard of Duncan's coming and determined for us the atmosphere which must colour the event:

> Come, thick night,
> And pall thee in the dunnest smoke of hell... (I, v, 49–50)

The two scenes are implicitly linked, for in the next this terrifying evocation is met with a sharp irony. The King declares,

> the air
> Nimbly and sweetly recommends itself
> Unto our gentle senses. (I, vi, 1–3)

and the smooth lilt of his speech must offend ears already attuned to Lady Macbeth's curt injunction, 'He that's coming/Must be provided for'. Furthermore, Banquo's aria on 'the temple-haunting martlet' seems painfully unaware of the 'raven' which Lady Macbeth imagined would croak their 'fatal entrance'. The calm of Duncan's lines is matched with his gracious progress down the stage, in contrast with the hasty departure of the conspirators. Thus the sequence begins tensely and with the quiet of approaching disaster, and the spectator's attention is held strongly as he senses the chasm between what is seen and what is known. The '*hautboys and torches*' contribute their own eerie suggestion.

Duncan's 'See, see! our honoured hostess!' (line 10) takes the eyes to the upstage door, and the presence of the Lady on the platform to welcome her guests raises the tension to flash-point. Meanwhile her speech cunningly slows the pace and loads with ambiguity every deceptive phrase.

> All our service
> In every point twice done, and then done double,
> Were poor and single business to contend
> Against those honours deep and broad, wherewith
> Your majesty loads our house... (14–18)

These cool lines are delivered according to Lady Macbeth's preliminary scheming, when she advised her husband to 'look like th'innocent flower,/But be the serpent under it' (I, v, 64–5). The audience knows it, and since the victim has turned upstage to face the dissembler, they receive the full flavour of perfidy. The scene is short. With a few more plausible overtures, the hostess gracefully leads off her guests, leaving the audience suspended.

However, the effect of the sequence is not ended. The stage surges with the preparations for banquet, in which we taste the poison in every passing dish. Immediately to the audience comes Macbeth himself, hissing the rapid sibilants of

> If it were done, when 'tis done, then 'twere well
> It were done quickly: if th'assassination
> Could trammel up the consequence, and catch,
> With his surcease, success...       (I, vii, 1 ff.)

His tones exactly catch the mood in the auditorium. Although printed as if it starts another scene, this speech properly marks the climax of what went before. The audience now hears the spirit of duplicity fully articulated. Macbeth's language embodies the mind of the wrongdoer in the shuffling of his conscience, in addition to suggesting the weight of his decision upon his soul. It fittingly caps in overt speech the spectator's unexpressed feelings about the pantomime he has just witnessed, and leads directly into the next major element in the action, the contest of wills between husband and wife. The unit of action is shaped within itself; it serves to realize the unit it succeeds; and it informs the unit it precedes. It does this wholly in terms of the audience's ability to link meaningfully one thought and sensation with another.

The objective of each dramatic unit is built into the particular element of action, and Shakespeare crystallizes his effects by particularities. What is the final purpose of that ugly little scene of the slaying of Cinna the Poet in *Julius Caesar*, III, iii? The first two casualties of Brutus's reasonable rebellion are the great

Caesar, whose guilt is contestable, and the insignificant Cinna, whose innocence is incontestable. After lengthy oratory, the brief glimpse of mob violence leaves an indelible impression upon the mind, fixing some of the real meaning of what has passed on the stage until that time. The dramatist is mounting another attack upon the audience, and this is immediately followed by a further brief scene, IV, i, in which death is dealt out by the Triumvirate itself. Shakespeare attacks again as he moves from the lowest to the highest. His strokes are usually direct and not glancing, but in the course of the action, the attack is upon the cells of an already living tissue. The skill of the actors in adeptly conveying the spirit and mood of characters in a particular situation—that is, the actors' attack upon the lines—corresponds exactly with the author's attack upon the sensibilities of the audience. Such a moment of emphasis in the progress of the action fertilizes the audience's image of the play and keeps it alive and growing.

The element of tension in each dramatic unit thus arises when the spectator watches in a state of prepared anticipation. In each instance the formula for tension is the ancient one. The playwright may first interest the audience in the fate of his character or the outcome of a situation, and when the spectator has sufficiently identified himself with him in the given predicament (will Coriolanus reject his mother and save his life?), Shakespeare then proceeds to stretch time to an appropriate length. The action is protracted (Volumnia pleads at length) while the spectator is caught between fear and desire (Coriolanus must not capitulate; yet, let the matter be settled).

A careful application of pressure characterizes the climaxes of the great tragedies, and any analysis of the sequences leading to the death of Othello, Macbeth or Lear must be an analysis of Shakespeare's rhythmic control of the impressions a spectator takes from the plays. The last act of *Macbeth* is planned minutely, notwithstanding the overwhelming speed of its events as retribution descends upon the hero. This speed is illusory, since only in the study is it possible to observe the reflective and premonitory slowness of Lady Macbeth's sleepwalking, v, i. This painful scene is itself a distracting preparation for the first swift appearance of the drum and colours of Macbeth's enemies, the power of their intent felt in the urgent speaking of Menteith, Caithness, Angus and Lennox. The dramatic impetus is passed to Macbeth himself, flinging questions to his servants in hot anger ('What soldiers, patch?...What soldiers, whey-face?', v, iii, 15 ff.), then sinking as quickly into momentary reveries ('I am sick at heart', 19 ff.). He calls for his armour before it is necessary,

> I'll fight, till from my bones my flesh be hacked.
> Give me my armour. (32–3)

and finally flings off without it. His irritable asides are interpolated within the rising shape of his speech:

> Throw physic to the dogs, I'll none of it.
> Come, put mine armour on; give me my staff;
> Seton, send out; doctor, the thanes fly from me;
> Come, sir, dispatch... (47–50)

The fire in his blood explodes before the servant can finish, and the armour is thrust away with violence ('Pull't off, I say') as Macbeth stalks out growling, 'Bring it after me.' The urgency is sustained in v, iv, through the calm decision of Malcolm and Macduff to camouflage their advance with boughs from Birnam Wood. Macbeth's reflections upon his Queen's death are the final stillness of despair before the hunt is on, when a sequence of ten successive entrances suggests the vigour of the combat. Such a structure of acceleration and deceleration and acceleration again catches up the audience and hustles it to the close.

### SHIFTS OF TEMPO, MOOD AND PERSPECTIVE

The constant adjustment of the pace and quality of the impressions the audience receives is at the heart of the experience peculiar to each play. It is also the most difficult to analyse because it is an effect of theatre in action. The depth at which the actor plumbs his audience, our sense of his weight and urgency, is partly dependent upon the rate at which meaningful word and deed are passed to us. Slow speech often suggests profundity of thought; yet racing action serves to quicken the growth of interest, and it is in the interplay of currents fast and slow that the spectator is stimulated. The acceleration of the handkerchief scene in *Othello*, III, iv, would have little force without the Moor's ponderous and incantatory hallowing of the trifle as its prelude. It is the full variety of tempo in a scene sequence which makes its impact, as if a charge of feeling must be accumulated before it may explode, while the shock of the explosion itself demands a period of recuperation and assessment.

Even in comedy such progression is fundamental; but perhaps it will never be possible to know with what effect in a play like *Twelfth Night* Shakespeare alternates the scenes of warm sentiment with the farcical scenes of Sir Toby Belch and company, moving at a lighter pace. 'What is love, 'tis not hereafter', sings Feste (II, iii, 49), taking up the mood of the love-lorn Orsino, Olivia and Viola, its feeling then drained by the crude singing of Toby's drunken catch, 'Hold thy peace.' What emerges when the melancholy madness of the Duke in II, iv, and of the Lady Olivia in III, iv, is coloured by the unwitting buffoonery and grotesque love-making of that other self-deceiver, Malvolio?

With a change in pace must always go a change in mood: they too are finally inseparable, the one controlling the other, together producing the desirable fullness of response. Such a shift occurs at the end of *Love's Labour's Lost*, when the pageant of the Nine Worthies is summarily brought to an end by the messenger Monsieur Mercadé, who announces the death of the Princess's father:

MERCADÉ. I am sorry, madam—for the news I bring,
  Is heavy on my tongue. The king your father—
PRINCESS. Dead, for my life!
MERCADÉ.                Even so; my tale is told.
BEROWNE. Worthies, away! the scene begins to cloud.

(V, ii, 715–18)

The change is so surprising that Shakespeare has to stress the new manner by all means at his disposal. After reality's rude interruption, the former lively repartee is sobered. 'A heavy heart bears not a nimble tongue', as the Princess explains (line 733). The speech paragraphs lengthen, a firm metrical rhythm is asserted and the frivolous posing of the lovers is brought to a strangely pensive close. Shakespeare's readiness to introduce such touches of reality and humanity into his sunny comedies—we may think of Shylock or Rosalind's moment of genuine grief or Viola's sincerity in love—alerts the spectator and adds to their impact as repercussive theatre. At *Much Ado About Nothing*, IV, i, 288, that absurdly shocking line 'Kill Claudio' crackles from the lips of a Beatrice from whom only flippancy was expected; Benedick's protestations of love are abruptly cut short; surprise is added to tension; the words suddenly reveal the loyalty of the woman and stress the real issues among the frivolities.

Thinking always of units of action in their sequence, Shakespeare commonly conceived an individual episode specifically to particularize a general impression through details of human behaviour in recognizable, often domestic, circumstances. So he keeps touch with the real world of the audience, and at the same time makes his point vividly. He may also press home his idea by making a burlesque of it, or by broadening the particular action to suggest a wider, symbolic reference.

The audience frequently hears a statement and then sees an illustration of it. Early in *1 Henry IV*, the King talks of his dismay when he sees 'riot and dishonour stain the brow/Of my young Harry' (I, i, 85–6), but Shakespeare promptly transports the spectator to Harry's lodging in order to demonstrate the actual situation: the audience finds the Prince in a happy joust with Falstaff, and emerging by no means dishonourably from it. In *The Winter's Tale*, Camillo early announces that the Kings of Sicilia and Bohemia have 'rooted betwixt them...such an affection, which cannot choose but branch now' (I, i, 22–3), and there follows the expository scene in which the friendship of

Leontes and Polixenes is shown to 'branch'—in an unexpected way—before the eyes of the audience. The scene enacts the speech.

Simple, human moments not only add life to, but also lend a perspective view of, the protagonists in Shakespeare. Even Leontes in the flush of his jealousy is allowed the touch of humanity. He wipes clean his son's nose:

LEONTES. Art thou my boy?
MAMILLIUS.             Ay, my good lord.
LEONTES.                        I'fecks!
  Why, that's my bawcock...What! hast thou smutched thy nose?
  They say it is a copy out of mine...Come, captain,
  We must be neat; not neat, but cleanly, captain.    (I, ii, 120-3)

The detail permits a visual and a verbal hint at the idea of cuckoldry, but with some charm it also fixes in the mind's eye the real values of a man who remains loyal to the domestic hearth, and this is important for our hope for his regeneration at the last. In a similar way, Brutus might have stayed a merely philosophical agent to explain the reasons for civil rebellion, were it not for the care with which Shakespeare constructs the action of the scene of Brutus with the conspirators (*Julius Caesar*, II, i), a scene remarkable for its gentle prelude and its sensitive close. The vigour of the political argument is mitigated by his courteous treatment of the boy Lucius, and its humanity heightened by his affection for his wife Portia with which it concludes.

> O ye gods,
> Render me worthy of this noble wife!    (302-3)

Such a sentiment makes in our eyes a real creature of the assassin who is summoning heart and mind to murder his leader.

Elements of burlesque may slip into a scene by a gentle modulation of the tone. When Shakespeare introduces such an element, it either derides some aspect of a theme in the play, or else, diplomatically handled, it lightly corrects a posture that is over-earnest. The absurdity of Pyramus and Thisbe, squarely placed at the end of a romantic fantasy, adjusts the spectator's final image of the lovers who started the lively dance in the moonlit wood. Pyramus himself is the great lover, 'a most lovely, gentleman-like man', according to Quince his director (*A Midsummer Night's Dream*, I, ii, 80); Thisbe is the soul of faithfulness; and both die unblinkingly for love. The mockery of would-be heroic values of the heart also ridicules the less unequivocal professions of undying love exchanged between the young ladies and gentlemen in the wood the night before.

It is not a far cry from this grotesque treatment of the theme in *A Midsummer Night's Dream* to the gentler mockery of the pastoral love-chase in the Silvius and Phebe scenes of *As You Like It*. At times Rosalind herself is pushed into the fray, so that her pining for Orlando suffers direct comparison with the groans of faithless Phebe and bloodless Silvius. At the height of the entanglement, Rosalind protests,

Pray you no more of this, 'tis like the howling of Irish wolves against the Moon.                                                                                            (V, ii, 104-5)

She echoes our verdict, but since her 'howling' has been as loud as the rest, the indictment is of herself too. It is as if Shakespeare is suggesting that all lovers are fit subjects for a little rallying, and in its mood of detachment the audience must agree.

However, in this play the most delicate criticism by burlesque occurs in IV, i. Shakespeare manipulates his Chinese boxes to particular purpose when he has his boy actor play the girl Rosalind who must play the boy Ganymede, and then has Ganymede play an illusory Rosalind in order to approach her real Orlando. Not only does this allow Rosalind to take the lead in the duel of love, a Shavian and anti-romantic situation in itself, but it helps Shakespeare supply what a girl thinks a man thinks a girl thinks in the matter of courtship and marriage. This play-within-the-play is happily complicated when Rosalind from time to time slips her mask, so that she responds now as a man, now as a girl, now as herself. In spite of Celia's normal alarm for the modesty of her sex, Rosalind will play the priest and the blushing bride too, and in the constant changing of her roles, in the switch between the pretence and the reality, not only is Orlando's love tested, but the audience gains a hundred little insights into the feminine mind. When at last Orlando has departed, Rosalind discards her masks completely, breaks her own rules of restraint and we are free to mock and adore her for herself.

### EXTENSION INTO SYMBOLISM AND RITUAL

Yet Shakespeare hardly needed such a device to expand the reference of his scene and push back the frontiers of the spectator's imagination. The Elizabethan play was always skirting the edge of the Renaissance world of allegory. The symmetry of the stage, the ceremonial of its theatrical tradition, its naked boards and its norm of poetic speech all encouraged the allusive qualities in Elizabethan drama. From time to time Shakespeare presses a symbolic value upon a scene, and coordinates speech, visual effects and all the resources of his art to distinguish it. At such times, the logic of plotting or verisimilitude may be neglected.

He attempted a simple symbolic scene in his first play. The scene in the Temple-garden in *1 Henry VI* is prompted by the tidy allegorical opposition between the white rose of York and the red rose of Lancaster. After several scenes of war in France, the stage is suddenly and surprisingly transported to an abstract realm, otherwise indicated as the garden of London's Temple Hall. There an angry group of English noblemen conveniently come upon two rose-trees, one red, one white. The Wars of the Roses had an immediate significance for the Elizabethans, and this symbolism was as straightforward as a national anthem played today.

PLANTAGENET. Let him that is a true-born gentleman,
   And stands upon the honour of his birth,
   If he suppose that I have pleaded truth,
   From off this brier pluck a white rose with me.
SOMERSET. Let him that is no coward nor no flatterer,
   But dare maintain the party of the truth,
   Pluck a red rose from off this thorn with me.    (II, iv, 27–33)

While the factions divide before the spectators' eyes, such parallel speeches taint them equally. Verbal play is made with the figurative notions of spilling red blood and of an enemy white with anger, and the new war is on. The symbolism of this scene seems to have been of Shakespeare's invention, but it is not hard to guess how it sprang to mind. The Earl of Warwick confirms the transparent intention:

> And here I prophesy: this brawl to-day,
> Grown to this faction in the Temple-garden,
> Shall send between the red rose and the white
> A thousand souls to death and deadly night.　　(124–7)

The unreality of the scene, which bothered the Elizabethan audience not a whit, grants the dramatist the opportunity for broad theatrical statement. A few years later, Shakespeare retreats into another garden to express in allegorical imagery another grim political situation, that of *Richard II* (III, iv).

The characters in such scenes enact a tableau, and although they speak, they carry the allegorical force of a dumb show. However, this kind of rigid patterning barely survives the early history plays. Shakespeare continues to invent scenes designed to carry symbolic action, but they are engineered with more regard for the less formalized norm of presentation. The formal opposition of the rival houses in *Romeo and Juliet* prompts a symbolism in those of its scenes where the young lovers are seen to defy their difference in blood. The Chorus-Prologue instructs us that they 'take their life' from 'the fatal loins of these two foes': their life-giving union shall 'with their death bury their parents' strife' and its sterile butchery. The marriage scene displays this ritual element:

> Do thou but close our hands with holy words,
> Then love-devouring death do what he dare.　(II, vi, 6–7)

The play's fatal end, set in a vault of the dead, contrives to bring together the enemies that they may gaze upon the pitiful havoc they have wrought:

> Where be these enemies? Capulet, Montague?
> See what a scourge is laid upon your hate,
> That heaven finds means to kill your joys with love!
> 　　　　　　　　　　　　　　　　(v, iii, 291–3)

The stage grouping emphasizes these concluding words of the Prince, the young bodies draped over the tomb upstage, the accusing evidence of a misbegotten feud.

The pictorial element of emblematic presentation all but disappears, but symbolic invention graces scenes from many later plays—a voluptuous Helen of Troy offering to disarm the warrior Hector at the end of her luxurious scene, III, i, in *Troilus and Cressida*; the bawd and the hangman comparing their lethal trades in *Measure for Measure*, IV, ii; the meeting of Macbeth with his demons the Witches in *Macbeth*, IV, i, realistic and allegorical figures brought face to face. Yet the two tragedies with the most straightforward stories seem to invite the greatest number of scenes carrying symbolic valuation. These are *Othello* and *King Lear*.

The corruption of the Moor and the disintegration of his marriage must wait till all are ashore in Cyprus, where he finds an 'enchafed flood' to welcome him. While Montano and two Gentlemen maintain the wild music of the tempest in their words, in turn Cassio, Iago, Desdemona and Othello have their arrival signalled by the storm. Othello greets his wife,

> If after every tempest come such calms,
> May the winds blow till they have wakened death!
>
> (II, i, 182–3)

The spectator, for his part, will not miss the traditional significance of the rage in heaven. Such an ironic introduction to Cyprus was not called for by the narrative line of the play: the storm is imposed upon the action to lend it a ritualistic pattern, as the fatal triangle of Othello, Desdemona and Cassio is grouped upon the stage under the eyes of Iago—'I'll set down the pegs that make this music' (198). After the temptation of Othello, the whole mode of the play shifts into ritual symbolism. Again, the plot is not furthered by the terrible scene of the 'closet lock and key', during which the spectator looks through the envenomed eyes of Othello at Desdemona as a common harlot and Emilia as her bawd:

Some of your function, mistress:
Leave procreants alone and shut the door;
Cough, or cry hem, if anybody come—
Your mystery, your mystery; nay, dispatch. (IV, ii, 27–30)

By such enacted imagery the Moor turns the divine blessing of his marriage into a hell inhabited by devils, and the allegorical slant to this searing scene exists to point the larger theme of the play, the corruption of the good by evil. If in this scene the Moor turns his wife's chamber into a brothel, he makes of it a temple at their last encounter. Desdemona herself has in IV, iii transformed her bridal sheets into a sacrificial shroud; now the bed on which she will die seems as an altar to him:

O perjured woman! thou dost stone my heart,
And mak'st me call what I intend to do
A murder, which I thought a sacrifice. (v, ii, 66–8)

In its incantatory preface and the slow ritualism of the smothering (no sudden death here), the lines of plot and theme meet and intertwine.

*King Lear* is also a play in which scenes are devised to mark out a symbolic action. Lear in his madness assumes the burden of mankind, and the play comprehends a vision of life. Simply to satisfy the plot, it was sufficient to send the old man out into the storm; for the storm scenes to include a meeting between Lear and a mad beggar (III, iv), and then a mock trial (III, vi), for Gloucester to take his imaginary leap from Dover Cliff, and then to meet Lear crowned with wild flowers (IV, vi), was, for the simple needs of the story, gratuitous. These scenes risk anti-climax, but on the edge of farce achieve visionary drama. The passage of the action into the realm of fantasy leaves Shakespeare free to emphasize in stage terms those issues which are most germane to his theme; having created the spatial dimensions of a storm in heaven and chaos in the mind, he may now explore the new territory. The scene before the hovel is therefore con-structed, not of narrative incident, but of symbolic incident designed to make three progressive advances into this other world of fantasy.

Lear first refuses succour natural to a man in his extremity; instead, he shakes off Kent and offers himself to the elements on others' behalf:

> Expose thyself to feel what wretches feel,
> That thou mayst shake the superflux to them
> And show the heavens more just.　　　(III, iv, 34–6)

This crisis of decision is followed immediately by the depiction of Poor Tom as the epitome of wretchedness, destitute, desolate, possessed of the devil himself. Lear now makes his second decision and confirms it before the startled eyes of the spectators:

Thou art the thing itself. Unaccommodated man is no more but such a poor, bare, forked animal as thou art. Off, off, you lendings! Come, unbutton here!　　　(106–9)

Pressed by the unexpected entrance of Gloucester his father, Edgar now pretends more madness than the mad, more extremes of repulsive and bestial misery than outside the theatre we may imagine:

Poor Tom, that eats the swimming frog, the toad, the tadpole, the wall-newt and the water; that in the fury of his heart, when the foul fiend rages, eats cow-dung for sallets, swallows the old rat and the ditch-dog drinks the green mantle of the standing pool...

(129–34)

Faced with this horrific chimera, Lear finally rejects the entreaties of Kent and Gloucester, and touches the leper—he puts his naked arm round Edgar's naked shoulders:

> First let me talk with this philosopher.
> What is the cause of thunder?　　　(154–5)

This is Lear's third and last step in this scene. The action reaches a climax almost ludicrous in effect, but overwhelming in meaning.

Still on this razor-edge of theatrical acceptance, Shakespeare next (III, vi) has Lear place two joint-stools to arraign them as his daughters, and invites the Fool and the madman to judge them. The scene of this mad trial is brief and shapeless and a kind of bedlam in itself; but its pathetic image is indelible, reflecting as it does that earlier image of a regal king passing judgment on his children in all apparent sanity. 'Is there any cause in nature that makes these hard hearts?'—this has been said before, but nature now includes the Gods and all of life, and the justification for such a scene is the expansion and the ferment in the spectator's mind which the deliberate echo from Act I is designed to stir. Such a scene, visionary, fantastic, grotesque in sight and sound, is Shakespeare's precursor to Artaud's hypothetical theatre of cruelty.

The meeting of the blinded Gloucester and the mad King, while also an engrossing scene of symbolic values, is, compared with the mad trial, relatively articulate, and, with Edgar's helpful asides, surprisingly lucid.

> O, matter and impertinency mixed!
> Reason in madness! (IV, vi, 173–4)

Shakespeare is wisely clipping the spectator's wings and imposing a new control. Lear in his assumed role as judge supreme passes judgment again, this time upon Gloucester his counterpart, a sinner in sins of the flesh. His compassion for mankind as a whole, 'this great stage of fools', is complete. When the blind man is addressed by the madman,

What! Art mad? A man may see how this world goes with no eyes. Look with thine ears: see how yond justice rails upon yond simple thief. Hark in thine ear: change places and, handy-dandy, which is the justice, which is the thief? (149–53)

Shakespeare has so transported his audience beyond actuality that actuality is seen with new clarity.

## AN 'EPIC' STRUCTURE

The peculiar sequence of imaginative, emotional and intellectual tugs which is characteristic of a Shakespearian play is due less to the individual scenes than to their planned sequence, and any account of the building of Shakespeare's stage action must put due weight on the continuity and contrast of his scenes, qualities felt best, of course, in performance. At his best he constructed his drama like an architect, with the whole work in mind, and the serial manner of his dramaturgy tells the story as directly as possible; but it is not the mere needs of the story which finally determine what the next scene is going to be. He is preoccupied with the sequence of contrasts in style, pace and even volume of sound, contrasts of subject, the political with the domestic, the masculine with the feminine—the range is unlimited. If he can make the narrative line and the rhythmic and imaginative line coincide, so much the better. The ironies created by the sequence of scenes passing across the stage thus tend to defy the causal dramatic logic characteristic of, say, Ibsen's social plays. Shakespeare trades in the direct and unreserved ironies of the sensuous imagination, dealing a series of shocks to body and mind, and to this end he manoeuvres his action.

There could be little place in this pragmatic scheme of theatre for the now discounted theory of 'scene alternation', which set a scene first at the front of the stage and then at the rear. Nor was Shakespeare likely to follow any automatic plan to satisfy the more hardy concept of 'scene rotation', which would have him ring the changes round platform, 'study' and balcony. Such formulae are too neat either for the variety of conditions under which the players had to work, or for the spirit of an intuitive drama. Shakespeare used an upper level or a discovery curtain as it was called for, and then only if he could get it. If the location of the scene was to shift, he relied upon the imagination to effect the change, and this did not mean that he had to search for another area of the stage for the actors to use. In any case, he is unlikely to have risked building the delicate structure of his play on the uncertain basis of a particular theatrical design. His first consideration in changing a scene was the pattern of mood and tone, and the contrasts possible in the action: for this, elasticity of staging was of paramount importance.

The break at IV, i in *The Winter's Tale* for 'Time, the Chorus' was exceptional, and it seems that the one factor Shakespeare could take for granted was that the stage action might flow uninterruptedly from first to last. All his effects of building scene upon scene depend upon this. Division into act and scene does not appear in the early quartos, which were probably taken from the players' prompt copies, and the effect of ironic shifts resulting from continuous action in performance confirms that for the most part Shakespeare wrote a drama without seams. Continuity of action did more than sustain the attention of an audience; it became the essential index of the particular rhythm of impressions each play was written to promote.

When Dryden came to rewrite *Troilus and Cressida* in 1679, he determined that he would have 'no leaping from Troy to the Grecian tents, and thence back again, in the same act, but a due proportion of time allowed for every action'. He signally failed to see to what advantage Shakespeare had put his Elizabethan opportunity, and he inflicted a mortal stroke upon a technique of dramatic writing which has hardly been revived in three hundred years. We see it now. The scene-changes never were arbitrary geographical leaps constituting an act of ignorance or defiance of classical principles. The audience is like a swimmer hit by the successive waves through which he passes.

In the transition from scene to scene, Shakespeare can provoke and engage his audience, expand the image of his play in the mind and change the emotional key in which it is being played. With what easy, yet striking, progression the stage passes from the pain of Ophelia's madness, through the grating hypocrisy of Claudius's honeyed words to Gertrude,

> Poor Ophelia
> Divided from herself and her fair judgment,
> Without the which we are pictures or mere beasts...
>
> (*Hamlet*, IV, v, 83–5)

(this from the poisoner himself), to the tumult at the doors whence Laertes bursts in, rebellious and angry: 'Where is this king?' The feelings of a harrowed spectator first find expression in Laertes's rage, before he is fired to wrath by Claudius's icy ability to master the young man. By this device, the pathos of the Ophelia scenes nourishes our hostility towards Hamlet's enemy. Pain on the stage must hurt in the auditorium.

Shakespeare binds us with the spell of his words, and by

the contrasts which follow exposes us to their full intrinsic effect. With

> Age cannot wither her, nor custom stale
> Her infinite variety...
>
> > (*Antony and Cleopatra*, II, ii, 35 ff.)

echoing in the spectator's ears, how sad is that little portrait of the inadequate Octavia which ensues in II, iii; and with what shock he next sees Cleopatra chastising the messenger who brings the news of Antony's marriage:

> Hence,
> Horrible villain! or I'll spurn thine eyes
> Like balls before me; I'll unhair thy head,
> Thou shalt be whipped with wire, and stewed in brine,
> Smarting in ling'ring pickle.                         (II, v, 62–6)

The scenes devised for Caesar, Octavia and the predictable world of Roman sobriety are in strict contrast with the capricious Queen, and by ringing the changes Shakespeare keeps his audience alert to the complexity of Cleopatra the woman, and the scale of Antony's final choice. The treatment of Cleopatra marks the peak of all those efforts in modulating from one manner to another, to exhibit Shylock the monster and Shylock the man, Hal the gay fellow and Hal the royal prince, Brutus the politician and Brutus the kind husband, Angelo the judge and Angelo the lecher.

Juxtapositions of scene regularly point contrasts in subject and theme, and extend the range of the drama. In a play like *Coriolanus*, the contrasting attitudes of two classes of people, plebeian and patrician, the humble and the proud, are set at the centre of the play. To present the hero, the stagecraft re-orientates the map by showing, for example, first the plebeian concern for intimate human rights (in II, iii), and then the higher command busy with the enemy at the gates (in III, i). To arrange this duality of viewpoint on the Elizabethan stage is no more difficult than to leap between Rome and Alexandria, or Sicilia and Bohemia. And just as this technique brought a refinement of judgment to the experience of *Coriolanus*, juxtaposition encouraged dry humour in a comedy of sentiment: to set Rosalind's pursuit of Orlando beside Touchstone's pursuit of Audrey in *As You Like It*, III, ii/iii, is to provoke a choice element of sardonic criticism.

Once these incongruities have been thought of, like Swift's 'big and little men' in Dr Johnson's dubious verdict, 'it is very easy to do all the rest'. It was a short step from having Falstaff seem to snore behind the throne of the King of England in the opening scene of *1 Henry IV* (doubtless the one old man was rousing himself as the other was shuffling off) to plotting an illuminating domestic scene between the fiery Hotspur and his wife:

LADY PERCY. But hear you, my lord.
HOTSPUR. What say'st thou, my lady?
LADY PERCY. What is it carries you away?
HOTSPUR. Why, my horse, my love, my horse.
LADY PERCY. Out, you mad-headed ape! (II, iii, 75–9)

This follows hard upon the other view of Hotspur as stern, courageous and hot-headed, and the powerful moving spirit behind the conspiracy against the throne. His genial indifference to his wife's anxiety touches in his character and even endears him to the spectator. Yet primarily the episode lends him some of Hal's sense of humour and makes him the more dangerous an enemy. The audience is to know that this will be one potential king fighting another:

PRINCE. Nor can one England brook a double reign,
Of Harry Percy and the Prince of Wales.
HOTSPUR. Nor shall it, Harry, for the hour is come
To end the one of us. (V, iv, 66–9)

The alternation of private and public scenes is adopted as a basic technique in the problem comedies, and it especially illuminates such moral themes as social appearances and personal decorum. In *Troilus and Cressida*, the disintegration of social and personal values in time of sterile warfare, and the dependence of the private life of the individual upon his society, are explored in several dimensions. The sexuality of the affair between Paris and Helen is presented as the cause of the internecine war,

Cressida's feminine hopes for security, affection and happiness are disrupted by the impersonal injunction that she change camps, the heroes Troilus and Achilles have their quality as soldiers sapped by personal appetite, public idealism is undermined by the actualities of life. The pathetic parting of Cressida from Troilus ('My lord, will you be true?') is immediately succeeded by that chilling scene of kissing the Greeks in public display (IV, iv/v), calculated to reveal Cressida's attempt to parry their frivolity and to stagger the audience.

The audience's sense of the theme and subject of a play by Shakespeare has much to do with their sense of the rhythm of contrasts in the ordering of events. When the news of Portia's death comes just after the empire-shaking quarrel between Brutus and Cassius (*Julius Caesar*, IV, ii), a political tragedy is translated into a personal one. When the tender fears of Virgilia for the safety of her husband are set against the mother's blood-lust in the first women's scene in *Coriolanus*, I, iii, and immediately succeeded by the '*drum and colours*' of Marcius and the army before Corioli, the theme of the stability of society is shifted on to human ground. An audience tries to reconcile such disparate elements in shaping its image of the play, and in so doing will delve to the roots of the play's conception, which may be ambivalent, many-sided and contradictory—like life itself. Civil war like that in *Julius Caesar* does resolve itself in personalities and human foibles which tend to transcend the major issues: the audience is given the insight that a private love in the life of a man can have equal value with a nation's welfare. In *Coriolanus*, the honour of a class, a family or a man can, in proving itself, destroy the greater values of human relationship, even the joy of life itself. These are some of the hidden themes in the Roman tragedies, explored at greatest depth in *Antony and Cleopatra*, where the abandon with which the play seems to mix its public and private ingredients urges upon our attention the conflict of duty to self and duty to society, and brilliantly justifies the stage technique.

Nevertheless, the most far-reaching theatrical effect of

Shakespeare's ordering of scenes by contrasts lies in its power to determine the mood and temper in the auditorium. All those intangibles which present themselves in the discussion of Shakespeare's audience response arise from these characteristic features—the ironies of his tragic conceptions; the nature of comic 'relief'; the delicate tone of humour in his earlier comedy; the spirit of criticism in his tragicomedy.

A tragedy of the simple order of *Romeo and Juliet* is built upon the fine lyrical verse of the lovers whenever they are together, but our sense that such idealized love is too much of a dream to last is saved from crude emotionality on the one hand and cynicism on the other by the comic presence of Juliet's Nurse, Mercutio and old Capulet in scenes interpolated judiciously through the play. Criticism of the artless antitheses of youth and age, innocence and experience, pure love and public irresponsibility, and the accompanying sentiment, is kept at bay by the perspective realism of their earthy sanity. Moreover, such scenes sharpen our sense of the lovers' special rarity. It is in the ascent from the normal to the ideal that the audience is alerted to a perception of the purity in the tragedy, something refined and unique, but within the bounds of human possibility. In the contrasting of tones the audience is required to measure one set of values against another.

Comic 'relief' in terms of the accumulation of scenes has a greater impact and meaning in the theatre than would appear in the text. It no more lowers the play's tension than does the introduction of Falstaffian comedy into *Henry IV*. The comic scenes in Shakespearian tragedy do not distract, but concentrate and illuminate. In *Romeo and Juliet*, the straightforward contrasts of the scene sequence IV, iii/iv/v, fairly illustrate the point. The original stage direction '*She falls upon her bed within the curtains*' warns that Juliet's distress is to be constantly before the eyes and in the mind during the boisterous preparations for her wedding with Paris. The bustle and the joking and the wedding-music reach a pitch in the bawdy of the speech with which the Nurse turns upstage to wake her mistress:

Mistress! what, mistress! Juliet! Fast, I warrant her, she.
Why, lamb! why, lady! Fie, you slug-a-bed!
Why, love, I say! madam! sweetheart! why, bride!
What, not a word? You take your pennyworths now!
Sleep for a week; for the next night, I warrant,
The County Paris hath set up his rest
That you shall rest but little. God forgive me!...   (IV, v, 1 ff.)

This racy but harmless prattling makes the innocent victim of
the situation, silent on the bed, a more poignant sight, and the
spectator must embrace the discord as one of the supreme ironies
of the play. The Nurse's artless language works to perfection in
this disarming experiment. Whether the archaistic mock rhetoric
in the scene of family lament which follows worked equally well,
we shall never know: to our ears it seems to overplay the irony.
At any rate, Shakespeare does not grope for an effect like this
again, which suggests that on rare occasions his judgment as a
craftsman went astray.

The mature tragedy of *Othello* again makes a useful comparison: with greater confidence and restraint Shakespeare
spices with humour the more extreme situation of Desdemona
in IV, iii. He caps that most painful song of Barbara's fate with a
discussion of the justification for a wife's unfaithfulness:

DESDEMONA. Wouldst thou do such a deed for all the world?
EMILIA. The world's a huge thing: it is a great prize for a small vice.
DESDEMONA. In troth, I think thou wouldst not.
EMILIA. In troth, I think I should; and undo't when I had done't.
  Marry, I would not do such a thing for a joint-ring, nor for measures
  of lawn, nor for gowns, petticoats, nor caps, nor any petty exhibition.
  But for all the whole world—ud's pity, who would not make her
  husband a cuckold to make him a monarch? I should venture
  purgatory for't.                                    (IV, iii, 67–78)

The casual realism of Emilia, which recites the common attitude,
indicates Desdemona's purity as exceptional. Her sober views
stretch the mind and curb the sentiment. Shakespeare has
tempered the wit to the smart of the wound, and it stings the
more.

Transitions of mood do not present such delicate problems

of handling an audience in the comedies. Within the chosen range of feeling in a play as airily fantastic as *A Midsummer Night's Dream*, it is easily done for Quince and company to vulgarize young love, or in *Twelfth Night* for Olivia's infatuation to be mocked by confrontation with the grotesque love-making of Malvolio (III, iv), or for Viola's breeches to be ridiculed in the farcical duel of the same scene. However, in those comedies carrying a more emotional charge, tone contrasts present as scrupulous a task as in the tragedies. It has never been possible to feel that the Italianate romance of Hero and Claudio in *Much Ado About Nothing*, at all times tottering on the edge of melodrama, mixes well with the Elizabethan repartee of Beatrice and Benedick. The home-grown subplot must forgo the centre of the stage before the end, but not before Hero has cut a too simple figure; the playgoer could wish that the heroine had borrowed a little of Beatrice's tongue.

The problem of mixing the froth with the salt becomes acute in the comedies which introduce an element of tragedy: they demand abnormal transitions of mood in abnormal frequency. However, Shakespeare did not bother with the subtleties of tonal gradation when in *The Merchant of Venice*, IV, i/ii he had to pass from the tensions of Shylock's trial scene with its incipient tragedy to a dénouement which united the couples and resumed the comedy. With an abrupt change, he writes a lyrical address to a romantic moon, makes casual reference to 'the wealthy Jew' and Shylock is forgotten. The contrast in tones has no dramatic force—is, indeed, a mere convenience.

By comparison, a higher order of dramatic skill is displayed in the alternation of scenes of idealism and bawdy satire in *Troilus and Cressida*. By such means, the heroism of the Trojan War is deflated, the romantic love of Troilus for Cressida debased, so that the play's cynicism is transmitted as much by its structure as by its characterization and story. In the final diffusion of its mood, at least, this play exhibits more 'unity' than either *The Merchant of Venice* or *Much Ado About Nothing*, and in post-war years has proved itself a success in a theatre ready to accept its satirical, alienating structure. The incongruous ingredients in this play pass the only true test—that of appropriate performance.

## THE AUDIENCE AND DRAMATIC FORM

The wish to provoke his audience increasingly affects Shakespeare's shaping of the play. The fluid verbal and visual action of the Elizabethan stage, and the opportunity for extreme conventions of anti-illusory extravagance and close naturalism, may be understood as technical elements with which to direct the spectator's imagination; and since the manipulation of the spectator must be sustained from first to last, the characteristics of Elizabethan theatre affect the growth and shape, balance and style, of the play as a whole. A study of these technical elements must bring us nearer to a radical criticism of the play-as-play.

The form of *A Midsummer Night's Dream* or *The Merchant of Venice* or *Twelfth Night* is based upon a series of ironic changes in manner and matter, both in the broad contrasts between Titania and Bottom, Portia and Shylock, and Viola and Sir Andrew, and in the subtler tonal differences between Titania and Hermia/Helena, Portia and Nerissa, and Viola and Olivia. *A Midsummer Night's Dream*, as a play about love and marriage and the suitability of partners, jumps wildly between the romancing couples and the little weaver who puts them all in their place, either as an ass or as Pyramus. The light-hearted way in which Portia gambles her love on a casket sets in harsh relief the grasping Shylock, the free spirit with the tied; until her abandoned

> Pay him six thousand, and deface the bond;
> Double six thousand, and then treble that...
> (The Merchant of Venice, III, ii, 300–1)

modulates with the reading of Antonio's letter,

My bond to the Jew is forfeit, and since, in paying it, it is impossible I should live, all debts are cleared between you and I, if I might see you at my death.
(318–20)

The irresponsible becomes the responsible Portia, charity confronts usury, and the trial scene not only blends the plots but contrasts opposing attitudes to life as well.

These confrontations are less on the stage than in the mind of the engrossed spectator, and Shakespeare increasingly leaves the conflict in the mind alone. The *Henry IV* plays extend the exercise to balance one sector of society with another, and a form emerges which illuminates both. The tragedies, less obviously, assume a shape which pits the hero against himself, the discord nevertheless made plain by changes in his tone and manner as the play grows. On occasion the tone changes so distinctly that when the Moor re-enters in *Othello*, III, iii, or when Timon makes a delayed entrance '*in a rage*' in the scene of the creditors (*Timon of Athens*, III, iv), the spectator recognizes a crux in the structure of the play.

The patterns of response are especially intricate in the problem comedies, for the reason that the dialectic of the drama has become a dialectic of mood. As a poem may make its points 'metaphysically' by a teasing and challenging verbal imagery, so a play may bandy a metaphysically arranged sequence of moods and attitudes. Again, the interplay of intellect and emotion is less in the characters on the stage than in the mind of the spectator. In *Troilus and Cressida*, scenes of love and war, of the idealistic and the practical, interweave like a cat's cradle, the facts of life militating ironically against affection and chivalry, so that the form of the whole constitutes in itself a steady questioning of values. In *Measure for Measure*, the true comedy lies, not in setting the chastity of Isabella against the lechery of Angelo and seeing which will yield, but in illuminating this rigid, puritanical antithesis by scenes which contrast, instead, Angelo with Lucio, Claudio with Barnardine, and Isabella with Juliet, and oppose a tragically narrow standard of justice with the generous one of comedy.

The audience thus enjoys the refreshment of entering into the spirit of the play and taking part in its moral discussion as a participator in an aesthetic experience. The spectator is goaded into activity by the dovetailing of Shakespeare's devices, each in the service of a larger effect, which it is never easy fully to identify. A play's structure is planned so that the spectator is granted, as it were, a double perspective on its subject. One assertion queries another, one area of experience is balanced against another. The pleasure of watching a Shakespearian play is the pleasure of both seeing and performing a tightrope dance— and the world seems richer when the experience is over.

On the romantic stage of the Elizabethans, the dramatist's final problem was to ensure that a chaotic centrifugality of impressions was not his sole result. The balance and unity of the audience's response is planned from the start. An audience will feel that the pathos of Ophelia's genuine madness (*Hamlet*, IV, v) is a retribution for the evasions of Hamlet's simulated madness before the King, IV, iii, for treating too lightly the precious jewel of the mind. The order of scenes satisfies our sense of a moral order. Or when an audience sees Timon in rags pressing gold upon Alcibiades to commit atrocities upon his countrymen, on the whores Phrynia and Timandra that they may infect them with their diseases, on three Bandits that they may cut their own throats, and on the Poet and the Painter to rid himself of hypocrites (*Timon of Athens*, IV, iii, and V, i), they can hardly fail to contrast the absurd generosity of the banquet scene, I, ii, and its motives. After the audience has been caught in a shuttle of judgment, the reversal of the mood redresses the balance.

A director's decision about the style of a performance of one of the plays—the relative degree of naturalistic and stylized speech and manner—is properly an estimate of what in that play will kindle his audience when in balance. It is this principle of diagnosing the final unity of the stage impressions to secure a complete reaction from an audience which also informs Shakespeare's intuitive preparation of signals. The 'meaning' of the play emerges and flowers as its structure unfolds, the rhythm of its scenes being felt only in the framework of time which conditions of performance create. The pendulum which moves between the intimate love of Romeo and Juliet and their environment of hate swings faster, until the fearsome race of time brings love and hate into collision and the pendulum to a shuddering stop. *Macbeth* chronicles a relentless agglomeration of horror, until retribution finds Macbeth all but as distracted and stampeded as the spectator. The meaning of such theatrical experience is inseparable from the ordained rhythm with which it hits the receiving mind. The pace at which such drama grows, the direction in which it pushes the spectator, the final frame of mind in which it leaves him—these contribute to its meaningful life.

It is the complex transaction between the stage and the audience that is the object of a study of Shakespeare's stagecraft. He starts along a new path each time, meets a fresh set of problems of mood and tone, and must engineer different balances and compensations; he was his own task-master, but the discipline was determined by his audience. The form and pressure of ideas and feelings in his play is their pressure on an audience. Its potential qualities of intimacy and immediacy have meaning only for a live audience. Its unity is the response of the audience. Shakespeare's sense of the stage is finally his feeling for other people.

### THE STUDY OF SHAKESPEARE IN THE THEATRE

The study of audience response is a study of the audience in conditions of performance; the test of Shakespeare's stagecraft is in the theatre in action. A beginning is being made, particularly in America, to reproduce the physical conditions of his stage, and this could enable us to make a fresh discovery of how his plays work.

This essay is not a doctrinaire call for a return to Shakespeare's own theatre, however. That is manifestly impossible when the times and the audience are different: 'a pie dish without the pie' was Gordon Craig's view of this idea in 1889.[1] Yet a director will better understand the elements of Shakespeare's stagecraft,

---

[1] *Index to the Story of My Days*, p. 99.

and therefore his purpose, on a stage nearer his own than in those proscenium theatres which continue to squeeze the playwright for a shape; and an understanding of his purpose must be the prerequisite for a production in any medium, stage or screen. The requirement of Shakespearian scholarship, whether the critic's or the actor's, is first to be able to read the texts through the eyes of an Elizabethan actor.

So much of the style and speech in Shakespeare's plays is alien to the ingrained naturalistic tradition born of Ibsen and Chekhov, Stanislavsky and Freud, the cinema and television, that a school of Shakespearian acting, too, is long overdue. Nor is this a demand for an Elizabethan style of gestic acting, like that envisaged by B. L. Joseph; for all its interest, such a style remains in any case hypothetical. At the simplest, this study urges the players to acquire a sense of the original function of Shakespeare's speech, and therefore of the stage behaviour which should accompany it. Granville-Barker asserted[1] that the speaking of the verse must be at the foundation of the study of his drama, and pleaded for the revival of a lost art. The actor 'must think of the dialogue in terms of music; of the tune and rhythm of it as at one with the sense—sometimes outbidding the sense—in telling him what to do and how to do it, in telling him, indeed, what to *be*'.[2] Yet even a correct speaking of the verse has little value without the intimate conditions for which its music was composed, and in which its full range of tone may be heard. A study of the voice is also a study of the stage conditions.

The conditions of spatial freedom and intimacy which promote the best exercise of the voice will only be reproduced upon an open stage, one not necessarily bare, but at most with those purely functional settings with which Granville-Barker set the standard for modern production at the Savoy Theatre in 1912 and 1913. Compelling speech and significant movement need all that the physical shape and dimensions of an open stage can lend them, and judgment upon their final effectiveness upon an audience is hamstrung without it.

[1] See *Prefaces to Shakespeare, First Series*, pp. xxiv ff.    [2] *Ibid.* p. 27.

This is not to deny the good Shakespearian occasions which the modern theatre has frequently created. Much of the drive and urgency of Shakespeare's dramatic situations averts the asphyxiation of the proscenium arch, and elements of scenic illusion perfected in the last two centuries cannot destroy the essence of a fully realized Shakespearian character relationship. Nevertheless, so many of Shakespeare's established techniques—the invitation to the actor to play to the audience, the 'attacking' north-to-south entrances, the intimate soliloquy, choric speaking to the audience, the use of the aside, the grouping of characters for liaison or repulsion—show the effort on his part to break down the barrier between actor and spectator; a proscenium arch artificially raises another barrier of which Shakespeare knew nothing. Picture-frame acting tends to divide the theatre into two worlds, an active world of self-sufficient and remote players, and a passive world of lazy playgoers. The Shakespearian experience was designed to coax the spectator and rouse an audience to participation. To this extent our knowledge of Shakespeare's notion of total theatre remains absurdly scanty.

Strange arguments have been put forward to suggest that a platform jutting out into the house encourages an undesirable proximity to the actors, one which dispels 'a sense of reality'. This might have a slim element of truth in it, but only if that reality is thought of in a non-Shakespearian way, a reality of a kind which the audience had only to sit and observe externally, a make-believe reality. The reality in which Shakespeare trades is that which arises from involvement, and which therefore exists in part in the spectator before the performance begins, and wholly after it is finished.

It is possible to abstract from a play the Shakespearian signals which point to this reality of involvement; not so easy to record their effects in performance. One thing is certain: they can be recorded only from the living art. Jack Isaacs reached this conclusion in his seminal paper, 'Shakespeare as Man of the Theatre' in 1927. In this he wrote that 'if we are to be more than amateurs in the study of Shakespeare, as I fear have been many eminent and erudite scholars, it would be well to devote at least part of our attention to that side of his work which shows Shakespeare as a practical man of the theatre'. He added wistfully, 'If a national theatre is permitted by the temper of this country it does not seem too much to ask that some part of its activity may concern itself with the basic elements of dramatic and theatrical effect as exemplified in the work of the greatest wielder of the English language.' The meaning, quality and ordering of the theatrical impressions discharged from Shakespeare's living stage as they penetrate the living imagination of an audience—these constitute the inexhaustible study.

# SELECTED BIBLIOGRAPHY

Adams, J. C. *The Globe Playhouse*, 2nd edition, London, 1961.

Adams, J. Q. *Shakespearean Playhouses*, Boston, 1917.

Baldwin, T. W. *The Organization and Personnel of the Shakespearean Company*, Princeton, 1927.

Beckerman, B. *Shakespeare at the Globe, 1599–1609*, New York, 1962.

Bentley, G. E. 'Shakespeare and the Blackfriars Theatre', in *Shakespeare Survey 1*, ed. A. Nicoll, Cambridge, 1938.

Bethell, S. L. *Shakespeare and the Popular Dramatic Tradition*, London, 1944.

Bradbrook, M. C. *Elizabethan Stage Conditions*, Cambridge, 1932.

—— *The Growth and Structure of Elizabethan Comedy*, London, 1935.

—— *Themes and Conventions of Elizabethan Tragedy*, Cambridge, 1955.

Brown, J. R., *Shakespeare's Plays in Performance*, London, 1966.

—— and Harris, B., (eds.) *Elizabethan Theatre*, London, 1967.

Chambers, E. K. *The Elizabethan Stage*, 4 vols., Oxford, 1923.

Coghill, N. *Shakespeare's Professional Skills*, Cambridge, 1964.

De Banke, C. *Shakespearean Stage Production : Then and Now*, London, 1953.

Flatter, R. *Shakespeare's Producing Hand*, New York, 1948.

Gerstner-Hirzel, A. *The Economy of Action and Word in Shakespeare's Plays*, Bern, 1957.

Granville-Baker, H. *Prefaces to Shakespeare*, 5 vols., London, 1927–47.

—— 'Shakespeare's Dramatic Art', in *A Companion to Shakespeare Studies*, ed. H. Granville-Barker and G. B. Harrison, Cambridge, 1934.

Greg, W. W. (ed.). *Dramatic Documents from the Elizabethan Playhouses*, 2 vols., Oxford, 1931.

—— *Henslowe's Diary*, 2 vols., London, 1904–8.

—— *Henslowe Papers*, London, 1907.

Harbage, A. *Shakespeare's Audience*, New York, 1941.

—— *Theater for Shakespeare*, Toronto, 1955.

Harrison, G. B. *Elizabethan Plays and Players*, Ann Arbor, 1956.

—— *Introducing Shakespeare*, 3rd edition, London, 1966.

Hodges, C. W. *The Globe Restored*, London, 1953.

—— *Shakespeare and the Players*, London, 1948.

—— *Shakespeare's Theatre*, London, 1964.

# Selected Bibliography

Hodges, C. W. 'Unworthy Scaffolds: a Theory for the Reconstruction of Elizabethan Playhouses', in *Shakespeare Survey 3*, ed. A. Nicoll, Cambridge, 1950.

Hotson, L. *The First Night of Twelfth Night*, London, 1954.

Hotson, *Shakespeare's Wooden O*, London, 1959.

Isaacs, J. 'Shakespeare as Man of the Theatre', in *Shakespeare and the Theatre*, The Shakespeare Association, London, 1927.

Joseph, B. L. *Acting Shakespeare*, London, 1960.

—— *Elizabethan Acting*, London, 1951.

—— *The Tragic Actor*, London, 1959.

Kernodle, G. R. *From Art to Theatre: form and convention in the Renaissance.* Chicago, 1944.

Knight, G. W. *Shakespearian Production*, London, 1964.

Lawrence, W. J. *The Elizabethan Playhouse and Other Studies*, 1st and 2nd Series, Stratford-on-Avon, 1912–13.

—— *The Physical Conditions of the Elizabethan Public Playhouse*, Cambridge, Mass., 1927.

—— *Pre-Restoration Stage Studies*, Cambridge, Mass., 1927.

—— *Shakespeare's Workshop*, Cambridge, Mass., 1928.

—— *Those Nut-Cracking Elizabethans*, Cambridge, Mass., 1935.

Lea, K. M. *Italian Popular Comedy : a study in the Commedia dell'arte, 1560–1620, with special reference to the English stage*, 2 vols., Oxford, 1934.

Marshall, N. *The Producer and the Play*, London, 1957.

Merchant, W. M. *Shakespeare and the Artist*, Oxford, 1959.

Nagler, A. M. *Shakespeare's Stage*, trans. R. Manheim, Yale, 1958.

Naylor, E. W. *Shakespeare and Music*, 2nd edition, London, 1931.

Nicoll, A. 'Passing over the Stage', in *Shakespeare Survey 12*, ed. A. Nicoll, Cambridge, 1959.

—— 'Studies in the Elizabethan Stage since 1900', in *Shakespeare Survey 1*, ed. A. Nicoll, Cambridge, 1948.

Noble, R. *Shakespeare's Use of Song*, Oxford, 1923.

Poel, W. *Shakespeare in the Theatre*, London, 1915.

Quiller-Couch, A. *Shakespeare's Workmanship*, Cambridge, 1918.

Reynolds, G. F. *The Staging of Elizabethan Plays at the Red Bull Theatre, 1605–1625*, London, 1940.

Saunders, J. W. 'Staging at the Globe, 1599–1613', in *Shakespeare Quarterly*, XI, 4, New York, Autumn 1960.

—— 'Vaulting the Rails', in *Shakespeare Survey 7*, ed. A. Nicoll, Cambridge, 1954.

Smith, I. *Shakespeare's Blackfriars Playhouse*, London, 1966.

—— *Shakespeare's Globe Playhouse*, London, 1963.

Southern, R. *The Open Stage*, London, 1953.

# Selected Bibliography

Speaight, R. *William Poel and the Elizabethan Revolution*, London, 1954.

Sprague, A. C. *Shakespeare and the Actors*, Cambridge, Mass., 1948.

—— *Shakespeare and the Audience : a study in the technique of exposition*, Cambridge, Mass., 1935.

Sprague, A. C. *Shakespearian Players and Performances*, London, 1953.

Stamm, R. *Shakespeare's Word-Scenery*, Zürich und St Gallen, 1954.

Sternfield, F. W. *Music in Shakespearean Tragedy*, London, 1963.

Stoll, E. E. *Art and Artifice in Shakespeare : a study in dramatic contrast and illusion*, Cambridge, 1933.

—— *Shakespearean Studies*, London, 1927.

Thorndike, A. H. *Shakespeare's Theater*, New York, 1916.

Watkins, R. *Moonlight at the Globe*, London, 1946.

—— *On Producing Shakespeare*, London, 1950.

—— and Lemmon, J., *The Tragedy of Macbeth*, London, 1964.

Wickham, G. *Early English Stages 1300 to 1660*, vol. 2, *1576–1660*, part 1, London, 1963.

Williams, R. *Drama in Performance*, London, 1954.

Wilson, J. D. *The Fortunes of Falstaff*, Cambridge, 1943.

—— *What Happens in Hamlet*, Cambridge, 1935.

# INDEX OF SUBJECTS

'above', 24

absurd, theatre of the, 146

acoustics, 16

acting, 14, 15, 21, 24, 30, 36, 46, 65, 69, 70, 94 ff., 195, 229

actor, 3, 15 ff., 38 ff., 53 ff., 72, 75 ff., 78, 81, 91, 96, 115, 123, 145, 147, 150, 152, 155, 157, 163, 166, 167, 169, 179, 180, 191, 197, 198 ff., 217, 229, 230

actresses, 41–2

address to the audience, 72 ff., 75 ff., 82, 83, 86, 94 ff., 98 ff., 130, 145, 157, 161, 165–8, 173, 199

alarum, *see* trumpets

Alexandrine, 54

allegory, 211 ff.

anapaest, 54

anticlimax, 121, 173, 214

'apron', 17

armies, 118 ff.

arras, 23

aside, 36, 58, 74, 77, 78, 82, 90, 94, 98 ff., 103–4, 125, 137, 157, 162, 173, 201, 206, 230

atmosphere, 38 ff., 46, 47

'attack', 117, 147, 199, 230

audience, 3, 14 ff., 36, 50, 60, 70–1, 73, 75 ff., 81, 83, 85, 94 ff., 98 ff., 103, 114–15, 119, 125, 127, 128, 129, 130, 142, 155, 156, 158–9, 164, 166, 167, 173, 190, 191, 195 ff., 200, 201, 202 ff., 206 ff., 216, 218, 221, 222, 225 ff., 228 ff.

auditorium, 9, 11, 12, 13, 14 ff., 42, 95, 118, 200

balcony, 12, 23, 24 ff., 31, 104, 119, 128, 129, 217

battle scenes, 17, 26, 37, 118 ff., 164

bear-baiting, 11

blocking, *see* grouping

bodies, 38

boy actors, 40 ff., 71, 80, 83, 106, 151, 210

'bridge' scene, 85, 88

bull-baiting, 11

burlesque, 29, 36, 130, 134, 208, 209 ff.

'business', 60–1, 62, 199

caesura, 145, 148

'centres of interest', 82–4

'chamber', 128

characters, characterization, 2, 19, 28, 38, 39, 41, 44, 46, 53, 56, 60, 69, 72, 78, 81, 82, 83, 84, 89 ff., 94, 100, 110, 121–2, 123, 136, 146, 148, 154, 155, 157, 158, 159, 165, 168, 172, 173, 178, 190, 205, 220, 224, 230

chorus, choric, 38, 39, 70, 82, 83, 96, 97, 98 ff., 133, 138, 230

cinema, 8, 72, 94, 122, 229

climax, 85, 87, 93, 114, 120, 132, 133, 153, 169, 182, 190, 204, 205, 215

clowns, 36, 74, 76–8, 79, 127, 159, 164, 165, 175, 199, 202

colloquial speech, 154 ff., 160, 175, 178

colour, 34 ff., 91, 133, 195, 196

comedy, 37, 38, 41, 72, 76, 82, 123, 125, 126, 134, 159, 174–5, 187, 207–8, 220, 222

comic 'relief', 222 ff.

commentary, 98 ff., 133, 202–3

conceits, 134

confession, 98 ff.

convention, 28 ff., 73, 94, 103, 123, 133, 167, 179, 225

costume, 2, 28, 30, 31, 34 ff., 44, 46, 64–5, 91, 103, 105, 118, 133, 134, 188, 197–8

couplets, 137

crescendo, 167, 183 ff.

crowd scenes, 17, 24, 25, 89–90, 93, 109 ff., 113, 114, 115 ff., 118 ff., 165, 173, 174

crowns, 32, 63–4

cruelty, the theatre of, 216

cues, 70, 78 ff., 97, 180, 199

curtain, 22 ff., 134–5, 136, 217, 222

dance, 2, 17, 54, 57, 59, 74, 81, 82, 89, 136–7, 195

daylight, 42 ff.

# Index

dénouement, 48, 189

depth of stage, 9, 16, 19, 21, 54, 55, 71, 81–2, 93

devils, 18

diction, 153

director, 53, 227 ff.

'discoveries', 22 ff., 136, 217

distancing, 97

doors, 11–12, 20 ff., 22, 23, 31, 66, 69, 73, 76, 80, 82, 93, 100, 123, 203

downstage, 61, 70, 72 ff., 81 ff., 87, 89 ff., 94 ff., 98 ff., 103 ff., 115, 118, 124, 128, 131, 132, 151, 202

duels, 17, 57, 72, 113, 114, 120, 123, 125–6, 161, 199, 224

duets, 175 ff.

dumb show, 123, 132, 133, 134, 136, 212

duologue, 67, 84 ff., 125, 164, 175 ff., 183, 185

eavesdropping, 82, 83, 103 ff., 124, 129–30

Elizabethan theatre, 7 ff.

end-stage, 16

end-stopping, 56, 148

entrance (*see also* successive entrances), 21, 53, 55, 65, 69 ff., 84, 89, 96, 97, 109 ff., 113, 120, 136, 199, 200, 203, 230

'epic' drama, 100, 216 ff.

epilogue, 36

exit, 21, 53, 54, 78 ff., 113, 120, 203

exposition, 67, 122, 167, 208

expressionism, 123

fantasy, 214

farce, 37, 69, 79, 125, 128, 161, 174, 175, 207, 214, 224

film, *see* cinema

flats, 22

'flying', 11, 27

Folio, First, 7, 143–4

folk-tale, 137, 162

'fourth wall', 17

galleries, 9, 11, 12, 15

Georgian theatre, 20

gestic poetry, 53 ff.

gesture, 2, 54, 55 ff., 58 ff., 61 ff., 84, 87, 89, 91, 95, 108, 111, 112, 132, 135, 136, 137, 141, 149, 155, 191, 196, 197, 198, 200, 229

ghosts, 19, 43

graves, 19

groundlings, 11, 128

grouping, 21, 81 ff., 84 ff., 89 ff., 94 ff., 99, 105 ff., 115 ff., 123 ff., 127 ff., 137, 213, 230

halls (banquet-halls, guildhalls), 7, 12, 24

'heavens', 11, 27

hell-mouth, 19

hiding, 103 ff., 129

history plays, 68, 126, 133, 134, 159, 187, 212

'houses', 12

iambics, 145, 162, 170

imagery, 32, 33, 46, 53–4, 59, 61, 63, 83, 89, 144, 147, 148, 156, 167, 170, 176, 182, 183, 186, 201, 212, 214, 226

immediacy, 73, 228

improvisation, 199 ff.

incantation, 163, 187, 207, 214

inn, 7

'inner stage', 22 ff., 54, 105, 128

intimacy, 14 ff., 18, 34, 36–7, 70, 72 ff., 83, 87, 94, 96, 128, 228, 229

intonation (*see also* tone), 143 ff., 151

irony, 98, 101, 108, 122, 125, 127, 133, 145–6, 150, 159, 172, 188, 190, 191, 198, 201, 205, 213, 217, 218, 222, 223, 225

juxtaposition of scene, 173, 219

kneeling, 61 ff., 89, 134, 146

laughter, 143, 199

lighting, 8, 19, 38, 42, 195, 196

lights, 42 ff.

localizing, 8, 19, 38, 42, 195, 196

machinery, 11, 27

magic, 135, 136

mansions, 14, 31

market squares, 7, 14

masques, 133, 134, 136

medieval theatre, 14, 16, 19, 24, 34

melodrama, 224

metaphor, 170

mime, 2, 58, 66, 67, 69, 81, 82, 128, 137, 195, 196

minor characters, 101

monologue, 100

monosyllables, 181, 199

mood, 3, 38 ff., 67, 69, 76, 78, 115 ff.,
 120, 121–2, 135, 137, 146 ff., 148 ff.,
 154, 161, 172, 186, 187, 188, 204,
 205, 206 ff., 217, 222 ff., 226, 227
movement, 3, 8, 45, 53 ff., 81 ff., 84 ff.,
 89 ff., 94 ff., 99, 103, 105, 109, 111,
 115 ff., 120, 123 ff., 137, 153, 158,
 164, 165, 196, 197, 200, 229
music, 2, 49, 82, 109, 122, 123, 133,
 136, 150, 157, 162, 197, 203, 206,
 221, 229
musical comedy, 24
musicians' gallery, 12, 25, 26
mystery plays, 34, 36, 37

narrative, 122–3, 217
naturalism (*see also* realism), 28, 36 ff.,
 47, 61, 118, 123, 165, 191, 195, 196,
 225, 227, 229
neo-classicism, 28
night, 40, 42 ff., 49, 122, 133, 203
noises-off, *see* sound effects
novel, 2, 195

open stage, 16, 229
opera, 151, 179

pace, 14, 54, 57, 70, 88, 89, 110, 112–
 13, 114, 137, 148 ff., 151, 161, 171,
 172, 180 ff., 182 ff., 186 ff., 199,
 203, 206 ff., 217, 228
pageantry, 17, 38, 133
pageants, 14, 24
parentheses, 143–4, 146
parody, 33, 159, 197, 223
pastoral, 129, 136, 160, 175, 210
patron, 7
pause, 37, 112–13, 114, 115, 141, 180,
 183, 187 ff.
pentameter, 181
'perspective', 206 ff., 222, 227
pitch, 89, 91, 144, 149, 151, 152, 186, 201
place (*see also* localizing), 28–9, 31, 38, 44, ff.
plague, 7
platform, 9 ff., 16 ff., 21–2, 29, 31, 55,
 65, 70, 72, 73, 76–8, 81 ff., 84 ff.,
 89 ff., 94 ff., 98 ff., 109 ff., 112 ff.,
 116, 120, 123 ff., 127 ff., 136, 137,
 151, 200, 217, 230
play-within-a-play, 94, 130, 210
plot, 123, 124, 211, 214, 224
poetic drama, 30, 95, 201

poetry, 2, 32, 39, 41, 83, 148, 153, 170–1,
 172, 201, 202
presenters, 100, 136
private theatres, 128
problem comedy, 220, 226
processions, 17, 55, 68, 91–2, 109, 133
producer, *see* director
prologue, 36, 100
prompt copies, 218
properties, 18, 22, 30 ff., 42–3, 59, 133
proscenium arch (theatre), 15, 18, 22,
 23, 24, 75, 89, 229, 230
prose, 137–8, 142, 153, 157, 158 ff., 173,
 174, 175, 199, 202
prosody, 141, 148
punctuation, 143–4

quartos, 218

radio, 14, 42
realism (*see also* naturalism), 21, 29, 30,
 172, 222, 223
repartee, 41, 178–9
repetition, 144, 148 ff., 154, 157, 182,
 183, 185–6
Restoration theatre, 20, 22, 42
revue, 16
rhetoric, 89, 109, 134, 141, 148, 149,
 154, 158, 162, 167, 176, 184, 223
rhyme, 71, 137–8
rhythm, 66, 101, 142 ff., 146 ff., 150, 152,
 154, 168, 172, 174, 178, 181, 184, 195,
 196, 205, 208, 217, 218, 221, 228, 229
ritualism, 21, 25, 36 ff., 56, 64, 135, 157,
 158, 184, 188–9, 201, 211 ff.
Roman tragedies, 221
running-on, 144, 148, 181

scaffolds, 11
scene, 142–3, 146
scenery, 8, 14, 22, 24, 30–1, 44, 196, 230
sequence of scenes, 19, 202 ff., 206 ff.,
 211 ff., 216 ff., 227
sets, setting, 19, 24, 42, 44 ff., 75, 84,
 104, 123
sex, 40 ff.
'shadowe', 11
short lines, 58, 64, 66, 180–1, 186
sibilants, 144, 204
sight-lines, 16, 18, 130
silence, 37, 55, 66, 70, 79, 80, 81, 82,
 132, 134, 135–6, 138, 153, 172, 184,
 187 ff., 223

silent figures, 105 ff., 111, 165
simplicity, 37, 153, 154 ff.
simultaneous staging, 26, 31, 70, 82–4, 123 ff., 127 ff.
single figures, 17, 90, 94, 173
situation, 39, 46, 60, 157, 169–70, 174, 178, 200, 205
soliloquy, 37, 70, 72 ff., 87, 89, 91, 94 ff., 98, 101, 163 ff., 174, 177, 199, 230
song, 2, 70, 142, 157, 188, 201
sonnet, 57, 197, 198
sound effects, 27, 43, 44, 49, 93, 112, 118, 133, 147
space, 17, 21, 66, 72, 81, 89 ff., 120, 123, 125, 129, 133, 191, 201, 229
spectacle, 133 ff.
spectators, *see* audience
speech, 15, 24, 29, 37, 53, 56, 64, 95, 96, 111, 141 ff., 146 ff., 148 ff., 151 ff., 157 ff., 163 ff., 172 ff., 175 ff., 180 ff., 195, 197, 207, 227, 229
spondee, 141
stage directions, 18, 20, 22, 23, 53, 75
stage posts, 18, 103
stanza, 137
steps, 11, 25
stichomythia, 157–8
stillness, 56, 86, 115
storms, 39, 40, 45, 161, 186, 197, 213, 214
street stages, 11
'study', 22, 128, 217
'subtext', 156
successive entrances, 114, 120, 206
'supers', 115, 119
surprise, 208
suspense, 49, 122, 129, 131, 132, 157, 163, 166, 180, 187, 188, 189, 192, 205, 208, 222
symbols, symbolism, 21, 28, 29, 30 ff., 34 ff., 42, 44, 49, 57, 61 ff., 84, 114, 118 ff., 133, 136, 149, 157, 159, 187, 208, 211 ff.

tableaux, 109
tautophony, 150
television, 37
tempo, 3, 47 ff., 109, 110, 116, 120, 171, 178, 186 ff., 206 ff.
tension, *see* suspense
tent, 31
theme, 100, 101, 136, 147, 149, 166, 167, 169, 172, 209, 214, 219, 220, 221

thrones, 27, 31, 73, 90, 132
'thrust' stage, *see* open stage
thunder, 19
time, 3, 28, 38, 47 ff., 86, 88, 89, 122, 205, 227
timing, 37, 199
tiring-house, 11, 12, 18, 21, 78, 94
tone, 3, 15, 57, 75, 83, 89, 91, 97, 99, 108, 113, 132, 133, 137, 141 ff., 146 ff., 150, 151, 170, 172 ff., 176, 177, 178, 186, 187, 188, 199, 201, 204, 209, 217, 222 ff., 226, 229
'top', 26–7
topicality, 34, 36
'total theatre', 195 ff., 201, 230
tragedy, 37, 38, 40, 126, 133, 153, 161, 168, 177, 205, 221, 222, 224, 226
tragicomedy, 175, 222
'transvestism', 42, 151, 178–9
traps, 11, 12, 18–19, 105
traverse, 23
trees, 18, 29, 31, 104, 105, 128
trumpets, 55, 70, 73, 111, 119, 120, 133, 147
Tudor drama, 19, 34

understatement, 156
unities, 28, 47
unity, 224, 227, 228
upper level, 12, 24 ff., 119
upstage, 69 ff., 73, 80, 81 ff., 84, 89 ff., 94 ff., 98 ff., 103, 114, 118, 123, 132, 134, 192, 198, 202

vernacular, *see* colloquial speech
verse, 56, 58, 66, 68, 141 ff., 146 ff., 154, 157 ff., 172, 173, 174, 181, 200, 222, 229
Victorian theatre, 8, 15, 16, 17, 22, 168
voice, 8, 15, 16, 45, 53, 81, 83, 91, 95, 109, 132, 141 ff., 146 ff., 148 ff., 151 ff., 157 ff., 170, 172 ff., 175 ff., 197, 199, 200, 229
vowels, 148, 154

weapons, 57, 61, 119
width of stage, 9, 16, 21
'window', 24 ff.
wings, 22
witches, 19

yard, 11

# INDEX OF PROPER NAMES

Adams, J. C., 9, 15, 18, 128
Appia, Adolphe, 187
Artaud, Antonin, 195, 216

Bell, John, 65
Blackfriars Theatre, 7, 14
Brecht, Bertolt, 28, 100, 127
Brooke, Arthur, *The Tragical History of Romeus and Juliet*, 39, 48
Buckingham, 2nd Duke of, *The Rehearsal*, 119
Burbage, Richard, 7

Chambers, Sir Edmund, 9, 11, 12
Chekhov, Anton, 127, 229
Cocteau, Jean, 2
Coleridge, S. T., 28, 60
Court, 7, 31, 42
Covent Garden Opera House, 16
Craig, Edward Gordon, 195, 228
Curtain theatre, 7, 11

Dekker, Thomas, 11
De Witt, Johannes, 9 ff., 17
Dickens, Charles, 195
Dryden, John, *Troilus and Cressida*, 218

Eisenstein, Sergei, 122
Eliot, T. S., 30

Fortune Theatre, 9, 11, 16
Freud, Sigmund, 229

Garrick, David, 65
Genet, Jean, *Les Nègres*, 197
Globe Theatre, the first, 9 ff., 23, 133
Globe Theatre, the second, 7
Granville-Barker, Harley, 1, 14, 49, 142, 229
Greg, W. W., 9

Henslowe, Philip, 9, 31, 34
Hodges, C. W., 9, 23
Holinshed, Raphael, 133
Hope Theatre, 9, 11, 18
Hosley, Richard, 23

Hotson, Leslie, 12

Ibsen, Henrik, 217, 229
Isaacs, J., 230–1

Johnson, Samuel, 28, 60, 220
Jonson, Ben, *Bartholomew Fair*, 17; *Every Man in His Humour*, 27, 119; *Every Man Out of His Humour*, 31; *Volpone*, 23
Joseph, B. L., 229

Kiechel, Samuel, 12
King's Men, 14
Knight, G. Wilson, 171
Kyd, Thomas, *The Spanish Tragedy*, 23, 31

Marlowe, Christopher, *Doctor Faustus*, 18–19, 32, 63
Massinger, Philip, *A New Way To Pay Old Debts*, 17
Medwall, Henry, *Fulgens and Lucrece*, 36
Mermaid Theatre, 16
Middle Temple, Hall of the, 13
Middleton, Thomas, *A Chaste Maid in Cheapside*, 22
Molière, J.-B. P., 199

Nagler, A. M., 9
Nicoll, A., 25
North, Sir Thomas, 62

Platter, Thomas, 11
Plutarch, 62, 101
Poel, William, 23

Quiller-Couch, Sir Arthur, 72

Racine, Jean, 199
Revels Office, 31, 34
Rhenanus, Johannes, 53
Rose Theatre, 31

Saunders, J. W., 25
Savoy Theatre, 229

# Index

Sheridan, R. B., *The Critic; or a Tragedy Rehearsed*, 72

Sidney, Sir Philip, *Apologie for Poetrie*, 118–19

Stanislavsky, Konstantin S., 229

Stratford-upon-Avon, 1

Swan Theatre, 9 ff., 18, 24

Swift, Jonathan, 220

Theatre, the, 7, 12

Theobald, Lewis, 63

Watkins, Ronald, 18, 91, 128

Webster, John, *The White Devil*, 17

Wickham, Glynne, 31

# INDEX OF SCENES

*Plays in approximate order of writing*

I Henry VI
I, ii 26, 109
I, iv 19, 26
I, vi 24, 26
II, i 24–5, 26
II, iv 211–12
III, ii 26
IV, ii 26
V, iii 19, 159

2 Henry VI
I, i 167

3 Henry VI
I, iv 63–4
II, v 20
III, ii 167–8
V, i 119
V, ii 98

Richard III
I, i 168
I, ii 60–1, 157
III, vii 26, 134, 197
IV, iv 110, 111, 157
V, iii 19, 43, 47
V, v 64

Titus Andronicus
I, ii 38
II, iii 38–9
V, ii 22

The Taming of the Shrew, 36
Induction, ii 26

The Comedy of Errors, 123,
159

The Two Gentlemen of Verona,
159
II, i 74
II, iii 74
IV, ii 26, 123–4

Love's Labour's Lost, 160
IV, iii 31, 104
V, i 79
V, ii 124, 134, 137, 207–8

Romeo and Juliet, 41, 48, 159, 161, 174,
202, 212, 222, 228
Prologue 100, 212
I, i 26, 110–11, 158
I, iv 45
I, v 45, 57, 76–8, 82–4, 154, 197, 198
II Prologue 100
II, i 176
II, ii 26, 37, 176
II, iv 35, 200
II, v 25, 65
II, vi 53, 212
III, i 48, 90–1, 112–13
III, ii 91
III, iv 48
III, v 26, 39, 45, 154–5
IV, ii 48, 143
IV, iii 22, 141, 143, 222
IV, iv 48, 143, 222
IV, v 222–3
V, iii 22, 42, 46, 113–14, 158, 212–13

A Midsummer Night's Dream, 37, 39–40,
159, 202, 224, 225
I, ii 153, 210
II, i 21, 45
III, i 29
III, ii 47, 127
IV, i 43, 127, 159–60
V, i 130, 209–10

Richard II, 158, 159
II, i 168
III, iii 25, 149, 153–4
III, iv 159, 212
IV, i 32, 56, 64, 105–6, 176

King John
I, i 146–7

# Index

*King John (cont.)*
II, i  26, 168
III, iv  168–9
IV, iii  25
V, i  64

*The Merchant of Venice*, 34, 38, 41, 42,
  208, 219, 224, 225
II, ii  74
II, v  21
II, vi  21, 26
II, vii  22, 134
II, ix  134, 189
III, ii  134, 162, 225–6
III, iii  149
III, iv  151
IV, i  45, 79, 189–90, 198, 224, 226
IV, ii  45, 224
V, i  56

*1 Henry IV*, 36, 37, 75, 142, 159, 165,
  199, 219, 222, 226
I, i  146, 208, 220
I, ii  75, 173, 208, 220
I, iii  68
II, ii  69, 128–9
II, iii  220
II, iv  23
V, ii  120
V, iv  172–3, 220

*2 Henry IV*, 36, 75, 142, 159, 165, 199,
  219, 222, 226
Induction, 17
I, ii  151
III, ii  143
IV, v  32

*Much Ado About Nothing*, 41, 160,
  224
I, i  160
II, i  105, 137, 151
II, iii  104–5, 178
III, i  105
IV, i  191, 208

*Henry V*, 15, 34, 38, 100
III Prologue 30
III, i  26
III, vi  151
IV Prologue 43, 119
IV, i  35, 43, 61, 150, 153, 197

IV, ii  43
V, ii  20, 120

*As You Like It*, 41, 42, 178–9, 202, 208,
  210
I, ii  34, 46, 98, 160–1, 187
I, iii  187
II, i  46, 187
II, ii  187
II, iii  187
II, iv  44, 69, 105
II, vii  40, 187
III, i  187
III, ii  18, 29, 187–8, 220
III, iii  220
III, iv  124
III, v  105, 125
IV, i  179, 210–11
IV, iii  155
V, ii  137, 182, 210
V, iv  109

*Julius Caesar*, 38, 40, 219, 221
I, i  17, 115
I, ii  32, 91–2, 115, 133, 161
I, iii  40, 161
II, i  35, 40, 42, 151–2, 209
II, ii  35
II, iii  40
III, i  45, 115–16, 169–71
III, ii  25, 116, 150, 161, 190
III, iii  115, 204
IV, i  205
IV, ii  84, 221
IV, iii  84–5
V, i  120
V, v  58

*The Merry Wives of Windsor*
III, iii  23
III, v  75

*Troilus and Cressida*, 161, 220–1, 224,
  226
I, i  147
I, ii  133, 153
I, iii  147
III, i  213
III, ii  74, 106
III, iii  96
IV, ii  106
IV, iv  106, 221

IV, v 80, 201–2, 221
v, ii 26, 129–30, 147–8
v, iv–x 121

*Hamlet*, 2, 34, 47, 91, 102, 142, 158,
     159, 162, 166, 176, 199
I, i 53, 67, 78, 80
I, ii 35, 46, 70, 75, 78, 90, 150, 153,
     165, 177, 182–3, 191
I, iii 78
I, iv 78
I, v 19, 59, 78, 158
II, i 35
II, ii 56, 70, 165, 172, 177
III, i 23, 103, 106, 161, 165, 172, 177,
     192
III, ii 11, 43, 100, 130–2, 137, 152
III, iii 66, 96–7
III, iv 23, 32, 41, 158, 183–4
IV, iii 227
IV, iv 165
IV, v 70, 218, 227
IV, vii 177
V, i 19, 33, 105, 109, 174–5
V, ii 34, 38, 57, 114

*Twelfth Night*, 13, 42, 161, 208, 225
I, iv 151
I, v 200–1
II, iii 35, 207
II, iv 207
II, v 31, 105
III, iv 18, 72, 125–6, 161, 199, 201,
     207, 224
IV, ii 199
V, i 109

*All's Well That Ends Well*
I, iii 55, 71, 155
II, iii 38, 137–8
II, v 20
IV, i 18

*Measure for Measure*, 41, 47, 165, 219,
     226
I, iv 143
II, ii 35, 85–7, 201
II, iii 155
II, iv 85–8, 166, 177–8
III, i 103, 173, 182
IV, ii 213
IV, iii 173

*Othello*, 41, 49–50, 102, 166, 175, 196,
     205
I, i 26, 42, 196
I, ii 35
I, iii 152–3, 161–2, 196
II, i 99, 162, 202, 213
II, iii 49, 74, 198
III, iii 63, 66, 67–8, 88–9, 92–3, 97,
     148, 184, 226
III, iv 33, 58, 71, 106–7, 151, 154,
     156, 186–7, 207
IV, i 63, 154
IV, ii 45, 46, 188, 213–14
IV, iii 46, 142, 188–9, 201, 214, 223
V, i 50, 142, 188
V, ii 23, 33, 42, 63, 99, 107, 109, 142,
     184, 191, 214

*Macbeth*, 34, 41, 42, 47, 102, 142, 163,
     166, 197, 202, 205, 227
I, i 19, 40, 54
I, ii 55, 71, 199–200
I, iii 19, 40, 173, 191
I, iv 28, 158, 163
I, v 28, 203, 204
I, vi 203–4
I, vii 204
II, i 32, 40, 163–4
II, ii 40, 66, 163, 180
II, iii 40, 44, 93–4, 109, 163
II, iv 40, 44
III, i 73, 163, 174
III, ii 46
III, iii 40, 42, 180
III, iv 19, 174
IV, i 19, 213
IV, iii 141, 152, 163, 190
V, i 42, 100–1, 163, 206
V, ii 55
V, iii 55, 206
V, iv 206
V, v 148, 191, 206
V, vii 38
V, viii 163

*King Lear*, 2, 40, 46, 102, 142, 151, 158,
     167, 205
I, i 64, 90, 155, 158, 162
I, ii 74
I, iv 162
II, iii 64
II, iv 111–12, 176, 184–6

*King Lear (cont.)*
  III, ii 172
  III, iv 42, 45, 56, 65, 81, 94–5, 99–100,
    126–7, 143, 162, 200, 214–15
  III, vi 156, 214, 215–16
  III, vii 29
  IV, vi 19, 69, 145, 200, 214, 216
  IV, vii 61, 62–3, 156, 197
  V, iii 114–15, 172

*Antony and Cleopatra*, 34, 41, 44, 102,
  151, 167, 197, 219, 221
  I, i 44, 97–8, 144
  I, ii 180–1
  I, iii 181
  I, iv 45
  II, ii 219
  II, iii 219
  II, v 219
  III, xiii 101
  IV, i 122
  IV, ii 122
  IV, iii 49, 60, 122
  IV, iv 60, 121, 122
  IV, v 121, 122
  IV, vi 101, 107, 121, 122
  IV, vii 121, 122
  IV, viii 121, 122
  IV, ix 49, 121, 122, 164
  IV, x 121, 122, 164
  IV, xi 121, 122, 164
  IV, xii 54, 121, 122, 164
  IV, xiv 54, 57
  IV, xv 25
  V, ii 35, 46, 156, 164

*Coriolanus*, 34, 61–2, 91, 166, 167, 205,
  219, 221
  I, i 79–80, 102, 117, 122
  I, ii 122
  I, iii 62, 107, 122, 221
  I, iv 26, 91, 122, 221
  I, v–viii 122
  I, ix 20
  I, x 122
  II, i 62, 102, 107
  II, ii 102
  II, iii 36, 91, 102, 117–18, 219
  III, i 118, 219
  III, ii 151
  IV, iv 91
  IV, v 102, 191

  V, i 62
  V, iii 62, 91, 107–8, 192, 198
  V, vi 62, 91

*Timon of Athens*, 91
  I, i 102
  I, ii 102–3, 136, 227
  III, iv 226
  IV, i 102
  IV, iii 19, 227
  V, i 18, 227
  V, iv 26

*Pericles*
  I, i 136
  II Prologue, 134
  II, i 19
  II, ii 134
  III Prologue, 134
  IV, iv 134
  IV, vi 41, 47

*Cymbeline*, 14, 34
  I, vi 178
  II, ii 23, 41, 43
  V, ii 123
  V, iv 27, 134, 136
  V, v 89

*The Winter's Tale*, 14, 219
  I, i 208
  I, ii 57, 58, 59, 81, 144, 181, 182,
    208–9
  II, iii 175
  III, iii 175
  IV, i 49, 217
  IV, iii 47, 49, 175
  IV, iv 136, 175
  V, iii 134–6

*The Tempest*, 14
  I, i 39
  I, ii 39, 41, 45, 56, 136
  II, i 136
  III, iii 27, 136
  IV, i 89, 136
  V, i 136

*Henry VIII*
  IV, i 133
  IV, ii 136
  V, ii 26